PRACTICAL
GARDENING

This is a Parragon Book
This edition published in 2001

Parragon
Queen Street House
4 Queen Street
Bath BA1 1HE, UK

ISBN: 0-75255-469-7 Paperback
ISBN: 0-75255-857-9 Hardback

A CIP data record for this book is available from the British Library.

Created and produced by
Foundry Design and Production, part of
The Foundry Creative Media Co. Ltd.
Crabtree Hall, Crabtree Lane, London SW6 6TY

Acknowledgements
Illustrations: Kate Simunek
Special photography: Andrew Newton-Cox

Special thanks to Jennifer Bishop, Katie Cowan, Josephine Cutts, Dave Jones, Chairworks, Clifton Nurseries, Draper's Tools Ltd, Idencroft Herbs Jardinerie and Queenswood Garden Centre for the loan of plants, props and tools.

Printed in China

PRACTICAL GARDENING

Deena Beverley

Special photography
by Andrew Newton-Cox

p

CONTENTS

INTRODUCTION

The aim of this book is to help people with relatively little gardening knowledge make informed choices about how to plan and maintain their gardens. The upsurge of gardening as a leisure activity during recent years has been phenomenal and as a result the demand for information on practical gardening and plants to be grown in gardens has developed rapidly.

Everyone has a unique vision for their garden, but many people, when confronted with a garden for the first time, feel intimidated by their lack of knowledge and the seemingly vast amount they think they will need to know if they are to succeed in managing their gardening. This book will show you that gardening need not be difficult – almost any garden, whatever shape or size, can be tailored to suit individual tastes, and as you gain confidence, you will quickly find your gardening horizons widening.

This book provides all the practical gardening information and techniques that you will need to begin the tasks of designing the structure, adding paths, patios and ponds, laying lawns and creating borders. Sections on propagation, pruning and working with plants and garden DIY contain simple step-by-step text and illustration sequences.

Whether you're a first-time home owner with a small urban plot or tiny balcony, or have a large rambling garden that is in need of renovation, this book will inspire you to turn your garden into your own personal haven.

BEFORE YOU BEGIN

To become a gardener is to embark on an exciting journey. Your garden will reward you for taking the time to understand its needs.

❀

Gardening is such a huge subject that it is easy to be daunted by it. Don't be put off. Gain experience by reading about the subject and simply by gardening.

❀

Do not be overwhelmed by all the information within this book. Dip into it to solve particular problems or to check the best way of handling something before you start planning a project.

❀

Reading through the relevant section before you visit a garden centre could save you a lot of money. The more informed you are, the wiser your gardening choices will be.

BASIC TECHNIQUES AND EQUIPMENT

In the rush to embark on the planting aspect of gardening, the non-planted elements (the 'hard side') are often overlooked when it comes to garden planning and implementation. However, these play a massively important supporting role. They form a constant backbone that should be installed and maintained properly if the garden is to look presentable from all angles throughout the seasons. Fences, paths, driveways, steps, shed, summer-house, pergolas, arches, gazebos, arbours, cold frames, greenhouses, path edging, seating and tables ... the list is extensive, and it is easy to see that if these elements are not properly considered and cared for, the overall look of the garden will suffer.

WHEN YOU DON'T 'DO IT YOURSELF'

EVEN if you will not literally be 'doing it yourself', it is well worth appraising yourself of the tools and techniques involved, so that you can plan works in the garden, choose materials and supervise work confidently, as well as make provisions for any future maintenance and upkeep, such as re-treating timbers before, not after, they start to deteriorate.

❀ Read about a project, and carefully consider what is involved, before setting out to the do-it-yourself (DIY) store. Most DIY tasks, even the smallest, benefit from at least some forward planning so that you do not end up wasting time, effort and money.

❀ Gauge how realistic it is to embark on a project yourself. For example, laying a large patio is hard, physical work. If you have a bad back it is not sensible to undertake such a strenuous task unaided, so call in a professional.

❀ Ask friends and neighbours for recommendations of reputable

contractors, and obtain a variety of comparative quotes before settling on a price. The more informed you are, the more in control you will feel. This is particularly important if you are employing someone to undertake a large-scale project, such as a circular driveway, which will temporarily render your entire front garden a muddy building site. Having this sort of work done is undeniably stressful, as well as expensive, and you will feel much happier if you have an overall awareness of what is happening and why.

RIGHT: *Unusual fencing materials are increasingly widely available, making it simple to create a highly individual garden style.*

HOW MUCH TO SPEND

HARD-side garden projects serve a variety of purposes, from fences that shelter you and your plants from the wind to barbecues beneath pergolas, which provide delightful opportunities for alfresco dining. The level of emphasis you place on these projects, and how much you spend, will depend on a number of factors.

❀ Economic necessity is obviously one, but you should also consider the importance of a particular feature – in relation to the garden as a whole, and to you.

❀ A flimsy, tubular rose arch is undeniably temptingly cheap, leaving you with money to spend on planting. However, if it occupies a prominent place in your front garden, straddling the path leading to the front door of your picturesque cottage, it will add little in terms of visual appeal and may never be really satisfying,

especially when the flowers have bloomed. Far better, in this instance, to invest in a really attractive structure in sympathy with its surroundings.

❀ Careful choice of hard-side items will add not only to your enjoyment of the house and garden, but can prove a sound financial investment should you come to sell your home. Conversely, choosing unwisely can detract from the resale value of your home.

❀ Think about whether you will want to take items with you when you move. If you know that you will be leaving your current home in a year or so, choose portable options unless installing them as investments, such as a wheeled, rather than brick-built, barbecue and a self-contained pond rather than a permanent one.

BELOW: *Adding sympathetic colour to the non-planted elements of a garden adds year-round interest.*

TOOLS

THE list of tools required for DIY applications seems extensive, but you need not invest in all of those suggested. A basic tool kit comprising robust, good-quality tools will be sufficient for most requirements. Check carefully through what is involved in a project before you start work. It is very annoying to get half-way through a job, only to find that you need a small but important tool to complete the task.

A BASIC TOOL KIT

Always use the tool appropriate to the job. It is just as pointless and dangerous to use a huge hammer to try to knock in a tiny nail, as it is to try and break up an old patio with a claw hammer. Pay attention to basic safety guidelines; choose the right tool for the job and you will save yourself a lot of frustration and minimise the risk of injury and damage. Large, infrequently used tools, such as cement mixers, are generally hired rather than bought.

Hammers

❀ Claw hammers are useful for levering out nails or tacks, particularly helpful if you are reusing wood from a previous project that has old ironmongery still present. The hammer part is obviously indispensable for a multitude of hammering tasks, but especially for driving in nails.

❀ A club hammer is great for heavy work, such as breaking up old paving, or knocking pegs into the ground. Sledge hammers are for heavier work still, such as knocking in posts or smashing up concrete.

claw hammer

Measuring tools

❀ A tape measure is indispensable and a level is essential for setting and checking levels. Various sizes are available to suit different applications. Obviously, it can be quite difficult to fit a full-sized builder's level on top of a tiny hanging basket bracket in a confined space, so a small level is a useful addition to the tool kit.

❀ Combination squares are useful, with the facility to measure angles and short lengths. A plumb line is

handy for finding true verticals. Beyond providing a visual guide for building level brick walls, a brick line has many garden uses, such as providing a level for installing fences.

wire

Saws

❀ A general-purpose panel saw is a good all-round investment as it will be suitable for cutting lengths of timber, the most common garden DIY wood-cutting task. Sheet materials are best cut with a tenon saw. You will need a hacksaw for cutting metal.

saw

Power drill

❀ Do buy a drill of appropriate power for the job. Cheap drills can be incredibly frustrating. If you are slightly built, and unfamiliar with DIY, you may feel that an inexpensive, low-powered, lightweight drill is the best choice. However, the opposite is true. The reason for using a power drill is that the motor should be doing the work, not you. Obviously, you will need to be able physically to hold and control the drill, but a good model will have a motor of sufficient power that you will actually be holding the drill for far less time than if you are trying to force a weak drill to undertake a heavy drilling job, which may end up breaking the motor, as well as exhausting you. Cordless drills are a great innovation for garden DIY. Make sure you have sufficient batteries so that your power does not run out half-way through a job. Look for a drill with a reversing action and variable speed setting, which is very helpful when putting in screws.

power drill

Bucket

❀ The humble builder's bucket is useful for all sorts of mixing jobs. Buy the most substantial you can find.

bucket

Paintbrushes

❀ Buy the best quality you can afford. Cheap brushes that shed their bristles as you work are incredibly infuriating.

paintbrush

Screwdrivers

❀ You will need a selection of screwdrivers, some for slot-, some for cross-headed screws.

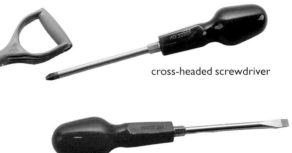

cross-headed screwdriver

slot-headed screwdriver

Shovel

❀ A shovel is required for the easy moving and mixing of loose materials.

shovel

Flat trowel

❀ A flat trowel is needed for grouting, pointing, laying bricks and smoothing cement.

flat trowel

Portable workbench

❀ This innovative bench enables you to work on a stable surface, even when in the middle of the garden. A basic workbench offers a facility for clamping pieces of wood firmly in place for cutting, as well as providing a range of measuring guides.

Wire cutters

❀ These make light work of cutting through the various types of wire used around the garden, and prevent you from using and damaging your other cutting tools.

wire cutters

portable workbench

GARDENING TOOLS AND EQUIPMENT

Care of even the smallest garden requires some specialised tools and equipment. Confronted with the range available at hardware and garden stores, it is easy to be bewildered into inappropriate purchasing, so spend some time considering your needs before venturing to the shops. The range of tools required will depend on the size of your garden and the type of gardening you plan to undertake. For example, a garden with a huge lawn may prompt the purchase of a sit-and-ride mower, while a tiny lawn will have far more modest mowing needs. Similarly, a keen vegetable grower will benefit from a range of cultivation tools, while a topiarist will need special shears.

A BASIC GARDEN TOOL KIT

WHATEVER the size of your garden, quality is of paramount importance when selecting tools – be they for cultivation, digging, pruning or cutting. These tools will be in regular use for many years and it is worth investing in the best quality available. A cheap fork that bends on contact with compacted soil is frustratingly useless and a complete waste of money. It can be galling to spend large sums on basic tools when there are so many other, more immediately exciting temptations on sale in the garden centre, but sturdy, comfortable and effective tools really will turn basic gardening functions into much more pleasurable tasks.

Spades and forks

❀ You will be using spades and forks regularly so it is vital to select models that are comfortable for you to handle. Great demands will be made on both items in terms of lifting and leverage, so look for designs that combine lightness with strength.

❀ Consider the material of the head carefully before purchase. Stainless steel does not rust but is expensive; coated steel blades are more affordable and will last well if kept clean, but beware of inexplicably cheap tools – the coating is likely to be so thin that it will lift away almost immediately.

❀ Non-stick coatings are available, and undoubtedly make cleaning the tool and working the soil easier, but may wear off after lengthy use.

❀ As with all tools, check that all the joints are secure – particularly where the head of the tool meets the shaft, as this joint will be under a lot of pressure in use.

ABOVE: A well-stocked and well-ordered garden shed with neatly stored tools is pleasant and efficient to use.

✿ For optimum strength ensure that the head and neck are moulded from a single piece of metal. Shafts may be of wood or metal, possibly covered with plastic. Both are generally strong. Wooden shafts have the advantage of being easy to replace and warmer to handle in winter than even plastic-coated metal. Ensure that the tines or blades are smooth, for ease of working and cleaning.

✿ Handle shapes differ so don't be afraid to experiment with the varying types – D-, Y- and T-shapes – in the shop, until you arrive at a model that feels right in the hand. The Y-shape, formed by splitting the shaft wood, may not be as strong as the D-shaped hilt.

✿ Although there are various sizes of spade and fork available – for example border (small, sometimes called 'ladies'), medium and digging (generally the largest) – do not feel that you need a whole selection for different tasks. A fork is useful for turning heavy soil, dividing or transplanting plants, spreading mulch, applying manure and lifting root vegetables.

✿ The addition of a tread on a spade makes digging easier, and less hazardous to footwear, but also adds weight and cost, which it may not be necessary to incur if you have only minimal digging requirements. Be guided by the head size, length and weight that feels most workable for your stature and strength.

fork

spade

shovel

EARLY GARDENS

THE earliest gardens we have pictures of are Egyptian ones, created over 3,000 years ago. In Egypt the narrow fertile stretch of the Nile is surrounded by desert. The idea of paradise was centred on an enclosed green oasis full of water and fruitfulness. In fact, water became the most important aspect of the garden, both for irrigation and as a symbol of the River of Life. All the irrigated gardens of Persia, Arabia and India developed from these Egyptian gardens. Their influence could be seen in ancient Roman gardens and was brought to medieval Europe by knights returning from the Crusades, and to Spain through the Moorish invasions from North Africa.

The Hanging Gardens of Babylon, built in 605 BC, were different. They consisted of a series of steep terraces planted with trees and shrubs, created by Nebuchadnezzar II for his Persian wife, who was homesick for the green hillsides of her home. They

ABOVE: *This picture of a man and woman ploughing and sowing seed shows the typical boundary of tall trees that lined ancient Egyptian gardens. It comes from a tomb in Thebes, dated about 1200 BC.*

were, basically, the first roof gardens and for many centuries they were considered to be among the Seven Wonders of the World.

Hand forks and trowels

❀ Essentially miniature spades and forks, these tools are used for small-scale jobs like light weeding, cultivating in rock gardens, raised beds and containers, and dividing small bulbs and plants. As before, choose the best quality you can afford, making sure the tool feels comfortable to hold.

❀ Hand forks have either wide and flat, or narrow, round prongs. The flat prongs are more suited to weeding since the weeds are more easily trapped and held between them; the round, narrow prongs are better for cultivating as they pass freely through the earth. A single, flat-pronged hand fork will be adequate for most gardeners.

hand fork
and trowel

Hoes

❀ Hoes are used for weeding around plants and cultivating topsoil. There are several types. The popular 'Dutch' hoe is used like a sharp-bladed spoon to skim along the surface of the soil, loosening weeds, which may then be sliced through. Turned so that the blade is at right angles to the ground, it may also be used to break up and aerate topsoil.

❀ The small, sharp head of the hoe is useful for making seed drills and marking out lines. Swan-neck, or draw hoes, used in a chopping motion for weeding, are less commonly used; other, specialised hoes include onion and triangular hoes.

Garden rakes

❀ A general-purpose cultivation tool, the garden rake can be used with its prongs facing down to break up the surface of the soil and collect stones, leaves and other debris. Inverted, it is used to level the ground. Choose a rake with a head of suitable width for both your own size and the scale of raking job you will most commonly undertake.

❀ Choose shaft length carefully, too. To avoid back strain, you should be able to rake without bending. A 1.5 m (5 ft) shaft suits most people, but taller gardeners may need a longer handle. The strongest rake head is made in a single piece, unlike the cheaper, riveted head with its individual nail-like prongs, which are more liable to distortion and loss. A lawn rake is an entirely different tool (see p. 38).

Gardener's knives

❀ The general-purpose gardener's knife is possibly the most essential garden tool. Use it to open bags of compost, cut twine and cane to length, and for taking cuttings, pruning small plants and deadheading. A plastic or wooden handle is not as cold to handle in winter as a metal one. Choose a carbon-steel blade for longevity, wiping it dry and rubbing it over with an oily rag after use.

❀ Specialist knives include budding and curved pruning knives; multi-purpose knives have several different types of blade folded into one handle.

garden rakes

gardener's knife

hoe

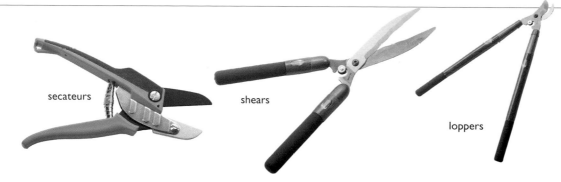

secateurs

shears

loppers

Secateurs

❀ For cutting that is slightly more demanding than deadheading and harvesting, a pair of secateurs is essential. Good ones will cut cleanly and easily through woody stems up to approximately 1 cm ($\frac{1}{2}$ in) in diameter. It is vital that the blades are sharp or you will achieve either a ragged stem, which will encourage disease in the plant, or a crushed stem.

❀ There are a confusing range of secateur types available. As always, your hands are the best guides. Select a pair that suits the hand you use most, since both left- and right-handed pairs are available.

❀ Bypass secateurs are a good, multi-purpose pair. They have a convex upper blade, which cuts in a scissor motion against a narrow, concave lower blade, and are comfortable for general use. If your hand span is small, or you do not have particularly strong hands, opt for ratchet secateurs, which make pruning thicker stems infinitely easier as the ratchet action makes the cut in several small stages, rather than requiring all your strength to make one powerful cut. However, the ratchet action is frustratingly slow if used for general cutting tasks.

❀ Other options include parrot-beak secateurs, which use a scissor action, and anvil secateurs, which have a sharp upper blade that cuts against a flat anvil. All secateurs have a safety catch, which should be easy to operate single handed.

❀ When choosing any pair of secateurs, consider how easy it will be to sharpen or replace the blades. Clean the blades after use to remove dried sap, and rub them with an oily rag.

❀ To use secateurs correctly, always place the stem to be cut well down at the base of the blades. This holds the stem securely, making an accurate cut much simpler to perform. It also preserves blade life as the blades are less likely to be pushed out of alignment.

Shears

❀ Shears are used for topiary, cutting back herbaceous plants and trimming hedges and small areas of long grass. Although some shears have a notch at the base of one blade to facilitate the cutting of the occasional tough stem, shears are best reserved for their specific, light 'hair cutting' work. Use proper pruning tools to tackle heavier stems and branches.

❀ A good pair of shears will be light, strong and comfortable to operate. Check their balance before purchasing, to ensure that the blades are not much heavier than the handles, which makes them tiring to use.

❀ As with all cutting tools, clean and lightly oil after use, and sharpen regularly. Specialist shears, such as topiary shears, are also available.

Loppers, tree pruners and pruning saws

❀ Cutting branches and stems thicker than about 1 cm ($\frac{1}{2}$ in) quickly damages secateurs and shears, and is dealt with most effectively by specialist tools.

❀ Loppers (long-handled pruners) are essentially secateurs with additional leverage and reach, making it easy to cut stems up to about 2.5 cm (1 in) thick and branches that are difficult to reach. Loppers should be well balanced so that you can use them comfortably at full stretch and overhead.

❀ Tree pruners also cut branches up to 2.5 cm (1 in) thick. The cutting device, operated by a lever or cord, is housed at the end of a long pole, sometimes an extending or telescopic one.

chainsaw

pruning saw

❀ For branches more than 2.5 cm (1 in) thick, use a pruning saw. A general-purpose pruning saw will be sufficient for most needs. Its small blade, usually no more than 46 cm (18 in) long, means that it may be used even in confined spaces.

❀ A Grecian saw has a curved blade, which cuts on the pull stroke only – particularly useful for pruning in a tight area. A small, folding pruning saw is ideal for those with limited storage space and pruning needs. However, it is not as strong and effective as a bow saw, which will cut through even thick branches quickly.

❀ All types should have heat-treated, hard-point teeth, which are tougher and stay sharper for longer than regular saw blades, although they still need regular sharpening to remain fully effective.

OTHER GARDENING EQUIPMENT

IN addition to basic cultivating, digging, pruning and cutting tools, you will need equipment for carrying, such as trugs and buckets, for watering and for propagating, for example a garden sieve, flowerpots, string, plant labels and canes.

Carrying equipment

❀ A folding wheelbarrow is useful where storage space is limited, although not as sturdy as a conventional barrow and its canvas can be damaged by careless handling.

❀ Choose a barrow that is well balanced, where the load is distributed chiefly over the wheel, rather than towards the handles, for good manoeuvrability. Metal barrows are more durable than plastic ones; a galvanised traditional barrow is a good all-round choice for most gardens.

❀ For very heavy loads, or for use on uneven ground, a builder's ball-wheeled barrow cushions the load and is easier to push, but the ball is susceptible to punctures.

❀ Bulky but light materials such as hedge trimmings can be easily collected and transported on ground sheets and in large bags, which can be conveniently folded flat for easy storage. Look for those made of woven mesh plastic material and with sturdy handles, which wear better than ordinary plastic.

Hose and watering can

❀ The humble hose is a vital piece of garden equipment. If not stored neatly on a reel it is vulnerable to kinks and punctures, as well as posing a tripping hazard.

❀ Many variants of hose are available, including the convenient flow-through type which allows water to be run through it even while it is stored on the reel. Always drain a hose fitted to an outside tap and bring it inside for the winter.

hosepipe

wheelbarrow

watering can and rose

LAWN EQUIPMENT

THE tools you purchase for your lawn will depend on its size and structure, whether it is sloping or flat, has intricate shapes to cut around or is a simple rectangle, and what type of lawn you require – be it a wild meadow or an elegant, striped bowling green-type lawn. For the former, which needs trimming only once or twice a year, a sickle or a power trimmer may be all you need. Your choice of equipment will also be governed by how much time and money you have available.

❀ A well-made metal watering can with a detachable rose will last for years. Always use a separate watering can for applying weedkiller, path clearer and other noxious substances that could cause plant damage if allowed to contaminate clean water. It is worth investing in a cheap, plastic watering can solely for this purpose.

Kneeling mat

❀ A cushioned kneeling mat is invaluable for gardeners of all ages and is inexpensive and easy to store.

❀ A more expensive and bulky option is the kneeling frame, which has the added advantage of supportive handles that make it easier to stand up and kneel down.

❀ This sort of frame is an excellent choice for the elderly, or indeed any gardener with back problems; used the other way up, it becomes a handy stool.

Lawnmowers

❀ Scarcely used today, the manual lawnmower is wonderfully quiet in use and easy to maintain, and is still a viable option for a small lawn.

❀ Electric or petrol-driven cylinder lawnmowers are heavy and tiring to use, but produce the clean, close cut desirable on a luxury lawn. They require good maintenance and are generally for those who enjoy spending time and energy on their lawns.

❀ Probably the most well-known power lawnmower is the electric hover mower, which glides above the lawn on a cushion of air. It is light, easy and quick to use but does not cut as closely as a cylinder mower and is not recommended where a really pristine, formal finish is required.

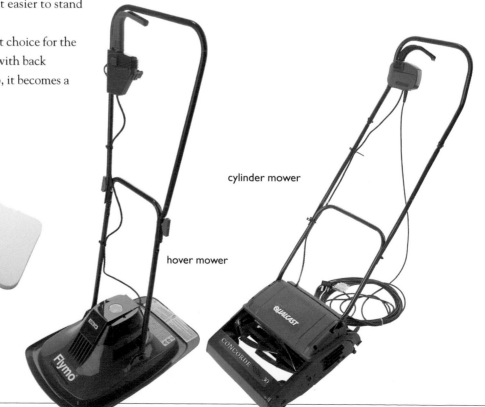

cylinder mower

hover mower

kneeling mat

Lawn edging and maintenance tools

❀ Often overlooked, edging tools add the finishing touch to lawns and are worth investing in.

❀ A lawn edging iron is essential for cutting away any rough edges where the lawn meets the soil of a border. Long-handled lawn edging shears are required for the long, untidy grass at the edges of a lawn.

❀ Power trimmers, driven by electricity or petrol, cut through grass and weeds using a fast-rotating nylon line. They are especially convenient to use in a confined area.

❀ Electric trimmers are cheaper and lighter than the petrol-driven equivalents, but need a power source close by and are not suitable for use on wet grass.

❀ A fan-shaped, spring-tined wire-headed rake is useful for removing lawn moss and leaves and also for aerating the lawn.

Tool care

❀ Regular cleaning and maintenance is essential for prolonging the life of tools. In addition, blunt blades will damage vulnerable plant tissues, and dirty tools simply do not function as well as clean ones. A mud-encrusted spade cannot cut into the soil as effectively as a clean one, making digging even more arduous. Similarly, grit works its way into joints and pivot points, causing moving parts to seize up and preventing blades meeting efficiently.

❀ Clean all tools after use and wipe metal surfaces with an oily rag to protect them against rust.

❀ Wipe electrical tools clean, and dry them thoroughly before storing. Have them serviced regularly – a label on the handle, indicating the date of the last service and a reminder of the next one, is helpful.

SAFETY IN THE GARDEN

THE garden can be a dangerous environment if some basic safety guidelines are not adhered to. Eyes are particularly at risk and safety goggles are advisable for jobs such as hedge trimming and lawn mowing, which involve a risk, not only from the tools themselves, but from spiky branches, loose stones thrown up by a mower, and other natural debris, which can move around unpredictably during such tasks.

strimmer

lawnmower

❀ Accidents also occur from tools – especially long-handled ones – left lying around the garden. Stepping on the head of an abandoned rake, for example, causes the handle to fly up with amazing force and speed. A tidy garden is therefore a safer garden.

❀ It is wise to wear sturdy boots when gardening, particularly when mowing. There is a wide range of gardening gloves available and you may need more than one pair – a fairly lightweight pair for light weeding, for example, and a stronger pair for pruning a large prickly, shrub.

Electrical safety

❀ Never use electrical tools in damp weather. Ensure they are scrupulously maintained and serviced, and check leads and connections regularly to ensure they are in good repair.

❀ Fit all electrical tools with a residual current device (RCD), which cuts out the electrical circuit in the event of the power being interrupted, for example by accidentally running over a mower cable.

PREPARING TOOLS FOR WINTER STORAGE

1 *All tools should be properly serviced before winter so that they will be ready for action in the busy spring months ahead. Clean away loose debris and encrusted soil from blades, around mechanisms and on handles.*

2 *Check fixings and moving parts and tighten any parts that have worked themselves loose during the summer and autumn months.*

3 *Lubricate any parts that have ceased to move freely. Sharpen tools or have them professionally sharpened.*

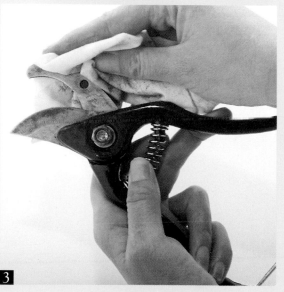

BASIC MATERIALS

ALWAYS buy the best-quality materials you can afford. 'Doing it yourself' is an economical and satisfying way of producing the unplanted elements of a garden, but it is not necessarily quick, so value the time investment you are putting in and use materials that will be long lasting and attractive. Treat surfaces with preservatives initially and maintain them appropriately. There is no point spending time and effort creating a marvellous gazebo if you use such poor-quality untreated timber that the whole thing disintegrates in a dispiritingly short time.

Wood is an important garden DIY material, used in the construction of fences, gates, outbuildings, plant supports, decking, steps and pergolas, to name but a few applications. Always buy wood that originates from sustainable sources. Salvaged wood, such as railways sleepers, is increasingly popular and an economical and ecologically sound alternative to buying new timber.

Softwood

❀ Softwood, such as spruce or pine, is generally softer and lighter than hardwood. It is cheaper and easier to work because its texture makes it simpler to cut and nail. It is available in rough or smooth planed finishes, and in a wide variety of thicknesses and widths. Always use tanalised softwood for exterior uses. This has been pressure treated with preservative, which is a much more effective weatherproofing than simply brushing on a non-penetrating preservative.

❀ Some softwoods, such as larch and western red cedar, are inherently more rot resistant than others, and are correspondingly more expensive.

Hardwood

❀ Hardwoods are cut from deciduous broad-leaved trees such as teak, mahogany or oak. Generally, hardwood is denser and harder than softwood, which makes it more difficult to cut and fix. It is also much more rot resistant and durable than softwood, so is an excellent choice for external applications – particularly those where the beauty of the wood grain is an important design feature, as in a pergola or a garden table. Iroko is a popular hardwood, as hardwearing as teak, but much cheaper, although not quite as smooth textured.

Manufactured board

❀ Manufactured boards, formed from wood chips or dust mixed with resins or glues that bond the fibres together, have become increasingly popular in recent times for their strength and value for money. Take care to use grades specifically designed for exterior use.

TREATING WOOD

SOFTWOOD is vulnerable to rot when used in the garden, particularly when it is in prolonged contact with the soil. Always buy pressure-treated timber if using softwood. If this is not possible, apply your own treatment. Choose from a weatherproof paint system or a preservative. Preservatives

BELOW: *The use of vivid colour can make a bold and dramatic statement in a children's play area.*

BELOW: *Pergolas are dramatic garden features even when unplanted, yet are relatively easy to build and install.*

are available in many colours and finishes, including transparent and imitation hardwood colours, as well as shamelessly synthetic, but none the less attractive shades, such as blue and lavender.

Applying treatments

❀ Most treatments are simply brushed on, but new wood will benefit from immersion in an appropriate treatment for at least an hour. Makeshift treatment baths are easy to improvise, using plastic sheeting supported on piled-up bricks.

❀ Always check that the preservative you are using is not hazardous to plants if you are applying it in a situation where it will be in direct contact with plants. Take appropriate safety precautions when applying treatments that are toxic and/or flammable. Work in a well-ventilated space. This may seem like unnecessary advice since you are working in the garden, but inclement weather may force you into an enclosed garage or other outbuilding, where it is all too easy for fumes to build up to a hazardous level.

❀ Wear gloves, goggles and a face mask when dealing with noxious substances, and have a good throughput of fresh air. Do not eat or drink while using chemicals.

❀ Ecologically friendly, water-based products are available but, unfortunately, most of the products that do a really effective, long-lasting weatherproofing job are still oil or spirit based, with the attendant problems of smell and toxicity.

BELOW: *Treating wooden fences not only makes them look better, but also protects your investment agains the elements.*

KNOWING THE CLIMATE

The climate in your garden is of critical importance in determining what you can grow, and how well it will do. Although some plants may tolerate a climate for which they are not ideally suited, they will never really thrive in it. For example, growing a sun-loving plant in a less-than-sunny spot will produce a plant that does not flower profusely, and may become straggly as it stretches out in an attempt to find the sun. It is far better, if you have a shady garden, to plant accordingly. Climate, of course, is not just about sunlight, but a complex blend of temperature, air humidity and wind, all of which affect the gardener's choices.

General climate

❀ The general climate is literally the climate general to your area. General climate is governed by latitude, altitude, proximity to the sea and the direction of the prevailing wind. Latitude affects temperature, thus gardens in the south are warmer than those in the north. As altitude increases, so the temperature drops, and rainfall and wind speed increase at high altitudes. Proximity to the sea increases rainfall and moderates temperature.

Local climate

❀ The local climate is a term used to describe the climate within your garden. The general climate may be modified within your own garden by a number of factors. For example, if you are generally in a very windy area but your garden is surrounded by bushes and trees, the level of wind within your garden is very much reduced from that outside it.

Microclimate

❀ Microclimate describes climate modified still further within your garden – the climate specific to particular areas of your garden. Although 'understanding and manipulating the microclimate' sounds quite technical, the concept is really very basic. Plan your planting according to existing microclimatic conditions for best results. For example, train fruit trees up a sunny, south-facing wall or fence. Having absorbed the sun's heat, a heat which is further retained by the wall and possibly added to by the heat generated from the house itself, the plant will flower and fruit well. A shade-loving plant would not flourish in this situation.

❀ As well as planting in harmony with the microclimate, it is possible to adapt and exploit it. For example, the sun may fall in one particular part of the garden only, perhaps in an awkward place and not on to the ground itself. Building a raised bed, possibly with a support behind it to further reflect and absorb the heat, will give you the opportunity to grow sun-loving flowers and food crops successfully.

BELOW: *If you live in an area of high snowfall, choose suitably sturdy plants that can withstand winter's worst.*

ABOVE: *Plants naturally accustomed to hot environments will need similarly sunny, dry conditions in order to flourish in the garden.*

Temperature and humidity

❁ Temperature and humidity are important factors in plant growth. Some plants need high temperatures and humidity in order to thrive. Dry, hot sites should be planted appropriately for best results. In very hot weather, some seeds will not germinate and plant transplantation is difficult as the soil dries out rapidly. Low temperatures bring their own problems, the most serious of which is frost.

Frost

❁ Frost is a weather condition that most gardeners quickly become aware and wary of. Late spring frosts are especially cruel to gardens. Just as the plants are starting into active growth and tender new shoots and buds are appearing, an unexpected frost can annihilate or very severely damage them. Ice crystals form within the plant cells. When the cell sap thaws, it expands. If the expansion is rapid, the cell walls split. Obviously, plants that are known to be tender (i.e. not frost resistant) will suffer most, and may be killed altogether. Half-hardy plants are of less certain frost resistance. They may or may not withstand frost conditions. To guarantee the survival of a half-hardy species in your garden, either protect it *in situ* or bring it under cover. Propagation is often undertaken to produce extra plants as an insurance policy against frost loss. Even supposedly frost-hardy plants may come under attack as their emerging, tender new top growth appears. In very severe frosts, woody plants may split their bark.

❁ In spring, every keen gardener watches the weather closely, trying to ascertain the magical moment in the season when the risk of frost has truly passed, so that bedding and tender vegetables can be safely planted out. It is soul destroying to see your healthy young plants, whether bought from the garden centre, or lovingly raised from seed or cuttings, blackened and shrivelled, possibly killed entirely, by a single brutal late frost. The only comfort is in knowing that every gardener gets caught out like this at least once. After planting out, pay attention to the local weather forecasts and keep a close eye on the weather, particularly as night falls. If frost is predicted, protect your plants accordingly. A general piece of advice is to delay planting for at least one week after you feel that it is really safe to plant out.

❁ Frost can affect plant roots, loosening the soil and lifting plants out of the ground, where their exposed roots are vulnerable to damage from low temperatures and drying winds (wind chill). Check for frost loosening and refirm affected plants.

BELOW: *Tropical plants require moist, fertile, sunny conditions that mimic their natural habitat.*

ABOVE: *Getting to know your garden in all seasons is vital: what may be a cool shady spot in summer may be prone to frost pockets in winter.*

ABOVE: *A beautiful garden equals a well-watered one, so be prepared for some hose-work if there is a sustained dry period.*

Frost pockets

❀ Because it is heavy, cold air falls so frost collects at the lowest point it can reach. This forms a frost pocket of air – an area particularly prone to all the risks associated with frost. Low sites, such as valleys and the land at the bottom of slopes, are potential frost pockets. If the cold air that forms in a valley cannot move freely away it will be forced back up the slope, increasing the area of potential damage. If the cold air descending a slope meets a solid barrier, such as a fence or a row of closely planted trees, it will form a frost pocket in front of it. Thinning out the trees or removing the obstacle altogether will allow the cold air to pass through. Vulnerable plants should not be grown in frost pockets unless you are prepared to protect them.

Rainfall

❀ Water is essential for plant survival. It is the main component of cell sap and is necessary for photosynthesis, the process by which plants manufacture food and transport nutrients. Seed germination and the development of shoots, roots, fruit, flowers and foliage all need a steady supply of water. Most garden plants depend largely on rainfall for their water requirements.

❀ Along with frost, drought is the other weather condition that gardeners will probably be most aware of and vigilant about in terms of plant care. A drought is a prolonged period – generally considered in the UK to be 15 consecutive days – without rain. However, plants can suffer in a much shorter time than this, particularly if they have been recently planted, so throughout the summer in particular, water your plants adequately in dry conditions. Some plants found in areas of low rainfall, such as cacti with their succulent, water-retentive tissues, are naturally adapted to drought conditions and are good choices for places where drought is a regular occurrence, or in particularly arid parts of the garden.

Wind

❀ Some wind in the garden is useful. It discourages disease, distributes pollen and seeds and reduces humidity. However, wind can also cause problems. On exposed sites, plants may be susceptible to damage such as wind scorch, which can kill new buds and blacken and wither leaves and stems. Of course, in very high winds such as in gale conditions plants can be partially broken or literally lifted out of the ground. Coastal sites are particularly prone to windy conditions and the wind from the sea is salt laden, which can further damage plants, even killing them if it reaches their roots.

❀ When planning a windbreak to ease the potential of plant damage, the temptation is to install a tall, solid barrier. However, this is counterproductive. A down-draught is caused in the lee of the barrier, resulting in increased, not reduced, turbulence. The solution is to allow approximately 50 per cent of the wind to permeate the windbreak. On a very exposed site, plan a series of windbreaks spaced approximately 10 times their height apart.

❀ Plant sympathetically. Harsh winds are very drying, so choose plants for a windy site that are well adapted to drought conditions. Plants of low-growing habit, planted closely together for more protection, will fare better on exposed sites than tall, vulnerable, willowy plants.

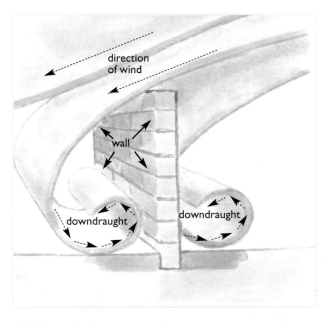

ABOVE: A solid wall or fence creates downdraughts on either side, which can harm plants.

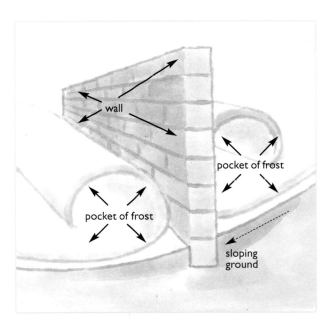

ABOVE: Potentially damaging frost pockets can occur on either side of a solid barrier on a sloping site.

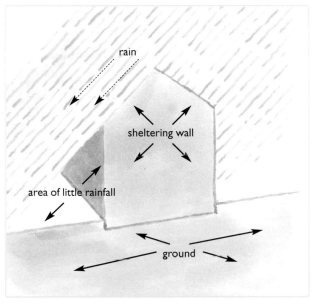

ABOVE: The area beside a sheltering wall receives little rain – this is the rain-shadow effect. Choose drought-tolerant plants for such a site.

KNOWING YOUR SOIL

Spend time assessing the type of soil that prevails in your garden. Some plants will positively thrive in particular types of soil, while others grown in the same soil will merely survive. Although you can alter your soil to suit particular plants by adding different topsoils, this is not generally recommended, particularly on larger areas of garden. It is expensive and labour intensive to implement and maintain. Contemporary garden thinking leans more towards planting in harmony with pre-existing conditions rather than artificially adapting them.

Soil types

❀ The character of soil is determined by the proportions of clay, sand and silt present within it. Sandy soil is virtually clay free, and composed of large, gritty particles, which make it free draining and easy to dig. Sandy soil warms rapidly in spring, but dries out quickly in drought conditions and both water and nutrients drain away freely.

❀ Silty soil also has a low clay content, but is more moisture retaining and fertile than sandy soil. It tends to compact, which means that water can run off its surface, making it difficult to feed adequately.

❀ Clay soil retains water well and is rich in nutrients, but becomes easily compacted. A dried-out clay soil is virtually brick-like and quite impossible to work. Even when not compacted, clay soil is heavy to work and slow to warm up.

BELOW: *Growing plants in conditions similar to their natural habitat leads to healthy specimens. These lupins are growing in well-drained, sandy soil, which mimics the conditions in which they grow wild.*

❀ Medium loam is the most desirable soil type for gardening, as it comprises approximately 50 per cent sand and 50 per cent silt and clay mix. It has a good crumb structure and holds food and water well.

Soil structure

❀ A cross-section of garden soil reveals three layers (or horizons) – topsoil, subsoil and a layer derived from the bedrock (parent rock).

❀ Generally, topsoil is dark because of its high organic content and is full of useful soil organisms.

❀ Subsoil is lighter in colour. It contains far fewer nutrients and less organic matter than topsoil and should not be brought to the surface when digging.

❀ If subsoil and topsoil are similarly coloured, the topsoil may be organically deficient.

❀ Some plots may have a soil pan, a hard horizontal layer on or beneath the surface of the soil, which prevents air and water moving freely to the area below.

❀ This impermeable layer can be caused by a number of factors, such as heavy rain on silty soil. It needs breaking up by double digging.

Soil pH

❀ The abbreviation pH stands for parts hydrogen and is used to indicate the level of acidity or alkalinity in soil – measured on a scale from 1 to 14. A reading of 7 indicates neutral soil; above 7, alkaline; below 7, acidic soil. It is important to ascertain the pH value of your soil, since pH affects the solubility of nutrients and therefore their availability to your plants.

❀ A good pH range for most plants is between 5.5 and 7.5. If your soil is dramatically acidic or alkaline, it is possible to adjust the pH, for example by adding lime to acidic soil.

❀ However, since maintenance of this adjustment is ongoing, it is more practical to select plants suited to extremes of soil pH, such as rhododendrons, which thrive on acidic soil, or fuchsias, which enjoy alkaline conditions.

TESTING FOR SOIL TEXTURE

1 Rub a handful of soil between your fingers. A sandy soil will feel gritty and granular and is impossible to form into a ball, even when moistened slightly.

2 A soil that feels smoother and more solid, and easily retains a shape pushed into it, has a high proportion of clay present.

3 Between these extremes fall the soil types that contain various minerals in differing proportions. Sandy clay is gritty and granular yet sticky and easy to mould.

TESTING SOIL pH LEVELS

1 Soil pH testing kits are in-expensive and easy to use. Add water to a small amount of soil in a test tube and shake well.

2 As the soil settles, the water changes colour to revel the level of acidity or alkalinity.

3 It is worth taking samples from various areas of the garden, as pH can vary within a single plot.

IMPROVING YOUR SOIL

Having assessed your soil, you will be aware of its properties and
possibly its problems. You will know its pH and its texture.
Even if you are not making drastic changes, but want to
improve drainage or moisture-retaining conditions, as well as
create a fertile environment for plants, soil improvement is
an important ongoing task.

IMPROVING SOIL STRUCTURE AND TEXTURE

DIGGING will improve soil structure, but for a significant improvement that will doubly repay the effort of digging over soil, add appropriate organic and inorganic matter at the same time.

The importance of humus

❧ Humus describes the partially decomposed organic matter that is full of micro-organisms. There are millions of bacteria and other organisms in a handful of earth, which break down leaves, dead roots and insects and transform them into nutrients, which feed living plants. Without humus, soil is essentially finely ground rock. Humus promotes good air flow through the soil and improves soil texture. It makes light soils more moisture retentive and heavy soil more workable. The humus balance is largely unchallenged in uncultivated soil, but garden planting makes demands on the humus content, which need to be regularly redressed.

Organic soil improvers

❧ Organic options include leaf mould, well-rotted farm manure, garden compost, peat, composted shredded bark and seaweed. All improve moisture retention and soil aeration. Some contain valuable nutrients and also stimulate the bacterial activity, which makes organic material into accessible plant food.

❧ Generally, matured organic matter is used since raw humus makers can damage plants: fresh manure emits ammonia and can burn plants; fresh leaves and straw increase bacterial activity, robbing the soil of nitrogen. Raw matter is best used before planting, or in areas well away from plant roots.

RIGHT: *Well-made garden compost is a fantastic soil conditioner, adding workability and fertility to the soil.*

Compost

❧ The satisfaction of applying your own garden compost to the soil is immense. Even the smallest garden should find room for a compost bin. Ecologically and economically sound, these may be constructed from scratch or purchased ready-made. Rotating bins are ideal for the smaller garden.

❧ Compost bins should never be regarded as rubbish dumps. Aim to produce a non-smelly, crumbly brown mixture that will enrich and improve your soil texture. Do not create problems for yourself by returning perennial weeds, diseased plants or plants treated with hormone weed killer to the soil.

Leaf mould

❧ Leaf mould is best composted separately as it breaks down slowly. It is not high in nutrients and is generally acidic so is not ideal for every soil or plant type, although acid-loving plants such as camellias and rhododendrons will love it. It is a good source of humus, improves soil texture and moisture retention, and is easy to make. Collect fallen leaves in autumn, particularly oak and beech leaves since these decompose quite fast. Store in a wire mesh bin or black plastic sack punctured with air holes and the leaf mould will be ready to use the following autumn.

Inorganic soil improvers

❀ Inorganic soil additives such as grit, gravel and coarse sand are useful for improving the workability and drainage of heavy soils.

❀ Fine sand can aggravate drainage problems by blocking soil pores, so use a coarser aggregate.

❀ Lime is often used on heavy clay soil to help bind the tiny particles together to a workable crumb. It also contains nutrients and acts on humus.

❀ Apply the soil improver in carefully measured doses, according to the manufacturer's directions, and only after testing the pH of your soil to assess whether lime is needed at all.

A COMPOST HEAP

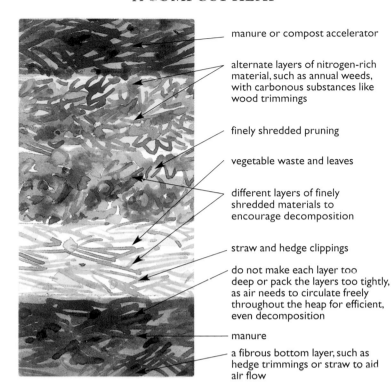

manure or compost accelerator

alternate layers of nitrogen-rich material, such as annual weeds, with carbonous substances like wood trimmings

finely shredded pruning

vegetable waste and leaves

different layers of finely shredded materials to encourage decomposition

straw and hedge clippings

do not make each layer too deep or pack the layers too tightly, as air needs to circulate freely throughout the heap for efficient, even decomposition

manure

a fibrous bottom layer, such as hedge trimmings or straw to aid air flow

MAKING A COMPOST BIN

The front of this box has removable sliding planks to give easy access to the front of the heap.

1 You will need four 85 cm (33 in) and two 80 cm (31 in) battens, plus ten 1 m x 16 cm (39 in x 6 in) and ten 60 x 16 cm (24 in x 6 in) planks, plus nails or screws. The wood should be water resistant.

2 To create the first side panel, place five of the 1 m x 16 cm planks across two of the 85 cm battens. Ensure the sawn ends of the plank are flush with the outside edge of the battens. There should be a 5 cm (2 in) gap between the bottom plank and end

of each batten. Using two nails or screws for each, attach the planks to the battens. Repeat to make the second side panel.

3 To create the back panel, hold these two side panels upright, one metre (39 in) apart, by nailing scrap wood to straddle their tops. Starting at the top, nail or screw five of the 60 x 15 cm planks onto the side panels, as shown in step 3. For the front panel, nail or screw the two 80 cm battens just inside each front upright to

create a housing for three of the 60 x 16 cm sliding planks, ensuring the planks fit between the battens.

4 To ensure stability of the bin when the front planks are removed, nail the two remaining 60 x 15 cm planks to the top and bottom of the front panel. You may want to nail a small piece of wood into the bottom in the space between each of the front battens to hold the sliding planks securely in place.

2

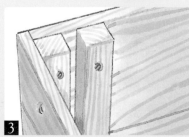
3

4

DRAINAGE

Adequate drainage is of vital importance in maintaining a healthy garden. Soil that drains too readily will require strenuous efforts to keep it adequately watered and fed, while very badly drained soil can actually kill some plants – their roots starved by a lack of oxygen caused by immersion in stagnant water. Healthy bacterial activity is slowed down in these conditions, while harmful organisms multiply readily, leading to diseases such as clubroot. Even if the roots are not killed by poor drainage, they will not be able to flourish. Root growth will be restricted and the resulting shallow root system will not be able to tap into deeper water sources in the event of drought.

ASSESSING DRAINAGE

THERE are varying levels of drainage problem, many of which may be remedied without recourse to major building works. Of course, there are some plants that thrive in both extremes of drainage condition. For example, alpines enjoy very freely drained soil, while bog plants love moist, marshy conditions. Thus you could choose to leave drainage conditions unaltered and plant accordingly.

❀ There is a simple, standard test for assessing the current drainage condition of a plot. It is worth performing at the planning stages of a garden. You will need to dig a hole approximately 60 cm (24 in) deep and 60 cm (24 in) square, and leave it exposed until heavy rain has fallen.

❀ If there is no water in the hole one hour after rain, your soil is excessively drained and you will need to take steps to conserve water, such as applying mulch. If there is no water in the hole a few days after rain, you have good drainage and need take no remedial action. If some water remains at the bottom of the hole a few days after rain, drainage is poor and you will need to take action to improve it, such as double digging and applying organic top dressings.

❀ If, after a few days, the hole is still quite full, even with additional water seeping in from the surrounding soil, drainage is impeded. Also observe the colour of the soil, especially towards the base of the hole. Soil with a blue-grey or yellow tinge, possibly with rust brown marks and a stagnant smell, indicates very poor drainage.

ABOVE: *Rather than trying to retain moisture in a naturally dry site, choose plants that enjoy arid conditions for the best results with minimal effort.*

DRAINAGE PROBLEMS

Excessive drainage

❀ Adding humus (partly decomposed organic matter) to the soil will help reduce water loss, as will non-organic mulches such as pebbles. The type of humus you choose depends on what you have available and what you want to grow. For example, mushroom compost is too high in lime to use on areas planted with rhododendrons.

Poor drainage

❀ Adding organic matter generously to the soil will improve conditions where drainage is not too severely restricted. Digging in lots of coarse sand or gravel will also help. Double digging breaks up the soil, producing a more readily drained soil structure. If surface water is the problem, it may be possible to shape garden surfaces so that water can run away freely into simple ditches or drains. You could also consider introducing raised beds, or adding more soil to heighten the soil level generally, to keep roots drier.

Impeded drainage

❀ Drainage will be severely restricted if your garden has non-porous rock close to the surface, a very high water table (the level at which water is held naturally within the ground) or a soil pan (hard layer below the surface). Artificial drainage methods then become necessary. There are several

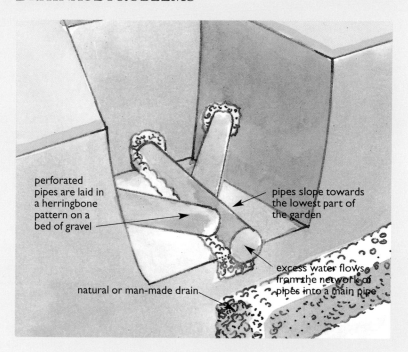

perforated pipes are laid in a herringbone pattern on a bed of gravel

pipes slope towards the lowest part of the garden

excess water flows from the network of pipes into a main pipe

natural or man-made drain

ABOVE: *If surface water is a serious problem in your garden and the water table is close to the surface, you may need to install a submerged drainage system.*

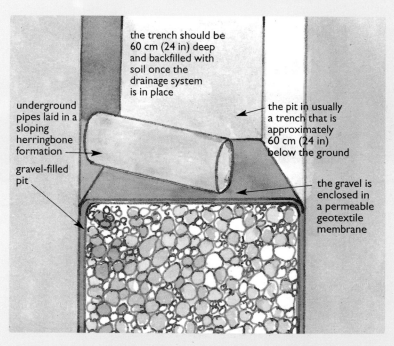

the trench should be 60 cm (24 in) deep and backfilled with soil once the drainage system is in place

underground pipes laid in a sloping herringbone formation

gravel-filled pit

the pit in usually a trench that is approximately 60 cm (24 in) below the ground

the gravel is enclosed in a permeable geotextile membrane

ABOVE: *A French drain is an unobtrusive solution to the problem of a badly waterlogged site.*

possibilities; the simplest is a French drain, a gravel-filled trench. More elaborate piped systems are generally best installed by professionals. If a piped system is planned on a flat site, the pipes will need to slope to allow water to flow away easily.

WATERING

All plants need water and the various watering requirements of different plants need to be considered when planning a garden. For example, if you live in an area of low rainfall or are gardening on a roof terrace exposed to drying wind, it is wise to consider planting to suit these conditions. Some plants cope well with dry conditions, for example succulents, which store water in their tissues, and silver-leaved plants, which are covered with fine hairs to help reduce evaporation.

Existing conditions

❀ Planting sympathetically to dry conditions significantly improves your chances of growing healthy plants, without necessitating an undue investment of time and effort in watering systems.

❀ Although it is possible to develop irrigation systems to deal with whatever conditions you face, it is more sensible to work on conserving the moisture available – for

BELOW: A sprinkler is invaluable for watering wide areas such as lawns and herbaceous borders evenly and gently.

example, surface mulching, adding moisture-conserving organic matter to your soil, and planting according to the level of moisture prevalent in your garden.

Effective watering

❀ Watering is a critical gardening task, so an accessible water supply is vital. Although an accessible kitchen tap and watering can will answer the needs of a very small plot, a garden tap is invaluable, along with a hose of sufficient length to reach the furthest part of the garden. Make sure that the tap and any exposed pipework is protected from frost in winter.

❀ Most novice gardeners water little and often, but this actually encourages shallow root growth and germination of weeds. Even a small garden will require a significant amount of watering in dry weather and a hose makes light work of this task. As a guide, an adequate level of watering in midsummer, on a fast-draining soil, would be approximately 10–20 litres per sq m (2–4 gallons per sq yd) – roughly two watering cans full. This demonstrates that simply sprinkling over the border with a single watering can full is inadequate, and will lead to plant problems. Never water in full sun as you risk leaf scorch, and the water will evaporate very quickly from the soil's surface.

Watering container plants

❀ Plants in containers lose water rapidly through evaporation. Group containers together to help conserve moisture. Make plans for watering if you are going away in summer or, at the very least, move containers to a shady place; otherwise you may arrive home to a collection of dead plants.

❀ Incorporating water-retaining granules into the compost at planting time is useful. These granules swell to form a gel capable of holding large quantities of water, which is gradually released into the compost. This is particularly useful for containers especially prone to rapid moisture loss, such as hanging baskets with their large exposed surface area yet small amount of soil, and terracotta pots, whose porosity allows for quick evaporation. Applying a surface mulch will also help retain moisture.

Automated systems

❀ If you garden on a particularly dry site and wish to grow thirsty plants, such as vegetables, or if you wish to simplify your watering duties, consider installing a permanent watering system.

❀ Drip-feed systems comprise tubes fitted with drip heads to trickle water on to particular areas, such as shrubs in a border or growing bags. Unless fitted with a timer, drip-feed systems can waste water, and they need regular cleaning to keep the tubes and heads clear.

❀ Seep hoses are another option. These are flattened hoses punctured finely along their length. They are useful for watering large areas such as lawns, and are ideal for watering rows of vegetables evenly.

ABOVE: *A watering can is a perennial gardening essential, and it is worth investing in a good quality metal one for long-term use.*

PLANTING A CONTAINER USING WATER-RETAINING GEL

1 *With the addition of a liner and drainage holes, an old basket can be used as a container for plants. To reduce the need for watering, mix water-retaining gel with the compost before you begin, following the manufacturer's directions regarding quantities. Place a layer of crocks over the base of the container, followed by a layer of compost.*

2 *Add the shrubs and larger bulbs of your choice to the basket.*

3 *Backfill with compost before adding smaller bulbs. Firm the compost gently and water.*

4 *For instant colour, fill the basket with some flowering plants.*

PLANT FOODS

Plants need a balanced diet of nutrients in order to thrive.
Plants use the essential elements in soil more quickly than they can be
replenished naturally, for example by the gradual decomposition of
fallen leaves. Substantial amounts of potassium, phosphorus and
nitrogen are lost when ground is cultivated. These major nutrients
are needed in large quantities to maintain good growth, so additional
feeding is required. Potassium promotes disease resistance and
produces healthy fruits and flowers. Phosphorus is needed for
good root development, and nitrogen for healthy growth and foliage.
The amount of nutrients required depends on the plants grown and
how intensively the soil is used. For example, an alpine rock garden
is much less hungry than a densely sown vegetable border.

Organic fertilisers

❀ Organic fertilisers are essentially matter derived from
living organisms, be they animal or plant in origin, such
as fish meal, bone meal or dried blood. They are natural
products, generally slow acting, and not as likely to
scorch foliage as inorganic fertilisers might if inapp-
ropriately used. Organic fertilisers generally provide
plants with a steady supply of food over a long period.

growmore

natural
manure

Inorganic fertilisers

❀ Inorganic fertilisers are not necessarily unnatural. Some
are derived from earth minerals, such as Chilean potash
nitrate; others are synthetically manufactured. Inorganic
fertilisers are very concentrated and fast acting.
Overdosing can result in scorched plants, so great care
must be taken to follow manufacturer's directions
accurately when applying. Inorganic fertilisers are often
used to give plants a quick boost of nutrients.

Soil conditioners

❀ Fertiliser feeds the soil, but does not alter the soil
structure. For example, it cannot make a heavy soil more
open. Soil conditioners such as animal manure add
nutrients, but the amount of food is minute in
comparison to the quantity of material which will need
to be applied. The benefit of adding manure and compost
to the soil is that in addition to their soil nutritional
qualities, they can improve moisture retention and soil
workability. In the longer term, they decompose to form
humus, the dead and live bacteria within soil which is its
life force, facilitating the effective absorption of plant
foods, promoting air flow and improving drainage.

bone meal

TYPES OF FERTILISER

FERTILISERS are available in different forms, including liquids, powders and pellets. The form chosen will depend on the type of plant, the season of application and the soil type.

Dry fertilisers

❀ These are nutrients in a dried form – granules, pellets or powder – which are sprinkled directly on to the soil. They are very concentrated and it is critically important to apply them evenly and in appropriate quantities, following the manufacturer's directions, to avoid plant damage.

Liquid fertilisers

❀ These may be bought either in liquid form, or as powder which is to be diluted in water before application. They are generally safer and easier to use than dry fertilisers, and are usually quick acting. Some liquid fertilisers are designed for foliar feeding. Application to the leaves means that the nutrients enter the sap stream quickly, which can be a useful technique if you are trying to resuscitate a sick plant.

Feeding container plants

❀ Container-grown plants need particular feeding care. The amount of soil in a container is limited, so any available nutrients are quickly exhausted by the plant. Regular watering also washes away nutrients through the drainage holes. Slow-release fertilisers worked into the compost when planting, or added as top dressing, are a good solution. If additional feeding is needed, for example if the plant shows visible signs of deficiency, this longer-term feeding programme may be supplemented by foliar feeding or by adding a quick-release fertiliser. Fertiliser spikes, small sticks that gradually release nutrients into the soil, are a convenient way of feeding container plants.

ABOVE: *Organic fertilisers include compost made from coconut husks, which can be used for potting and seeding.*

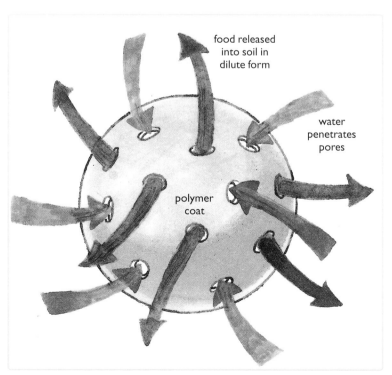

food released into soil in dilute form

water penetrates pores

polymer coat

ABOVE: *The food-releasing pattern of slow-release fertiliser is hard to assess as it is affected by the soil's moisture content, pH level and temperature. However, it is an undeniably simple way of feeding plants and is becoming increasingly popular.*

ABOVE: *There are many general-purpose fertilisers on the market; these are suitable for most conditions and uses.*

DIGGING

❦

Digging may not be the easiest or most exciting garden task, but it has many important functions, particularly on soil that is being newly cultivated. Digging improves the texture and workability in two ways. The spade physically breaks up compacted soil initially. Frost and drying winds further break up the exposed clods. Digging also offers an opportunity for incorporating substances into the soil that can help its fertility, humus-making ability, drainage and moisture retention. What you add will depend on the type of soil you have. Digging also makes it easy to remove perennial weeds and bury annual ones.

HOW TO DIG

IT IS all too easy to injure your back when digging. Digging is hard physical exercise and needs to be taken as seriously as any physical workout. Digging is usually done in autumn, when the weather has become colder; yet each year, thousands of gardeners embark on a bout of heavy digging without warming up their muscles gradually. Combine this sudden shock to the chilled body with a careless digging technique and you have a recipe for severe back pain.

❀ Wrap up warmly for digging. Acclimatise your body to exertion gradually by embarking on some more gentle gardening tasks before starting to dig. Do not overestimate the amount you will be able to dig, especially on your first session. You could all too easily hurt your back so badly that you will not be able to complete the task at all. Finally, and crucially, take care to use the correct posture when digging, treat your body with respect and never lift more weight than you can comfortably handle.

USING A SPADE CORRECTLY

1 *Press one foot down evenly on the blade and insert the spade vertically into the soil. The handle of the spade will be sloping slightly away from you if the blade has been inserted at a true vertical, giving you valuable additional leverage.*

2 *Pull the handle towards you. Slide one hand down the spade towards the blade. Holding the spade on the ferrule with this hand, and*

with the other hand still at the top of the spade, bend your knees and evenly lever out the soil. Work smoothly, not with jerky, sudden movements, which can jar your back.

3 *Gradually lift the soil on to the spade, taking the strain by gently straightening your legs, not jerking your back up suddenly. Never lift more soil than you are comfortable with at one time.*

DIGGING TECHNIQUES

AUTUMN and early winter are the best seasons for digging. At this time of year the soil is generally in an ideal condition – neither baked hard dry by the sun, nor saturated with water. The turned clods will also gradually be broken down by the elements over winter, to improve soil texture. Never dig when the ground is frozen or waterlogged as this will severely damage the structure of the soil, and always use the correct tool for the job. Your spade should be comfortably sized, so that it is not an effort to lift it, and an appropriate length for your height, to reduce the risk of back strain.

Although digging has many significant benefits, its role has gradually been viewed as being of diminished importance in recent times. For many years, garden experts prescribed complex and labour-intensive digging methods such as trenching (digging three spits deep). Simple, single and double digging are the techniques widely used and recommended today. Contemporary thinking generally veers towards double digging newly cultivated soil only once. Keen vegetable gardeners may repeat this double digging every few years, but most gardeners will use the single digging technique in subsequent years.

Simple digging

❀ Simple digging is the easiest and quickest digging technique. Since it does not involve any trench work, it is the only really practical way of digging in the sort of confined space created in a garden border filled with many permanent plantings.

❀ Simple digging literally involves simply digging. A spadeful of soil is picked up and turned over back on to its original position, then briskly chopped up with the spade.

❀ When you have dug the soil, leave it alone for approximately three weeks before growing anything in it. This will allow newly buried annual weeds to die, and give the soil time to settle. The weather will act on the soil surface to break it down into smaller clods. The soil will then be much easier to cultivate to the fine tilth needed for planting or sowing.

ABOVE: *As you lift the soil from the trench, slide your hand towards the blade and straighten up slowly without jerking your back.*

Single digging

❁ Single digging is a methodical way of ensuring that an area is cultivated evenly and to a specific depth. The ground is dug to a single spade's depth as you work systematically to produce rows of trenches. As each trench is dug, the soil being lifted is placed in the neighbouring trench.

❁ Although a spade is generally used, a fork may be a more comfortable choice when working on heavy soil.

RIGHT: *Digging over the soil before planting improves soil structure and allows you to incorporate the humus-making substances, such as manure, which are so beneficial to plants.*

SINGLE DIGGING

1 *Starting at a marked line, drive the spade vertically into the soil to the full depth of the blade. Remove the soil and place in a wheelbarrow, ready to carry to the opposite end of the plot.*

2 *Dig along the line to produce a trench 30 cm (12 in) wide, and the depth of the spade.*

3 *Dig a second trench parallel with the first. Fill the first trench with the soil from the second trench, incorporating organic matter as required. Twist the spade to aerate the soil as you place it in the first trench.*

4 *Continue digging trenches until you reach the other end of the plot, filling the final trench with the soil from the first trench.*

Double digging

❀ This deep form of digging improves drainage by breaking up any hard subsurface pan in the soil. Double digging is generally regarded as necessary for previously uncultivated soil prior to sowing or planting, and wherever drainage is poor. In double digging the soil is literally dug to double the depth of the spade or fork, and the trenches are twice as wide as those produced for single digging.

❀ It is critically important not to bring subsoil to the surface, as this will adversely affect soil fertility. You will need to ascertain the depth of the topsoil before starting to double dig. If the topsoil is more than two spade depths (known as 'spits') deep, then you have no problem. You can simply transfer the soil from one trench to the other as for single digging.

❀ If the topsoil is only one spit deep, you will need to ensure that the topsoil and subsoil are kept separate and distinct so that the subsoil goes back on the bottom of the neighbouring trench, with the topsoil on top – not mixed together or the other way around.

❀ You will need both a spade and a fork for double digging. Always dig at the right season for your soil. Dig medium and heavy soils in autumn and early winter; dig over very heavy soil before winter sets in.

❀ Sandy soil may be dug in winter or early spring. If you dig too early you may encourage a fine crop of weeds. Always make sure that the soil is not saturated with water, nor frozen solid, before planning to dig. Similarly, it is not prudent to dig when the soil has dried hard after a prolonged period without rain.

DOUBLE DIGGING

1 Mark out the plot with a garden line. Dig the first trench approximately 60 cm (24 in) wide, and as deep as the head of the spade. As with single digging, collect the soil from this trench in a barrow, ready to take to the opposite end of the plot when the barrow is full.

2 Standing in the trench, break up the soil at the bottom of the trench to the depth of the fork tines. Incorporate organic matter such as manure if required.

3 Mark out another trench parallel to the first. Dig out this trench, placing the soil from here in the first trench.

4 Fork the bottom of the new trench and continue to the next trench. Work your way across the plot until you reach the opposite end. Fill the final trench with soil removed from the first trench.

TOP DRESSINGS
AND MULCHES

Top dressing describes the superficial application of fertiliser and other additives, such as sand, to the surface of the soil or lawn. It is also used as a general term, encompassing any sort of superficial dressing of the soil, including mulching. Top dressings and mulches are applied to the surface of the soil for several reasons. They all help plant growth in one or more ways. All help reduce moisture loss by evaporation. Some add nutrients to the soil, enrich the humus content of the soil and improve soil texture and workability. Some, such as gravel, have no nutritional value but are used to aid drainage, regulate soil temperature, deter pests such as slugs, and suppress the growth of weeds, moss, lichen and other undesirable organisms on the surface of the soil. In addition, a simple gravel top dressing is also very decorative in its own right.

USING TOP DRESSINGS
AND MULCHES

Top dressings and mulches may be the unsung heroes of the garden border. They don't look terribly exciting in the garden centre, but they have an immense amount to offer every gardener – from the apartment dweller with a solitary window box dressed with an attractive, moisture-retaining, weed- and pest-deterring aggregate, to someone with a large vegetable garden using plastic sheeting for purely practical reasons.

ABOVE: A natural mulch, such as shredded cedar bark, helps suppress weed growth and conserve moisture, yet is an attractive, unobtrusive material.

Applying mulch

❀ Always apply mulch to warm, moist soil. If mulch is
applied to a frozen or dry soil, you will find that it just
works against you, simply sealing in the problems.
Similarly, if organic mulch is applied to a soil rife with
weeds, the weeds will benefit as much as the desirable
plants, reaping the benefits of an enriched soil and
improved moisture retention, and growing even more
profusely than in an unmulched soil. The overall
guiding principle of applying mulch, therefore, is to
think carefully before using it, taking care not to seal
in any problems, which will be aggravated by the
insulating properties of all mulch.

❀ Apply a generous layer of mulch, approximately 7.5 cm
(3 in) deep, spreading it out from the plant to cover
roughly the same area as the potential growth spread of
the plant itself. Apply up to, but not touching plant
stems, as this can encourage rotting.

ORGANIC MULCHES

MULCHES can be divided into organic and inorganic
types. They share many attributes, some organic
mulches having the added benefits of nutritional value.
This is not always desirable, however, as described
above. For example, garden compost has many good
properties, but it also provides a perfect environment
for germinating weeds. It is therefore not the best choice
for weed suppression.

Bark

❀ Available in a variety of scales, from finely shredded to
large chunks, bark is a popular mulch. It improves
surface drainage and suppresses weeds. Coarsely
shredded bark takes a long time to break down,
repaying the initial investment, as it should last two
years before it needs replacing.

❀ Bark is also sufficiently heavy not to blow about the
garden. It is very attractive, and is often used to top
dress borders. Bark is slightly acidic, a quality that
diminishes when it begins to decompose, so only
apply composted (matured) bark as a mulch. Soil
dressed with bark will need supplementing with a
nitrogenous fertiliser.

woodchip mulch

leaf mould mulch

dried bark mulch

Cocoa shells

✿ Cocoa shells smell wonderful, as if applying a blanket of grated chocolate to the soil. Apart from this sybaritic benefit, a cocoa shell mulch is very attractive, making it the next most popular ornamental border mulch after bark. Cocoa shell's are slightly acidic, so soil dressed with them will need to be supplemented with fertiliser. Until cocoa shells settle, they are also very lightweight and susceptible to being distributed around the garden by wind and birds. They are also quite expensive.

cocoa shells

Farmyard manure

✿ Once popular, farmyard manure has lost popularity as a mulch in the flower border. It does help the humus content of the soil and has some nutritional benefit, as well as its moisture-retaining and soil-texturising properties. However, it is not attractive, is often smelly, and its fertility promotes weed growth. It must be used only when well rotted, or it may damage your plants.

farmyard manure

woven black plastic

ABOVE: *Mulching helps keep weeds at bay while young plants are becoming established.*

INORGANIC MULCHES

INORGANIC mulches, especially sheet types, are excellent at retaining soil moisture. They are also superb at suppressing weeds because light is excluded totally from the soil, preventing weed germination. Obviously, they do not assist humus production or add nutrients to the soil. If you do need to enrich the soil beneath sheet mulch, pierce it and apply soluble fertiliser through the holes.

Woven black plastic

✿ Excellent for mulching between rows of vegetables, this is initially expensive but it is reusable.

Fibre fleece

✿ Used mainly to raise soil temperature, this is often used as a 'floating' mulch and pest barrier. It is used almost like a cloche – applied over, not around, crops.

fibre fleece

Black plastic

✿ This cheap mulch raises soil temperature and suppresses weeds, but is not attractive unless covered with a more decorative substance such as gravel. It is popular in vegetable plots.

Grit

❀ Grit is useful for improving drainage and is very attractive. To keep weeds at bay, grit is best applied over plastic sheeting. Coarse grit is often used as a slug and snail deterrent, since these creatures dislike moving across its sharp surface.

grit

Pebbles/gravel

❀ This is an attractive and popular inorganic choice. Choose well-washed products, free of soil particles that might bind the stones together, hosting weeds.

gravel

pebbles

TOP DRESSINGS

Some materials are used on the soil around plants, or on lawns, not for their mulching properties, but to improve the soil nutritionally and texturally. Always follow the manufacturer's directions precisely when applying top dressings. Keep solid dressings off foliage and plant stems, since fertiliser can scorch.

Lime

❀ Lime is available in many forms, such as chalk, ground limestone and magnesium limestone. The most popular form is hydrated (slaked) lime. Lime is a plant food, and makes other plant foods available by acting on humus to free the elements necessary for good plant growth. Lime removes sourness from the soil by neutralising acidity. Few plants thrive in very acidic conditions. Lime also breaks up heavy soil and encourages beneficial bacteria and organisms such as earthworms to flourish. A pH test will determine whether or not you need to lime your soil. Even a neutral soil will benefit from reliming every few years, since rain washes lime from the soil. Alkaline soil must not be limed, as it already has sufficient lime. Lime is generally applied after digging, in the autumn.

Fertiliser

❀ Fertilisers contain one or more nutrients in a concentrated form, and are added to the soil to feed plants. They must not be confused with humus makers, since they do not share their important attributes. Fertilisers should not be used in isolation. Without humus makers, the plants cannot utilise the food provided by the fertilisers. Fertiliser as a top dressing is usually applied in the spring.

Humus makers

❀ Bulky organic matter is used as a top dressing to improve soil texture and build up the bacterial population, thereby releasing nutrients to the plants. Humus makers do not have a significant amount of nutritional value compared with their bulk, and so need to be used in conjunction with fertilisers for optimum benefits. Organic top dressings are usually applied in the autumn.

PLANT PROBLEMS AND WEED CONTROL

Viewed as a whole, this section can appear daunting – depressing even, with its litany of weeds, pests and diseases. However, with careful planting and garden maintenance there is no need to suppose that your garden will play host to all the ailments and problems listed here. Good-quality, healthy plants, given optimum growing conditions, will stand an excellent chance of resisting disease and throwing off pest problems. Practise careful hygiene and vigilant observation, so that you can tackle problems as soon as they occur.

PREVENTION

THE maxim 'prevention is better than cure' applies particularly to gardens. Increasingly, gardeners are turning away from the chemical control of problems, recognising that to rely on chemicals, for example in pesticides and fungicides, can create more problems than they cure. Helpful predators may be eradicated along with the pests, leading to an even worse pest problem.

❀ You may be a gardener who has diligently sprayed your garden against aphids for years, and wonder why, one long hot summer, your garden is plagued with aphids, while your neighbour's unsprayed plot is aphid free. The reason is that you have gradually wiped out the predators who are now so obligingly policing your neighbour's unsprayed garden. Of course, the wider global issues of pollution and the potential dangers from chemicals, as well as the matter of slowly destroying the ecosystem within your own garden, are also of concern when thinking about how to tackle plant problems.

ABOVE: *Some diseases, such as clubroot, can quickly affect an entire crop, so it is worth being vigilant about plant health.*

Keeping problems in perspective

❀ The first thing to consider, before becoming hysterical about pests and diseases and automatically reaching for the nearest chemical spray, is to get matters into perspective. Some pests may be unsightly, but are actually not as hazardous to a plant as other threats, such as inclement weather. In fact, in general, weather issues are a much bigger risk to plant health than individual pests – something it is worth bearing in mind when you first spot a single caterpillar perched on your precious cabbages.

❀ The second biggest plant enemy is bad gardening practice. For example, overcrowding your plants leaves them prone to infection. Poor hygiene is another plant hazard. If you do not remove diseased material and burn, deeply bury or compost it well, you are inviting further plant troubles.

❀ This gives you some idea of the responsibility you have as a gardener. Your aim should be to maintain plant

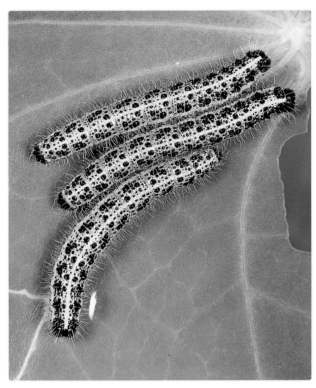

ABOVE: *A group of honeysuckle aphids cluster on the denuded axial of a leaf.*

ABOVE: *Large white butterfly caterpillars, pictured here on a damaged nasturtium leaf, are pests common to brassica crops and some ornamental plants.*

health, rather than allow problems to occur and get out of hand; and then curse the pests, who are in fact way down in the ranks of plant difficulties.

Minimising problems

❀ Keeping your garden healthy by careful and consistent adherence to gardening basics will go an enormous way towards preventing pests and diseases from overwhelming your plants. With the huge variety of plants on offer, it makes sense firstly to choose healthy looking specimens of disease-resistant strains, and plant them appropriately.

❀ A plant grown in the particular type of soil it needs, and where it can receive the amount of light it requires, has much more of a chance of surviving without problems than a plant grown without respect for its natural demands. Take care to provide the appropriate level of water, remembering that too much can be just as injurious as too little.

❀ Spacing is an important consideration. Plants grown too close together will compete for nutrients, and the congested, humid conditions will encourage fungal disease. Follow the guidelines for optimum spacing that appear on individual plant labels.

❀ Garden hygiene is a factor often overlooked as being of serious concern in preventing problems. After all, muck is muck – at least visually. However, it is all too easy to transfer disease through poor hygiene, for example by planting in uncleaned pots, which may carry disease spores, or by propagating using a knife that has not been sterilised.

COMMON PESTS

THERE are a number of common pests that are a widespread problem for gardeners and attack a wide variety of plants.

Aphids

✿ Aphids are widely thought of as the ultimate garden scourge. They suck sap and excrete the excess as a sticky residue, which falls on foliage where it can turn mouldy. Emerging shoots and leaves can be damaged, and affected plants can become distorted and disfigured. Aphids can spread viral diseases between plants such as roses, lilies and tulips. Sooty mould often accompanies aphid attack, since the fungus lives on the 'honeydew' secreted by aphids.

✿ Ladybirds and hoverflies are the best organic control for aphids. Attract them by planting poached egg flowers (*Limnanthes douglasii*) and *Convolvulus tricolor*. Physically place ladybirds on affected leaves.

✿ Companion planting can help in other ways. You could plant sacrificial crops. For example, nasturtiums planted near broccoli are likely to suffer from aphid attack, leaving the broccoli clear. Chives deter aphids and are a pretty edging plant, making them an excellent choice for the herbaceous border.

✿ Spraying with a soft soap – not detergent – solution works well, too. In the greenhouse, parasitic controls are useful. In all cases, simply removing the aphids by hand is also effective and organically sound.

✿ The non-organic approach, possible on vulnerable non-food crops, uses selective systemic insecticides, which leaves beneficial insects unharmed.

Earwigs

✿ The distinctive pincers of the earwig are not generally seen during the day, since they feed at night. They shred the leaves and eat the flowers of plants such as dahlias, chrysanthemums and clematis. Earwigs are not all bad, however. They do eat quite a number of aphids, so if your plants are not being damaged, do not automatically operate a 'search and destroy' mission. To check whether earwigs are responsible for decimated flowers and leaves, investigate by torchlight.

✿ Inverted flowerpots, stuffed with straw and suspended on canes, will attract and trap earwigs, which can then be removed and disposed of.

Slugs and snails

✿ Slugs and snails attack many types of plant, including bulbs, herbaceous perennials, vegetables, strawberries,

ABOVE: *Earwigs shred the leaves of certain ornamental plants such as dahlias and can also attack food crops, but since they eat some aphids and codling moth eggs they are not generally considered a serious garden pest.*

ABOVE: *Aphids are a garden scourge, wreaking havoc on a wide variety of plants by damaging and distorting new leaves and shoots, as well as weakening the plant as a whole.*

ABOVE: *A shiny red lily beetle* (Lilioceris lilii) *on a damaged lily leaf.*

ABOVE: *An adult cock chafer* (Melolontha melolontha) *devours fresh green buds on a leaf.*

climbing plants and young seedlings. Although most live on top of the soil, some attack the underground parts of plants such as bulbs, as well as tubers like potatoes. Slugs and snails feed primarily at night or after rain.

❀ Some plants are particularly susceptible to slug and snail attack, such as hostas, delphiniums and all young seedlings. Plants known to be vulnerable should be protected with physical barriers, such as crushed eggshells, sawdust, wood ash or sharp sand.

❀ Slugs have sensitive skin and do not like crawling over these surfaces, but be aware that the barrier is only effective as long it is unbroken. Rain can easily break down these barriers, so either check regularly and replenish or choose a very effective (though not very attractive) barrier method – a ring 10 cm (4 in) high, cut from a plastic bottle and pushed 2.5 cm (1 in) into the ground.

❀ Slug 'pubs', containers of tempting fermenting beer sunk into the soil, are also a popular way of disposing of slugs without recourse to chemicals. However, these traps also drown beneficial creatures, unless you provide twiggy ladders in each one for ground beetles and the like.

❀ Inverted grapefruit skin halves are also used. The slugs congregate within, ready for you to dispose of as you see fit – either by removing them to a distant place, or drowning them. However, you will need quite a number of traps to catch the quantities of slugs that congregate in most gardens, especially in moist conditions. Dedicated gardeners may be driven to seeking out slugs by torchlight, before giving them a burial at sea.

❀ Apart from mechanical and barrier methods, another organic option is a parasitic nematode, which can be watered on to the soil to kill slugs and snails.

❀ Methiocarb or metaldehyde slug pellets can affect animals higher up the food chain, such as birds and cats, and should be regarded as an absolute last resort. Aluminium sulphate pellets should harm only slugs and snails, but could leach aluminium salts into crops. Organic gardeners would not use these types of control.

BELOW: *Slugs are notoriously hard to eliminate but any effort to do so is worthwhile since, like snails, slugs cause damage not only to seedlings, but to all parts of a wide variety of mature plants.*

ABOVE: *Caterpillar damage on cabbage leaves.*

ABOVE: *This cabbage is displaying classic club root symptoms.*

Caterpillars and chafers

❀ There are many types of caterpillar, the most notorious of which is the caterpillar of the cabbage white butterfly. Caterpillars eat foliage, stems, flowers and fruits. Some caterpillars conceal themselves by curling up in young leaves or protecting themselves in a silk-like webbing, so if you see curled leaves and webbing, unroll them to investigate further. Leatherjackets are greyish-brown caterpillars, the larvae of crane flies. These soil-dwelling caterpillars eat the roots of young seedlings, immature plants and lawn grass.

❀ Remove any caterpillars by hand as soon as you notice them. There is an organically acceptable bacterial control, *Bacillus thuringiensis*, suitable for cabbage white caterpillar attacks. Alternatively, you can use special sticky bands of grease designed to prevent flightless pests like caterpillars climbing up the plants.

❀ Although, if left unchecked, caterpillars can munch their way unattractively through ornamentals, such as nasturtiums, as well as food crops like cabbages, the problem is not always critical. Nibbled leaves may look less than lovely, but often, only the external leaves are affected, the caterpillars having departed before the cabbage starts its main growth spurt.

PLANT DISEASES

THE general guidelines for good garden hygiene apply particularly to keeping disease at bay. Remove potential sources of infection by disinfecting pots, trays, canes and other equipment at the end of each season. Diligently remove and dispose of decaying, diseased or dead material by pruning out problem areas. Clear away plant debris that falls naturally, as these leaves and twigs may harbour fungal spores, which would reinfect plants the following spring.

❀ Practise crop rotation. This means not growing the same bedding plants or vegetables in the same spot each year. Overwintering pests and diseases emerge in spring to find that their target has vanished.

❀ Choose disease-resistant plant species where possible and plant them at the appropriate spacing. Keep the garden weed free, well watered and mulched.

Mildews

❀ These fungal diseases attack stressed plants, particularly those that have become dry at the roots and are in stagnant air conditions. Avoid overcrowding plants and keep them consistently watered and mulched in order to prevent this disease, which devours affected leaves and shoots from the outside. Downy mildew is more serious than powdery mildew, as it can penetrate the leaves and eventually kill the plant.

❀ Planting alliums in generous quantities near plants known to be susceptible to mildew is said to offer increased protection. Since alliums look spectacular paired with roses, this is a companion planting suggestion well worth trying but, as always, careful attention to spacing and watering of vulnerable plants is of prime importance.

❀ Remove affected areas to reduce the spread of mildew. There are some organic sprays available, such as those made of nettles or garlic, which claim to improve mildew resistance.

❀ The non-organic approach is to spray with a chemical fungicide, in addition to following the general guidelines on plant hygiene and care.

Grey mould *(botrytis)*

❀ Another fungal disease, which thrives in cool, damp conditions, *botrytis* is an unsightly grey mould, which covers leaves, stems and fruit. Poorly ventilated conditions, such as inside inadequately aired greenhouses or cloches, encourage the condition, as does overcrowding. Strawberries are particularly vulnerable to grey mould. Improve air flow and provide drier conditions to prevent and arrest the problem. Remove and destroy all affected parts of the plant.

❀ In addition to these measures, fungicides can also be used to control *botrytis* – there are organically acceptable ones available.

Rusts

❀ Rusts are a collection of fungal diseases that discolour leaves and encourage them to drop prematurely. They flourish in similar conditions to those that harbour mildews – that is, dank, overcrowded environments. Prevention guidelines are similar to those given for mildew. Take care to provide good ventilation and plant at appropriate spacings. Remove affected areas. Organically acceptable fungicides are available.

Wilts and rots

❀ Soil-dwelling organisms can cause plants to wilt – particularly chrysanthemums, clematis, tomatoes and carnations. Good plant hygiene and garden husbandry will help prevent wilt, which affects weak and generally unhealthy plants. Use fresh, sterile compost for seeds and cuttings, as wilt often attacks new seedlings. In the border, incorporating good quality garden compost will help plant health as the beneficial organisms it contains will help control any bad ones.

COMMON PLANT DISORDERS

1. *Uneven germination caused by damping off in lobelia seedlings.*

2. *A shot hole caused by bacterial canker on cherry leaves.*

3. *A viral disease on a Pelargonium, causing leaf venation.*

4. *Coral spot fungal fruiting bodies on the dying wood of an ornamental tree mallow.*

5. *Grey mould damage on the leaves of a Pelargonium plant.*

6. *Powdery mildew affecting the foliage of Achillea ptarmica 'The Pearl' in late flowering.*

7. *Close-up of the underside of a rose leaf, showing black teliospore pustules.*

PLANT DISORDERS

SOME plants may appear to have suffered pest or disease damage, but are actually displaying signs of nutritional deficiency or a physiological disorder. Common sense plant care will go a long way towards preventing these problems. For example, planting an acid-loving plant such as an azalea in a heavily alkaline soil is not going to produce a happy, healthy plant, unless the soil local to the plant is regularly adapted to its needs. Such a plant, grown in an alkaline soil, would show stunted growth and yellowing leaves, the symptoms of lime-induced chlorosis (manganese/iron deficiency). Protecting plants from weather damage, be it frost or drought, is also a basic element of garden practice that will give your plants the best possible chance of healthy growth. You will do well to learn to recognise the common plant disorders.

Nitrogen deficiency

❀ Pale green plants that eventually turn yellow, with weak, thin, pinkish-coloured stems and stunted growing tips can indicate a nitrogen deficiency. Older leaves turn yellowish-red along the veins and die off. The whole plant will have its growth checked and generally become spindly and unhealthy looking. Growing plants in restricted conditions where they are inadequately fed, or in poor, light soil can cause nitrogen deficiency. This is the commonest plant disorder as nitrogen is so readily leached out of the soil. Make sure your plants have a soil that is adequately fertile, regularly dressed with well-rotted manure and balanced fertilisers. As an emergency remedy where deficiency has been noticed, a high-nitrogen fertiliser or liquid feed can be applied.

Waterlogging

❀ When plant roots suffer a lack of oxygen, the plant becomes waterlogged (unless it is a bog plant). Although there is obviously plenty of water, the plant will wilt as if it was being under watered and its leaves will yellow. If you lift the plant, you may see black, even rotten roots, as the plant starts to die back. To prevent this condition, provide adequate drainage by regularly digging in plenty of organic matter to improve the soil structure. If the problem occurs in containers, there may be inadequate drainage holes, or they may have become clogged with debris. If you have localised areas in the garden that are particularly prone to waterlogging, then you might want to consider growing plants in raised beds. If the problem is more widespread, consider installing drainage pipes, or grow plants suited to boggy conditions.

ABOVE: *Potato plants, showing the effects of drought in a dried-up vegetable patch.*

ABOVE: *The effects of leaf scorch on daffodil plants, causing fused leaves and flowers.*

Drought

❀ When plants suffer a prolonged water shortage, they wilt and collapse, with dried out, curling leaves. Eventually, the plant will die. Container-grown plants are especially vulnerable, as are young plants on light soils. To reduce the potential for drought damage, incorporate plenty of well-rotted organic matter into the soil, and add water-retaining granules to containers. Water really adequately each time, rather than watering little and often, as this can lead to surface rooting, which will only aggravate the problem.

Frost damage

❀ Frost damage is sickeningly familiar to many gardeners. The blackened, dying remains of what was fresh new growth all too often serve as a reminder of how a late spring frost can take the gardener, and the vulnerable young plants newly planted out, unawares. In especially cruel frosts, even woody plants can split their stems. Almost any plant can suffer from frost damage if conditions are harsh enough – even plants that are generally accepted as being hardy. If particularly low temperatures are anticipated (below 0°C/32°F), protect vulnerable plants using fleece, cloches or cold frames. If you live in an area where frosts are common, plant accordingly, using plants that can usually survive in harsh weather conditions.

Manganese/iron deficiency

❀ This deficiency is commonly seen where lime-hating plants such as camellias or rhododendrons have been grown in a very alkaline soil. The leaf veins remain green, but the rest of the leaf turns pale and yellow, and the leaves may brown along the edges. The plant will generally have checked growth and will fail to thrive. The simplest form of prevention is to plant according to the particular soil requirements of a species. If you have a burning desire to grow a plant that would not do well in your garden soil, then restrict yourself to growing it in a container, where you can provide the acidic conditions it needs, using ericaceous compost. If beds or borders are showing this deficiency, you could correct it in the short term using sequestered iron. In the longer term, apply good-quality compost and well-rotted manure regularly.

ABOVE: *Very cold weather can cause damage to vulnerable plants. Protect precious specimens and knock heavy falls of snow off plants before it freezes.*

ABOVE: *The tell-tale symptoms of manganese deficiency showing on a rose leaf.*

WEED CONTROL

WEEDS are simply plants growing in the wrong place. This is worth remembering before you automatically reach for the weed killer or scythe. Some plants are considered weeds by one gardener, who works hard to eradicate them, yet are admired by another, who may propagate them from seed, or buy them as fully grown plants at the garden centre. Mind-your-own-business (*Helxine soleirolii*) and poppies (*Papaver*), for example, are plants that can be viewed as attractive, desirable cultivars or irritatingly pervasive weeds, depending on their location and the preference of the individual gardener. Mind-your-own-business can enliven dull paving with its lush, low-growing green carpeting effect, but can wreak havoc in what is meant to be a perfect lawn.

❀ The organic gardener appreciates the value of weeds as free sources of fertility, and works with weeds, rather than directly against them. Weeds are mineral accumulators, rendering minerals accessible to crops. For example, nettles accumulate potassium. Nettles have many other useful attributes, particularly in association with fruit and vegetables. In a large garden the keen organic gardener will find an appropriate place to give over to nettle growing – as good companions for plants such as redcurrants and blackberries, as hosts to many species of butterfly and to make into nettle sprays, which protect leeks from leek flies and moths.

❀ These positive attributes aside, good weed control undoubtedly has a vital role to play in maintaining a healthy garden. Weeds compete with desirable plants for nutrients, water and light, and can play host to diseases, which can spread to other plants. For example, groundsel often harbours greenfly, mildew and rust. Weeds are often extremely tough and pernicious, and can quickly colonise cultivated areas if left untamed.

Annual weeds

❀ Common annual weeds include groundsel, chickweed, nipplewort, shepherd's purse, annual nettle.
❀ Annual weeds grow from seed when the soil is moist, warm and exposed to light, thus mulching (covering the soil in order to block out the light, as well as for other reasons) or deep burying will prevent germination of annual weeds.

❀ Hoeing is often recommended as a control for annual weeds. The roots are severed from the stems to prevent further development. Walk backwards when hoeing, so that you do not tread the weeds into the soil. Hoe before the weeds have set seed. Allowed to germinate, the resulting weeds are quite easy to kill, but if left unchecked they can become more resilient.

Perennial weeds

❀ Common perennial weeds include ground elder, bindweed, dandelion, stinging nettle, horsetail.
❀ Mulching is less effective at controlling perennial weeds. Many perennial weeds such as dandelions have long, fleshy roots, which ensure the survival of the plant even if the top growth is killed off. These weeds will need to be dug out entirely. Some will regenerate if even a tiny portion of the root is left in the soil. Systemic weed killers are often used to control perennial weeds – particularly those that are very difficult to dig out completely, such as horsetail, which can develop roots that grow to depths of at least 1.8 m (6 ft). When a system weed killer is applied to leaves and stems, it is gradually absorbed by the weed and transported through the entire plant via the sap, eventually killing the whole weed.

ABOVE: *Regular hoeing is an efficient way of controlling annual weeds.*

Mulching for weed control

❀ Covering the soil around desirable plants with material that blocks out light and moisture has grown in popularity as a way of controlling weeds without recourse to chemicals.

❀ Although organic mulches have the added benefits of improving soil fertility and structure, they are not as effective as inorganic mulches at suppressing weed growth. Organic mulches need to be at least 10 cm (4 in) deep in order to be effective. Black plastic, however, is a very effective weed-suppressing mulch. Simply cut a cross in the plastic and plant desirable specimens through it. Conceal the unattractive plastic with bark or gravel.

Planting ground cover for weed control

❀ Ground cover plants will help keep weeds down by competing with them. However, they will not win the battle unless they are given a head start, by being planted in weed-free soil in sites suited to their individual needs. Planting ground cover through a plastic mulch, and concealing the plastic with gravel or bark, is an excellent and attractive way to keep weeds to a minimum.

❀ Good ground cover plants include periwinkle (*Vinca*) and lady's mantle (*Alchemilla mollis*).

COMMON GARDEN WEEDS

1. *Young nipplewort plant.*

2. *Annual nettle plant in flower.*

3. *Groundsel in flower.*

4. *Thistle in full bloom.*

5. *Flowering dandelion in grass.*

6. *Bindweed choking other plants.*

7. *Young ground elder plant.*

8. *Field buttercups in full flower.*

SEASON-BY-SEASON WORK PLANNER

The following planner is designed to make garden maintenance easier, by providing a guide to the optimum times throughout the year for undertaking particular tasks. Climate has a huge bearing on when some jobs may be undertaken wisely. There is no point planting out too early, just because the calendar proclaims it is the first day of spring, if the weather is so frosty that your plants have no hope of survival. Be guided by your prevailing local weather conditions for optimum chances of success.

SUITING YOUR REQUIREMENTS

DO NOT be put off by the number of tasks listed here – they will not all be relevant to every gardener. Use the planner to suit your personal gardening needs and priorities. For example, if you have many tender plants that you enjoy throughout the summer, propagating back-up stocks and overwintering the existing plants safely, all the guidance on this area of planting will be of note. However, if water gardening is your passion, then you will probably prioritise tasks related to this.

ABOVE: *Mulch the soil in beds and borders with compost or manure in spring to encourage healthy plant growth.*

SPRING

SPRING is a busy time for gardeners. Daylight hours increase noticeably and the sun shines more. The garden leaps into life; trees unfurl new foliage and bulbs give a cheering burst of colour after the grey of winter. Much sowing, planting, pruning and fertilising is undertaken, and attention is paid to weeds and pests such as slugs, which are particularly active now. Do not be deceived by early breaks in the weather into spending too much money – and time – on tender plants that have little hope of survival should wintry conditions return. When the weather looks sufficiently kind to risk planting, keep a careful eye on the forecast – a sudden late frost can annihilate plants at a stroke.

ABOVE: *A wild woodland garden in spring is vibrant with colour, with tulips and honesty groundcovers.*

General tasks

❀ Feed any plants that have been heavily pruned over winter and apply a generous layer of mulch.

❀ When the soil is moist and weed free, mulch borders and beds.

❀ When the soil is not too wet, prepare it for planting by digging appropriately, removing and disposing of perennial weeds.

❀ Clear weeds from driveways and paths.

❀ When the weather warms up, be vigilant in attending to watering requirements throughout this important growth period, especially during dry spells.

Annuals and biennials

❀ When the soil has warmed sufficiently, sow seeds of hardy annuals such as sunflowers and candytuft (*Iberis*) directly into their final planting sites.

❀ Sow biennials in a seed bed, ready for next spring.

❀ When the threat of frost has passed, plant out half-hardy annuals such as morning glory and busy Lizzies (*Impatiens*).

❀ Plant out sweet pea seedlings that were sown last autumn.

Perennials and bulbs

❀ Apply slow-release fertiliser to flowerbeds and borders and rake in.

❀ When the weather and soil conditions allow, plant perennials.

❀ Deadhead tulips and narcissus when they have gone over, removing the flower head only, not the whole stalk. Leave the foliage to die down naturally, as it produces the food reserves necessary for good flowering next year. Move the bulbs to a less prominent position in the garden while the foliage dies down if the unsightly yellow, withered leaves are too conspicuous. Do not tie the foliage in knots.

❀ When the flowers of aconites and snowdrops have faded, lift, divide and replant.

❀ Divide perennials as soon as new growth begins.

❀ Stake tall perennials such as delphiniums while they are still at an early stage of growth.

❀ Lift and divide ornamental grasses such as bamboo and purple moor grass.

❀ Plant summer-flowering bulbs, dahlia tubers and nursery-grown plants.

❀ Divide summer-flowering alpines.

❀ Protect plants from slugs, paying particular attention to those especially attractive to slugs, such as delphiniums. Take immediate, appropriate action, especially in warm and humid conditions.

❀ Weed.

ANCIENT ROMAN GARDENS

In AD 79 Pompeii was buried by volcanic ash from the eruption of Vesuvius. Wall paintings of gardens found during excavations show how the buildings were placed to take full advantage of the wider view – including that of Vesuvius – and how box and other green shrubs were clipped into disciplined shapes.

About 40 years later, the Roman emperor Hadrian had a villa built for himself at Tivoli, on ground lying between two valleys. In it he aimed to re-create the many famous buildings and sites he had visited on his travels, reinforcing the idea of the garden as an imaginary place. The site was enormous and the buildings were all linked along straight lines.

RIGHT: *A fresco found at Pompeii of a Roman garden scene with bird, fruit tree and lattice fence, from around AD 2– 40.*

Shrubs, trees and climbers

❀ Remove winter protection when weather allows.

❀ In early spring, prune slightly frost-sensitive plants such as lavateras.

❀ In mid- to late spring, take softwood cuttings.

❀ Layer climbers and shrubs, particularly those that do not root easily from cuttings, but which produce new plants naturally from layering, such as magnolia and rhododendrons. Their flexible stems make this a simple procedure.

❀ Regularly guide climbers along their supports and tie in to protect against wind damage. Handle fragile stems, such as those of large-flowered clematis hybrids, gently.

❀ Check and adjust ties.

❀ Remove suckers.

❀ To produce colourful winter stems on *Cornus* and *Salix*, cut back last year's growth almost to ground level.

❀ Prune large-flowered clematis.

❀ Cut out flowering shoots of winter-flowering shrubs such as jasmine.

❀ Plant hedges.

Roses

❀ If stems were earthed up for winter protection, remove this extra soil from the base of the stems.

❀ When the ground is warm and dry enough, plant bare-rooted roses in early spring. Spring, along with autumn, is also a good time to plant container-grown roses, although it is possible to plant them at any time.

❀ Prune repeat-flowering climbers, bush, shrub and miniature roses in mid-spring. Burn prunings. Do not prune ramblers and weeping standards.

❀ Lightly rake rose fertiliser into the topsoil in mid- to late spring.

❀ When the ground is warm and moist add an organic mulch.

❀ Remove suckers. Remove enough soil to trace the sucker back to its origin on the root and pull it off at this level. If you cut suckers off at ground level, their growth will be encouraged.

❀ Be alert for pests and take prompt action in the event of attack. Greenfly attack is a particular threat in late spring/early summer.

❀ Weed.

Lawns

❀ Lay turf or sow seed to make new lawns when weather conditions allow.

❀ Rake over and reseed bare or worn patches.

❀ After mid-spring do not cut summer-flowering meadows.

❀ In late spring, weed, feed and, if necessary, apply moss killer.

❀ As soon as grass starts active growth on established lawns, start mowing, with the blades set approximately 2.5 cm (1 in) high.

Herbs

❀ Clear away dead growth and debris from the soil.

❀ In frost-free weather, plant out hardy herbs grown indoors from seed.

tulips

narcissus (*pseudo-narcissus*)

❀ Sow hardy annual and biennial seed directly into the soil if it is not too wet.

❀ Most herbs can be divided now.

❀ Cut back lavender and rosemary to encourage bushy new growth.

❀ Plant nursery-bought container-grown herbs.

❀ Pinch out the growing ends of young shrubs to produce a neat shape.

❀ Apply a mulch of compost or other organic fertiliser.

❀ Begin weeding the herb garden.

❀ Stake and support trailing plants.

❀ Towards the end of spring, move tender and half-hardy plants to a sheltered place to harden them off.

Vegetables

❀ Prepare the soil for sowing by digging. Apply fertilisers and manures.

❀ Apply slow-release fertiliser to perennial vegetables.

❀ In warm, moist soil, sow maincrop vegetables. Accelerate soil warming by covering them with cloches, fleece or plastic film.

❀ For a continuous, rather than glut production, sow small quantities of vegetables in succession.

❀ Sow tender vegetables such as sweetcorn and outdoor tomatoes under protection.

❀ As the weather gets warmer, start to sow salad vegetables outdoors.

❀ Protect germinating vegetables with floating mulch or fleece.

Fruit

❀ Apply slow-release fertiliser.

❀ In frosty weather, cover early fruit blossom with fleece.

❀ Mulch early-cropping strawberries and protect them against frost with fleece.

❀ Continue pruning top fruit and soft fruit.

Pools and water features

❀ Remove pool heater and reinstate the pump after its winter service.

❀ Clean out overgrown or dirty ponds and pools in late spring.

❀ Remove decayed foliage that may have been left on marginal plants for winter protection.

❀ Plant aquatic plants.

❀ Lift and divide aquatic plants as necessary.

Under glass and indoors

❀ Plant containers for summer displays.

❀ Sow perennials, tender vegetables and half-hardy annuals.

❀ Harden these off towards the end of spring.

❀ Take softwood cuttings of tender perennials for container displays.

❀ Sow half-hardy annual seeds.

❀ Harden off earlier-sown half-hardy annual seedlings in a cold frame, protected against frost by additional insulation.

snowdrops (*Galanthus elwesii*)

daffodils and hellebores

SUMMER

WATER conservation and attending to the watering needs of all plants becomes the key gardening concern as temperatures rise. Consider how your plants will fare while you are on holiday. Move containers to a shady place and, if possible, arrange a mutual holiday water watch with a gardening friend.

General tasks

❀ Plant up containers in early summer. Move containers prepared in the greenhouse outside.

❀ If not using a slow-release fertiliser, feed your containers regularly.

❀ To encourage new flowers and reduce the spread of disease, deadhead spent blooms regularly.

❀ During prolonged dry spells, water plants that have not yet become established, including shrubs and trees planted within the previous two years. Be observant and water plants that are showing signs of stress, such as rolled leaves, wilting and leaf fall.

Annuals and biennials

❀ In early summer, sow a second batch of annuals in the form of plant plugs, to ensure a good display once the first sowings have started to fade.

❀ Deadhead regularly to keep annuals flowering.

❀ Weed.

❀ Sow biennial seeds in a nursery bed ready for next year's display.

❀ Plant geraniums (*Pelargoniums*) for summer bedding.

❀ Sweet peas will flower continuously if picked regularly and not allowed to form pods.

Perennials and bulbs

❀ Do not be hasty to remove bulb foliage. Allow it to die back naturally.

❀ Remove spring bulbs from containers, where their dying foliage is unsightly, and allow them to die down in a less conspicuous part of the garden.

❀ Lift, dry and store tulip bulbs when the foliage has died down.

❀ As soon as bearded irises have bloomed, lift and divide.

❀ Collect seeds.

❀ Deadhead lilies.

❀ Remove yellowing foliage from perennials and dead-head regularly.

❀ Take softwood cuttings of plants that may be under threat during the winter, such as penstemons.

❀ Order spring-flowering bulbs. These will arrive in the autumn.

Shrubs, trees and climbers

❀ Prune late spring- and early summer-flowering climbers and shrubs when they have finished flowering.

❀ Check climbers regularly. Tie in any straggly growth.

❀ Trim topiary, coniferous hedges and evergreens. Remove dead or damaged shoots.

❀ In late summer, take semi-ripe heel cuttings of trees, evergreens and shrubs.

❀ In late summer, order the shrubs and trees required for winter planting.

Roses

❀ Look out for mildew and black spot, and for signs of greenfly or other pest attack. Treat appropriately.

beech hedge with summer flowers

rock rose at the height of summer

❀ Deadhead faded blooms to encourage new growth.

❀ Apply a summer dressing of rose fertiliser.

❀ Order new roses for the autumn.

❀ Weed.

Lawns

❀ In very dry weather, raise mower blades and remove the grass-collecting box so that the clippings act as a moisture-conserving mulch.

❀ Feed lawns regularly.

❀ Make the first cut of a spring-flowering meadow.

❀ Mow regularly, and trim lawn edges after each cut.

Herbs

❀ Begin to harvest.

❀ Trim dwarf hedging.

❀ Towards the end of the summer, harvest and preserve.

❀ Collect seed as it ripens, label clearly in envelopes.

❀ Continue to weed.

Vegetables

❀ If a slow-release fertiliser was not applied in spring, feed regularly.

❀ Continue successive sowings.

❀ Plant out vegetable seedlings.

❀ Look out for pests, such as root flies on carrots and onions and blackfly on broad beans. Treat appropriately.

❀ Hoe to keep weeds in check.

❀ Lift onions and shallots when tops have died down.

❀ Harvest regularly.

❀ Feed tomatoes regularly. Remove side shoots and yellowing leaves from tomato plants.

❀ Thin out vegetable seedlings.

❀ When runner beans reach the top of their supports, pinch out the growing points.

Fruit

❀ Protect fruit against birds.

❀ Harvest regularly.

❀ Tidy up strawberries after fruiting.

❀ Towards the end of summer, harvest fruit for winter consumption.

❀ Summer-prune trained fruit trees.

Pools and water features

❀ Plant, or lift and divide aquatic plants such as water lilies.

❀ In hot weather, keep a close eye on water levels and top up if necessary.

Under glass and indoors

❀ Keep a close eye on plants for signs of pest attack. Treat appropriately.

❀ Be vigilant about providing adequate and appropriate shade and ventilation.

❀ In late summer, thoroughly clean, disinfect, fumigate, tidy and, if necessary, paint the greenhouse and any frames in readiness for autumn. This will reduce the risk of pests and diseases becoming a problem over the winter.

mallow shrub in full flower

Lilium 'Journey's End'

AUTUMN

ALTHOUGH the days are growing shorter and the plants are starting to look tired, in many ways autumn marks the start, not the end, of the gardening year. Planting bulbs, roses and shrubs is a forward-looking task, when most of the work in the garden revolves around tidying and disposing of dead and decaying plants.

General tasks

❀ Turn the compost heap.

❀ Spread well-rotted compost over borders and beds for winter protection.

❀ Dig heavy, clay soil and leave the clods unbroken. Winter frost will break these up to improve the soil texture.

❀ Collect fallen leaves for making leaf mould.

❀ Clear summer bedding from containers and plant up winter containers.

Annuals

❀ When annuals have finished flowering, clear them away, leaving ornamental seed heads in place.

Perennials and bulbs

❀ When perennials become straggly and unsightly, cut them back. Shred or chop the debris and add it to the compost heap. Lift, divide and replant perennials.

❀ Protect perennials of uncertain hardiness against the worst of the winter weather by applying a thick organic mulch.

❀ After the first frost has blackened the foliage of dahlias and other tender, bulbous plants, trim back the stems to 15 cm (6 in) and gently lift the tubers. Discard damaged roots and excess soil. Invert the tubers for a week or so to drain away excess moisture. Store them upright on a layer of peat that covers the roots, not the crowns, in a dry, cool, frost-free environment.

❀ As soon as your order of spring-flowering bulbs arrives, plant them in pots or in the garden.

Shrubs, trees and climbers

❀ Before the soil is cold, take hardwood cuttings, just after leaf fall.

❀ As the dormant season begins, plant trees and shrubs.

❀ Screen slightly tender woody plants with matting, conifer branches or bracken for winter protection.

Roses

❀ Continue deadheading roses, which are generally still blooming as autumn commences.

❀ Prune rambling roses and weeping standards.

❀ Dig to prepare soil for new plantings.

❀ Continue to observe and treat disease appropriately.

❀ Take cuttings of all rose types except hybrid teas, which do not transplant satisfactorily.

❀ Plant bare root roses. Although container-grown roses can be planted at any time of the year, autumn, along with spring, is a particularly good time.

❀ Tidy up rose beds, hoeing mulch and collecting up and burning fallen leaves and debris.

Hamamelis x intermedia 'Sunburst' and 'Diane'

Hydrangea anomala petiolaris 'Hilbam House'

❀ Prepare plants for winter. Cut back long stems to avoid damage by wind rock if your garden is very exposed. In particularly cold areas, earth up stems with approximately 10 cm (4 in) of soil.

Lawns

❀ Scarify, spike and top dress lawns.

❀ If the weather is sufficiently mild, a new lawn can be established from turf or seed.

❀ If lawns have suffered during the summer due to heavy use or drought, apply autumn feed early in the season.

❀ Cut spring- and summer-flowering meadows.

Herbs

❀ Fork over the soil and fertilise permanent plantings.

❀ Plant container-grown herbs.

❀ If you are planning a new herb bed on previously uncultivated soil, prepare by double digging.

❀ Plant hardy herbaceous herbs.

❀ Plant invasive herbs in sunken containers to prevent undesirable spreading.

❀ Transfer tender herbs such as basil and pineapple sage to a conservatory, windowsill or greenhouse.

❀ Grow chives and parsley in pots. Overwinter under glass for a good supply throughout the winter.

❀ Cut back larger shrubs such as rosemary.

❀ Plant low hedging such as rue, lavender and hyssop.

❀ Protect herbs that will be spending winter in the garden by earthing up a generous layer of straw, soil or compost around their roots.

Vegetables

❀ Continue to harvest.

❀ String up onions for winter storage.

❀ Sow green manure.

❀ Clear away, clean and store redundant stakes.

❀ Cut down asparagus.

❀ Earth up celery and leeks.

❀ Protect outdoor tomatoes with cloches to help hasten ripening.

Fruit

❀ Continue to harvest and store for winter consumption.

❀ Prune summer-fruiting raspberries and soft fruit bushes.

❀ Plant strawberries, fruit trees and bushes.

❀ Apply bands of grease to fruit trees to protect against pests.

❀ Take hardwood cuttings of currants.

Pools and water features

❀ Remove the pump in late autumn; clean, service and store until spring.

❀ Clear away dying foliage. Skim off fallen leaves and other debris.

Under glass and indoors

❀ Before the frosts arrive, bring tender plants inside.

Aster amellus 'King George'

Aster 'Grandchild'

WINTER

PROTECTION is the chief concern of the gardener in winter. Frost, heavy snowfalls, gales and hail storms all threaten. Make sure that plants are protected accordingly. Even in winter, there is work to be done in the garden, such as some weeding and planting, but the load is much diminished. Take this time to plan next year's garden. Observe the garden without its lively summer colours and consider the overall structure. If there are large areas that seem bare, plan next year's winter colour as well as thinking about the broader picture. Changes of height and the general dynamics of the garden design are much asier to plan when you do not have the distraction of too much colour.

General tasks

❀ Take root cuttings of fleshy-rooted perennials.
❀ Replace faded, broken and absent plant labels.
❀ Prepare for spring sowing. Clean propagators, pots and seed trays.
❀ While plants are dormant, maintain paths, trellis, fences and other garden structures.
❀ Continue to tidy up flowerbeds and borders, cutting back spent plants and clearing away debris.
❀ Continue to collect fallen leaves.
❀ Plan any major changes to the garden.

Perennials and bulbs

❀ Check stored bulbs for rot and mould. Discard affected bulbs.

Shrubs, trees and climbers

❀ Even if the weather is slightly frosty, prune roses, shrubs, trees and climbers.
❀ Inspect woody plants for diseased and dead wood. Remove and destroy infected or dead branches and stems.
❀ Knock heavy snow from conifers and hedges before it turns to ice and breaks or distorts branches. It may also cause top growth to blacken and die.

Roses

❀ Check that the roots of autumn-planted roses have not been loosened by frost and firm up if necessary.
❀ Check that the supports of climbing roses are in good condition.

Lawns

❀ Rake up leaves.
❀ Service mowers and trimmers. Ensure that blades are sharp, ready for the first spring cut.
❀ Keep off the lawn in frozen conditions.

Herbs

❀ Remove soggy herbaceous growth and annual growth as

Asplenium scolopendrium hit by frost

ornamental cabbage

it dies back. Leave healthy perennial growth to provide winter protection for other plants.

❀ Keep the herb garden neat and tidy.

❀ Consider next year's planting. Order seeds.

❀ Plan new herb gardens or consider whether alterations are necessary to existing ones.

❀ Towards winter's end, sow seeds of tender herbs indoors.

❀ Pot-grown hardy herbs may be planted out in frost-free weather.

❀ Keep an eye on bay trees. Move them inside if the temperature dips below -15°C (5°F), as bay is particularly susceptible to frost, which scorches the leaves.

Vegetables

❀ Order seeds for planting next year.

❀ Plan the rotation of crops for the vegetable garden.

❀ Lift parsnips and leeks.

❀ Cover soil with cloches to prewarm it, ready for early plantings in spring.

❀ Plant garlic.

Fruit

❀ Prune fruit trees.

❀ Mulch established fruit trees.

❀ Disinfect canes before storage.

❀ Force rhubarb.

❀ Plant container-grown fruit trees and bushes.

Pools and water features

❀ Install a pond heater or float a plastic ball on the surface of the water to keep an area free of ice. If you have fish, this is essential to their survival.

Under glass and indoors

❀ If you have not brought tender plants inside, do so now.

❀ Bring in tender container plants.

❀ Insulate cold frames against frost, using layers of hessian or old carpet, secured with ties or heavy pieces of wood. These opaque materials will need to be removed during the day so that the plants are not deprived of light. Transparent materials such as several layers of clear plastic sheeting may be left in place day and night. While not totally clear, the plastic does transmit some light.

❀ Insulate the greenhouse using plastic bubble wrap, which allows a reasonable amount of light through. Add polystyrene base cladding – polystyrene panels placed along the lower glazing panes to significantly reduce heat loss. These will need to be removed before planting summer border crops as polystyrene does not allow light transmission.

❀ Continue to ventilate the greenhouse to prevent a build-up of stagnant air.

Hamamelis 'Zuccariniana'

Eranthis hyemalis

GETTING TO WORK

Even the smallest garden has a high proportion of non-living elements. All the 'hard-side' elements need to be as carefully considered, installed and maintained as the plants in your garden if it is to work well.

Before embarking on any major projects, research your options thoroughly to avoid making costly mistakes.

Make an assessment of your garden, your practical requirements and the style of the house, then read the relevant sections in this chapter before you start work.

If you choose well, your plot will look well-integrated; if you choose badly, the resulting mishmash may be a disappointment.

FINDING SOLUTIONS FOR PROBLEMS

Every garden, large or small, has problem areas that irritate
or embarrass its owners – be it a shady dry spot where plants
steadfastly refuse to grow, a corner of the garden overlooked by an
unsightly building or a compost heap that dominates the otherwise
perfect potager. Some problems are immediately obvious, such as a
garden with a steep slope or incredibly boggy area, while others become
apparent with time, or as a garden metamorphoses with changing
use. Perhaps your garden was perfect when you had no children,
but now that you have toddlers with excess energy to run off,
and play things to store, it no longer suits your needs.

Assessing the situation

❀ Every now and again, perhaps in autumn, which is the
start of the dormant season, take time to look at the
garden without the distraction of a multitude of flowers.
Take a long, dispassionate look at what worked, and what
did not, during spring and summer.

ABOVE: *Al fresco eating generates a diversity of difficult-to-store items, such as
barbecues, tables, chairs and parasols.*

❀ Assessing which plants grew well, and which ones
suffered, will help you build an increasingly accurate
picture of the conditions that prevail in the
microclimates around your garden. You can then
plant accordingly, or shift the environment subtly to
suit. For example, add windbreaks to areas where plants
have otherwise flourished, but have suffered due to
wind exposure.

ABOVE: *Trellis forms an effective yet inexpensive screen that also provides an
excellent support for colourful climbing plants.*

The garden room

❀ You can also assess how well your garden has worked for you as a whole during the warmer months. Was there anything that became a constant annoyance, like a pile of outdoor games that slowly accrued, but which had no storage place, leading to a permanent fruitless attempt at tidying up.

❀ Did your local council install new wheeled bins, which now dominate the front garden? Perhaps you bought a barbecue and ate outside almost every night, but had nowhere to accommodate the barbecue itself, the charcoal, insect-repellent candles, lanterns, table, parasol and chairs that gradually took over the patio.

❀ The garden is increasingly regarded as an outside room, an additional living space, and it deserves to be planned as much with comfort and function in mind as your kitchen or any other room within your home.

Hiding an ugly view/adding privacy

❀ Privacy is an important garden attribute. A garden should be a sanctuary, a place where you can recharge your batteries away from the stresses and demands of the outside world. It is never going to be easy to relax if your garden is overlooked, or has an unsightly view.

❀ The solution is to screen out the problem, while retaining as much light within the garden as possible. In some situations, it may be possible to erect quite a high barrier without affecting the amount of light transmitted, but if your garden is already quite shady, use baffle screens, which diffuse rather than totally occlude, instead of solid screens.

❀ Trellis is a brilliant way of adding instant height, without excluding light totally, and is available in many shapes, sizes and designs – from rustic, twiggy panels topped with arching branches for a pretty, rural look, to elegantly formal geometric shapes in smooth, painted wood, perfect for a smart urban courtyard.

❀ Always support trellis properly, and use a grade appropriate to the task. Thin, expanding trellis may be temptingly cheap, but will quickly collapse under the weight of a heavy climbing plant like honeysuckle, and will look skimpy. It will also need constant propping up and repair, which are difficult things to do when the trellis is clothed with foliage.

❀ Where trellis is installed as a major feature, either as a freestanding screen or on top of a fence or wall, buy the best quality you can afford, pretreated with preservative; install it well and maintain it properly for a screen that will be as attractive as it is functional. Planting will further soften the effect. Scented plants will add another dimension.

ABOVE: *The effect achieved by the use of wooden decking and the wooden struts of the pergola is of a contemporary living area with a Japanese feel to it.*

THE ART OF CONCEALMENT

SOME elements of the garden are necessary, but not particularly attractive. With a little careful planning, every part of the garden can be visually acceptable, even appealing in its own right. All hard-working areas of the garden deserve to be as well thought out, installed and maintained as the purely decorative elements.

Compost areas

❀ Compost areas are an essential part of the well-maintained, ecologically sound garden, but their contribution is definitely functional rather than ornamental.

❀ The compost heap offers so much to the garden that it should be treated with more respect than it tends to receive in most gardens. All too often, the compost heap is just that – a literal heap, not of sweet-smelling, rich brown earth, but of rotting household rubbish, as well as old branches and weeds.

❀ Consider the functionality of any problem area first, and consider concealment later. Putting a fence in front of a badly installed and maintained compost area will only shield the problem.

❀ Perhaps install a proper compost bin, or pair of bins, appropriate to the size of your garden and the amount of composting you feel able to do. A shredder might be a worthwhile investment, since it will enable you to cut prunings into manageable pieces that degrade more quickly, and also take up less space in the compost area. Put only appropriate materials on the compost pile. Maintain the compost heap well, turning it regularly and keeping it covered, and you will have much less of a problem to conceal.

Concealing unsightly areas

❀ Assuming your compost area, bins and other functional, but unappealing, areas are in good general repair, and are designed and used properly, all you need to do is conceal them from view.

❀ The type of concealment used will depend to some extent on the purpose of the area. If you regularly need to wheel your bin from its usual resting place

RIGHT: A neatly kept rubbish area will look tidy and reduce the possibility of vermin attack.

to the front gate, you will need a permanent housing for the bin, that also allows easy access. A three-sided brick area is a popular way of hiding a large rubbish bin, and can be softened externally by planting.

❀ Obviously, a compost area will require sufficient access around it so that you can turn the heap, and add to or remove the compost, but the whole heap stays in one place, so all-round access is not so critical. Trellis clothed with climbers, hurdle fencing or another natural barrier could all be used to screen the area prettily, effectively and inexpensively.

Planting in difficult areas

❀ Always work with the natural garden environment, not against it. Although you can adjust some conditions, for example by planting windbreaks to shelter plants in exposed sites, some areas will never accomodate certain plant types with any real success.

❀ Respect the various microclimates around your garden and plant accordingly (see opposite). Although your choice of plants may be limited in some areas, sympathetic planting will mean that what you do grow, thrives.

❀ A thriving collection of plants, even in a limited range, will always look more attractive than a diversity of straggly, sick, struggling plants.

ABOVE: A functional corner of the garden between fencing and the door of the garden shed becomes a pretty nook to sit in, with the help of a strategically planted climbing rose.

ABOVE: *Euphorbia enjoy dry, shady conditions.*

ABOVE: *Succulent plants will thrive in hot, sunny conditions.*

Plants for moist, shady sites

- Astrantia
- Camellia
- Dicentra spectabilis
- Hamamelis mollis
- Helleborus
- Hosta
- Mahonia aquifolium
- Rhododendron
- Sarcococca humilis
- Viburnum davidii

Plants for dry, shady sites

- Anemone japonica
- Aucuba japonica
- Bergenia
- Euphorbia
- Ilex
- Pachysandra terminalis
- Pulmonaria
- Skimmia
- Vinca

Plants for dry, sunny areas

- Achillea
- Agapanthus
- Cistus
- Echinops ritro
- Geranium
- Iris germanica
- Nepeta
- Santolina
- Senecio
- Verbascum
- Yucca

Plants for acidic soil

- Azalea
- Camellia
- Pieris
- Rhododendron
- Skimmia

Plants for alkaline soil

- Buddleja davidii
- Clematis
- Cotoneaster
- Dianthus
- Lavandula
- Paeonia
- Scabiosa
- Syringa
- Verbascum

Pollution-tolerant plants

- Aucuba japonica
- Berberis
- Chaenomeles
- Cotoneaster
- Ilex
- Philadelphus
- Syringa
- Weigela florida

BELOW:. *Many plants will thrive in shady and dry areas of your garden.*

BELOW: *Choose plants that enjoy acidic conditions rather than trying to permanently modify the pH of the soil.*

ESTABLISHING BOUNDARIES

Boundaries are an important consideration in garden planning.
Not only do they mark the limitations of your property, they also
provide the opportunity to screen out noise and unsightly views and
to afford privacy. Conversely, your garden may enjoy a wonderful
view and have no issues of privacy or noise pollution. Thus, marking
the boundary may consist of a visually minimal delineation, such as
sinking a line of stones into the soil that terminate at ground level,
or installing a chain-link fence. Within the garden itself, fences,
walls and screens offer a way of marking out distinct zones of activity,
such as play areas and vegetable plots, as well as providing vertical
surfaces for planting and concealing ugly but necessary parts of
the garden, such as compost bins and recycling areas.

BOUNDARY TYPES

THE issues to consider when choosing a type of
boundary are straightforward, and governed by
common sense as well as visual preference.

Tall, solid boundaries

❀ If you need to enhance the level of privacy in your
garden, you will be considering solid, tall options, such
as high walls or closeboard fencing. Walls will block out

noise, as well as prying eyes, better than fences. In both
cases, remember that tall, solid screens also block out
light and can seem claustrophobic in small areas, so
plan carefully before purchasing and installing.

❀ There may also be local, as well as national, planning
restrictions on the type and height of boundary
marking that may be placed on your property, so do
research any such limitations at the outset.

❀ A final point of consideration is that, contrary to popular
belief, a solid wall or fence does not offer the best
protection on an exposed site, and can even lead to
problems such as the creation of a plant-damaging frost
pocket, instability of the barrier itself, and turbulent, plant-
harming wind conditions on either side of the barrier.

Partially open boundaries

❀ Where a solid wall or fence would be inappropriate,
a partially occluded screen may be the answer. For
example, a wattle fence appears almost solid but actually
allows some air to penetrate, and so makes an effective
windbreak in exposed situations where an impenetrable
barrier would cause problems.

❀ Certain types of partially open boundaries also offer a
degree of privacy and security, while allowing some light
to pass through them, for example walls topped with
screen blocks, or fences headed with decorative trellis.

LEFT: A partially occluded screen such as a decorative trellis can be used to
create a boundary without building a solid wall or fence, and serves as a
decorative feature as well as creating a feeling of space.

Open boundaries

❀ Some boundary markings are just that – a way of delineating the extremities of your property, without affording marked additional degrees of privacy, sound reduction or security. There are various options available, some more decorative and practically useful than others.

❀ Prices also vary widely. For example, a cast-iron fence can be highly ornamental and offers some security enhancement if it is sufficiently tall and of an intricate and pointed design that is off-putting to the casual fence-climbing intruder. Such fences can be expensive and will need ongoing maintenance in order to retain its elegant good looks, whether purchased new or from a specialist in architectural salvage.

ABOVE: *Fencing materials define the borders of a plot and need to be sympathetic to the overall theme of the garden, such as this bamboo, used to reinforce a Japanese style.*

RIGHT: *A tall, solid boundary such as closeboard fencing can be used to enhance the privacy of your garden, but remember that it will also block out light.*

WALLS

WALLS are more permanent structures than fences and, correspondingly, need thorough planning before building begins. They are very effective at noise reduction, and of course offer maximum privacy. High walls may seem to offer an increased level of security, since it is obviously more difficult to climb over a wall than to step over a chain-link fence. Bear in mind, however, that an intruder can work unseen and unheard behind the useful concealment of a high wall, so a lower wall may be a better option where security is a more important consideration than privacy.

Choosing a wall

❀ Walls are generally made of brick, concrete or stone, and may be solid or pierced, as in the case of a wall made of screen blocks. Always choose materials that are sympathetic to those used in the construction of your home, and appropriate to the style of wall prevalent in your area.

❀ For example, an old cottage built of stone would look very uncomfortable surrounded by a wall of concrete blocks. Similarly, a stark, modern home would look very awkward partnered by an overly rustic dry stone wall. Observe the materials and styles used in other gardens around your own, and make a note of what works and what is less successful.

BRICKS

❀ Clay bricks are attractive, and are available in a wide variety of colours, textures and degrees of weather resistance. Ordinary facing bricks are fine for most garden walls, but 'special' quality bricks will be required for applications where increased water resistance is needed, such as on exposed walls in coastal regions.

❀ Salvaged bricks are not necessarily a cheaper option than new bricks, but may be the best choice for producing a wall that tones in well with the brickwork of your home.

ABOVE: *Walls can be prettified considerably with planting. Here, the fan-trained pears are attractive as well as productive.*

ABOVE: *The severity of a solid brick wall is softened by a round window and arched doorway.*

❀ If you have any spare house bricks available to take to the builder's merchant for matching, so much the better. Always obtain a sample to take home to assess whether the tone, texture and colouring really work well *in situ*. Building a wall is a costly investment in terms of time and money, and mistakes are all too glaringly obvious when replicated in row after row of inappropriate brick.

BLOCKS

❀ Blocks are obviously quicker to lay than bricks, since they are so much larger. However, the foundations of a block wall are just as important, so do not regard building a block wall as any less serious an undertaking as laying a brick wall.

❀ The all-too-common garden sight of a shoddily built collapsing concrete wall bears testimony to the fact that block walling is seen by many people as a speedy and inexpensive alternative.

Natural blocks

❀ Stone walling is very attractive, and indigenous to some areas. Indeed, some districts even have planning regulations that necessitate the use of local stone for new walls. Granite, limestone and sandstone are all used for wall building. Flint and slate are also used, often in combination with other materials.

❀ It makes economic sense to buy from a local quarry or salvage company. Garden centres often have a selection of appealing stone, but to buy there the sort of quantities needed for a run of walling, rather than isolated pieces for a small rockery, would be prohibitively expensive.

Concrete blocks

❀ Standard structural blocks are inexpensive and easy to lay, although they are not attractive and their use is generally limited to areas where they will be later disguised by a coat of rendering or plastering. A zigzag pattern on their surface provides a key to encourage adhesion of these materials.

❀ Facing blocks have a decorative face and end, and are used for the external surface of cavity walls, backed by plain, structural blocks. They are available in a wide range of finishes to tone in with local stone, are cheaper than reconstituted stone blocks or natural stone, but much less visually convincing than either.

❀ Reconstituted stone blocks use crushed stone in place of aggregate, and are moulded into a range of shapes from smooth to rough hewn, and in colours to suit most local stone types. Although more realistic than facing blocks, they do not have the same lack of uniformity that characterises natural stone.

❀ Screen blocks are concrete blocks pierced with a decorative pattern, and are generally used to form walls produced in a stack-bonded pattern – literally piled up in columns rather than being offset. This produces a weaker wall than traditional bond patterns, so screen walls need supporting piers at each end for additional strength.

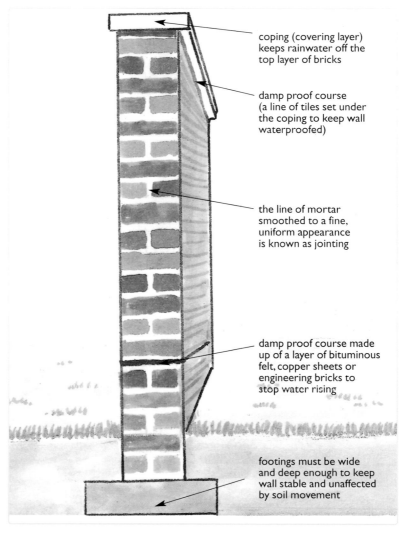

coping (covering layer) keeps rainwater off the top layer of bricks

damp proof course (a line of tiles set under the coping to keep wall waterproofed)

the line of mortar smoothed to a fine, uniform appearance is known as jointing

damp proof course made up of a layer of bituminous felt, copper sheets or engineering bricks to stop water rising

footings must be wide and deep enough to keep wall stable and unaffected by soil movement

TYPES OF FENCE

FENCES come in a wide range of styles and use a variety of materials, namely wire, concrete, plastic and timber. Forms of fencing available include such options as two or three lengths of sturdy wire threaded through upright posts, chain link fencing and ready-made wooden panels, among many others; and prices vary considerably, according to the type of fence chosen.

Post and chain fencing

❀ Post and chain fencing marks a boundary and deters people from straying from a path on to a lawn or flowerbed, but affords no additional privacy or enhanced security.

❀ Lengths of metal or plastic chain, which are available in several link types and colours, are suspended between wooden or metal posts. The most commonly used arrangement is a black-painted metal chain of oval links, alternating with diamond spikes, hung from white-painted posts.

Trellis fencing

❀ Trellis fencing has become increasingly popular in recent years. Used to divide the garden into separate areas, conceal unsightly views or top a solid fence, trellis is comparatively inexpensive, easy to install, wonderfully compatible with planting and suitable for many situations, since it allows light and air to pass freely through it.

❀ Trellis comes in many styles, sizes and variants – from rustic larch poles, which give a quaint, country cottage feel, to sophisticated shapes in smooth wood.

❀ The method of installing trellis will depend on the type used. Insubstantial concertina-fold trellis needs to be housed in a stout holding frame for added stability, whereas split larch poles, nailed on to sturdy posts and rails properly installed in the ground, produces a stable and attractive fence.

Closeboard fencing

❀ Closeboard fencing consists of vertically overlapped wooden featherboard strips, nailed on to horizontal rails. Cedar is the best quality wood for this, and is correspondingly expensive. Softwood is the more affordable option.

❀ Both types are attractive and strong and provide a high degree of privacy. Because the strips are vertical, the fence is not easy to climb, deterring children from attempting to scale it. Closeboard fencing is a good but expensive option for adding privacy to a sloping garden. It can be erected *in situ* – or made from 'off-the-peg' panels.

Picket fencing

❀ Picket, or palisade fencing, particularly when painted white, immediately conjures up images of country cottages and old-fashioned charm.

❀ Narrow vertical pales are spaced approximately 5 cm (2 in) apart, attached to horizontal rails. The tops of the pales may be pointed, rounded, or cut into decorative shapes such as Gothic-style finials. This fencing is highly decorative and is used primarily as an ornamental way of marking a boundary rather than to provide privacy, since it is open, and is also usually no more than 1.2 m (4 ft) high.

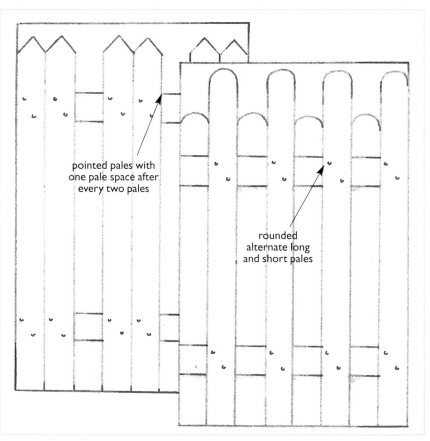

pointed pales with one pale space after every two pales

rounded alternate long and short pales

Ranch-style fencing

❀ As its name suggests, ranch-style fencing brings to mind the wide open spaces of the American plains. It is simply constructed from wide horizontal rails attached to stout boards. Made in soft- or hardwood, it may be painted or simply treated with weatherproofing.

❀ Low-maintenance plastic ranch-style fencing is also available. Removed from a large-scale, ranch-style context of bordering a field, this type of fencing can look somewhat oversized and municipal, and affords no privacy.

❀ This style of fencing is also irresistible to children as a ready made climbing frame and to passing adults as a convenient leaning post and makeshift seat; these are points worth considering if your boundary lies next to a bus stop or telephone box. Finding that you have spent a considerable amount of time and money in installing what is in effect a public bench could prove very irritating.

ANATOMY OF A FENCE

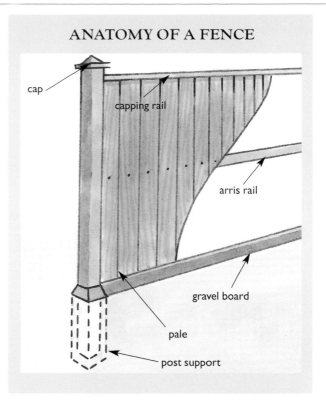

cap
capping rail
arris rail
gravel board
pale
post support

BUILDING A PICKET FENCE

Fence posts must be extremely sturdy and firmly positioned when constructing a fence.

1 *Sink each post at least 60 cm (24 in) into the ground for good stability. Metal post spikes remove the need for digging and concreting as they are simply hammered into position, but are suitable only for firm ground. If you are not using metal spikes, you will need* to dig a hole, fill the bottom with compacted hard core, then concrete the fence post in place. Chamfer off the concrete just above ground level.

2 *Fix the arris rails to the fence posts. Fix the pickets* to the arris rails, taking care to place them evenly.

3 *Use a picket to act as a spacing guide. Keep the top of the pickets level by working to a string line suspended between the fence posts.*

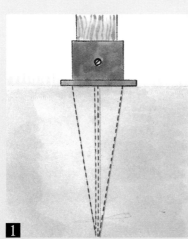

1

2

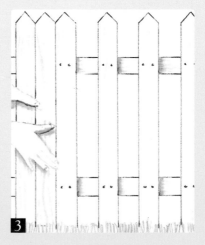

3

PANEL FENCES

Fences made from ready-made panels nailed between wooden posts are popular because they offer a reasonable level of privacy at relatively little expense, and are quite simple to erect. Various types are available.

Interwoven panels

❀ These are made of thin wooden strips woven between vertical stiffeners to produce a closed, but not totally occlusive fence. Choose good-quality interwoven panels with strips that fit tightly against each other, since the wood may shrink back in the summer and leave unsightly gaps.

Hurdle fencing

❀ Hurdle fencing is another type of interwoven panel, made from strips of flexible branches such as willow woven horizontally around sturdy upright wooden poles. It is an effective windbreak, since some air is allowed to pass through it.

❀ Hurdle fencing has become increasingly popular in garden design because it gives instant rustic appeal at comparatively low cost, and is made from natural materials from renewable sources.

ABOVE: *Ready made panel fences are a popular choice, since they are reasonably cheap to buy and easy to erect.*

❀ Although not as permanent an investment as a brick wall or closeboard fence, hurdle panels will last for several years, and make very pretty garden screening. Short hurdle fences are perfect for edging borders, and can be made *in situ* or bought ready-made.

Horizontally lapped panels

❀ Slightly more expensive than interwoven panels, these are more durable and offer greater privacy, since there are no gaps for prying eyes to peep through. Strips of wood, usually larch, are overlapped horizontally, and held between a sawn timber frame.

❀ The strips may have a smooth, straight edge or, for a more informal feel, are available with undulating edges with or without the bark attached.

Vertically lapped panels

❀ Self-descriptive, these panels of overlapping vertical strips, attached to a frame, make a durable, peep-proof fence, which mimics closeboard fencing. Choose good-quality panels that are well overlapped so that gaps do not appear as the wood shrinks with changing weather conditions.

Interlap fencing

❀ Interlap fencing consists of square-edged boards nailed to horizontal rails, and fixed on alternating sides. It is a popular choice for an exposed site, as it is sturdy, yet wind is allowed to pass through the gaps between the boards.

LEFT: *The appearance of panel fencing is greatly improved by sympathetic planting.*

❀ Where wind is not a problem the boards may be spaced as you wish – overlapped for more privacy, or spaced more widely to allow light to pass through. The construction method means that interlap fencing is equally attractive on both sides – another reason for its popularity.

Chestnut palings

❀ Sold by the roll, this consists of a series of parallel chestnut stakes, fixed together top and bottom with lengths of twisted wire to form a cheap fence.

❀ Attached to sturdy posts at 1.8 m (6 ft) intervals, chestnut palings produce an effective barrier, but do not offer increased privacy. Although not particularly attractive, this type of fencing is light, easy to transport and install, and blends quiet inconspicuously into its surroundings, especially if softened by planting.

Post and wire fencing

❀ Post and wire fencing comprises two or three lengths of sturdy wire stretched between strong posts of wood, concrete or steel and kept taut by straining bolts.

❀ The posts must be firmly fixed and well supported. The end posts will need supportive struts. Although privacy and security are not improved by this type of fence, it is an inexpensive, unobtrusive way of marking a boundary while a hedge is growing, as it also offers good support for the hedge itself.

Chain link fencing

❀ Chain link fencing comprises plastic-coated or galvanised wire mesh, attached to firm posts of wood or concrete. Choose a mesh colour that tones in with its surroundings.

❀ This fence type is familiar in municipal settings. Not the most attractive boundary option, it does offer optimum light transmission, some measure of additional security and is comparatively cheap and easy to install.

Wire picket fencing

❀ Plastic-coated wire hoops are linked together and fixed on to posts to make a discreet fence, which does not improve security or privacy but is a popular, inexpensive way of marking out boundaries and, in particular, flower borders and beds.

❀ The posts need to be sturdy and well fixed, and the wire panel held taut between them. Miniature versions are available for edging borders and paths at ankle height.

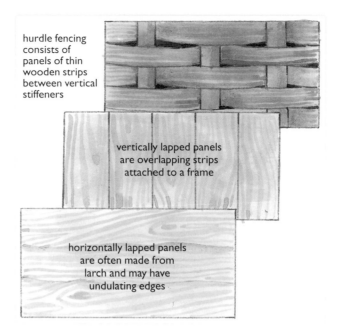

hurdle fencing consists of panels of thin wooden strips between vertical stiffeners

vertically lapped panels are overlapping strips attached to a frame

horizontally lapped panels are often made from larch and may have undulating edges

Concrete fencing

❀ This fence is a popular choice in municipal applications, valued for its minimal maintenance requirements and ease of installation compared with a brick wall.

❀ Slabs of interlocking concrete are slid horizontally between grooves in pre-formed concrete posts to make a solid, masonry wall that does not need foundations as brick walls do. It is difficult to climb, so enhances security, but blocks out light, is brutally unattractive and is also quite expensive.

BELOW: *A white painted heavy wooden wall can reflect the light in strong sunshine.*

ARCHES AND PERGOLAS

ARCHES and pergolas offer great opportunities for adding height to a garden, as well as providing additional planting surfaces and helping to divide the garden visually, so that the whole vista is not taken in at a glance.

ABOVE: *A pergola clothed in flowers adds height, drama and a valuable additional planting surface to the garden, as well as providing shade on hot days.*

BELOW: *The simple shape of the pergola can be greatly augmented by planting flowering climbers at each of the four corner bases.*

Which to choose

❀ Arches are comparatively narrow, while pergolas are essentially a single wide arch, or several arches linked together to form a garden corridor.

❀ Both arches and pergolas can encourage the eye to move through the garden more slowly by offering varying heights and making much more of the available space. These versatile structures can also encourage the eye to linger when appropriate, giving added visual impact, for example by placing a statue beneath an arch placed in front of a hedge.

Siting arches

❀ Always place arches so that they appear to have a definite purpose. All too often, an arch is purchased as an impulse buy, with little thought given to its appropriate site, and it ends up placed awkwardly in the middle of a lawn.

❀ As a rule, arches look most natural if they appear to lead somewhere, such as from a flower garden into a vegetable plot. Alternatively, arches can be used as a kind of picture frame, emphasising a particular feature, for example an arch fronting a scented flowering hedge, with an attractive seat placed thoughtfully below it.

Siting pergolas

❀ Pergolas need to be placed with equal sensitivity. A large pergola in the middle of nowhere can simply look like the skeleton of an unfinished building, instead of the striking garden feature you envisaged.

❀ Used for centuries to adorn long pathways, and often clad in wisteria or roses in large-scale formal gardens, pergolas have enjoyed a recent renaissance in more domestic settings. This is partly due to the increased availability of do-it-yourself pergola kits and because pergolas provide the sort of semi-covered environment ideally suited to al fresco eating.

❀ Lean-to pergolas are increasingly popular, as they form a visual link between the house and the garden and, when planted, can shade a patio used for entertaining.

Choosing arches and pergolas

❀ There are many materials and styles of arch and pergola available, including simple, inexpensive tubular metal curves, more ornate wrought-iron structures in Gothic-style shapes, and a variety of natural materials such as willow and the ever-popular rustic arch, consisting of split lengths of wood fixed to wooden poles in a trellis formation.

❀ Wooden arches and pergolas are also available in kit form. These are not expensive, and they save a considerable amount of laborious calculus. The selection of wooden components at most garden and do-it-yourself stores can be quite bewildering, and it

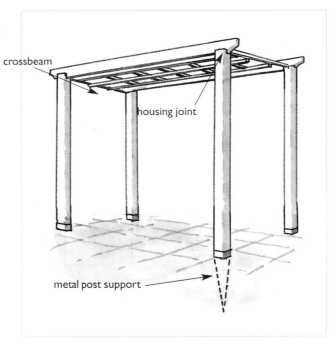

ABOVE: *Although imposing, pergolas are essentially very simple structures comprising vertical posts linked by cross beams, using halving joints at each intersection.*

crossbeam

housing joint

metal post support

can be difficult for the busy gardener to plan and translate such pieces into a single three-dimensional structure.

❀ Plant arches are very attractive, but obviously take time to become established – for example box hedging cut into archways, or willow planted and trained to form a living arch.

❀ Moon gates are circular arches popular in Oriental gardens, which are slowly becoming fashionable internationally, especially when used in conjunction with water as a striking visual feature. Brick and stone archways usually form part of a wall, and are often seen in large, formal gardens. They are an expensive and permanent option.

❀ Always make sure that you choose an arch of sufficient width to allow for a smooth passageway through it, even when it is covered with mature planting. As a rough guide, a reasonable internal height is 2 m (7 ft), and 1.2 m (4 ft) will be a sufficient internal width.

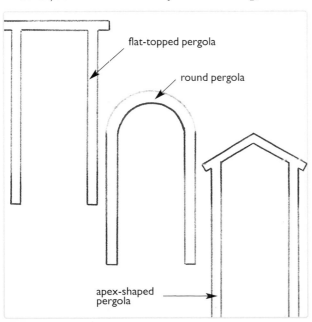

flat-topped pergola

round pergola

apex-shaped pergola

LEFT: *Pergolas are usually flat-topped, because this shape is simple to manufacture, but rounded and apex-shaped pergolas are also available, and can look much softer than the square profile.*

PROTECTIVE FINISHES, CLEANING AND MAINTENANCE

FENCES and other boundaries can be such a dominant part of a garden that it is important to maintain them properly. A collapsing, rotten fence is not the sort of visual highlight you want to draw attention to. Happily, if care is taken at the time of installation and, where appropriate, maintenance is carried out routinely, most fences and walls should remain attractive and functional for many years.

WOODEN FENCING

Fences are often neglected until a problem occurs, for example parts of it blowing over in a gale. Careful installation obviously helps to prevent such accidents. Ensuring that a fence is properly supported by appropriately secured posts at the outset will save a lot of remedial work.

Choosing a fence

❀ Choosing a fence that suits your needs will also determine the level of maintenance needed. For example, with an inadequately supported solid fence on an exposed site, it is almost inevitable that, sooner or later, panels are going to get damaged and displaced by high winds, which cannot move freely through the impenetrable barrier.

ABOVE: *The increasingly wide range of paints and preservatives available for exterior use has made it possible to unleash your wildest flights of decorating fancy in the garden as well as on the living-room walls.*

Stopping the rot

❀ Rot is the chief enemy of wooden fencing. Treat wood with an appropriate preservative annually, or at least every two years. Well-maintained wood should last for between 15 and 25 years. Softwoods, such as pine or larch, are obviously not as durable as more costly hardwoods like oak and beech.

❀ Water-based treatments should be chosen where the fence is in contact with plants. Manufactured fences and panels are generally sold already treated with preservative, but if you are creating your own fence from bare timber, you will need to treat it yourself.

❀ Pay special attention to particularly vulnerable areas, such as post ends, end grain and all parts of the fence that are at, or will be below, soil level. It is worth soaking the parts of the fence that will be below ground in

LEFT: *Applying the right protective finish to a well-prepared surface can prevent your garden buildings from becoming unsightly and unstable.*

preservative for at least 10 minutes, and preferably for an hour or so. To immerse whole lengths of timber, use an old bath, or make a temporary bath out of heavy-duty polythene sheeting supported by piled-up bricks.

Types of preservative

❀ As well as the preservatives in colours designed to replicate the shades of pricy hardwoods on inexpensive softwoods, a wide range of other colours is now available.

❀ Gardeners have increasingly come to consider the garden more as an outdoor room than as a separate entity, and judicious use of colour on hard surfaces, as well as in planting, can harmonise the soft and hard elements of the garden, as well as linking the garden visually with the house.

❀ Soft blues work surprisingly well in combination with planting, and the whole spectrum of greens is obviously a natural and discreet choice. Clear preservatives are popular, too, allowing the natural grain of the wood to show through. Most preservatives offer protection against insect attack, as well as warding off fungal disease.

Brick and stone walls

❀ If you are planning to paint masonry, always leave at least three months after installation before applying any

further treatment, so that the wall has a proper chance to dry out. Impatience may lead to all your carefully applied paint or plaster falling off the wall as it dries.

Efflorescence

❀ Do not be alarmed if you see white deposits defacing the surface of new brickwork. This is the water-soluble salts within the bricks coming to the surface as the wall dries out. The salts crystallise and form a white film on the wall's surface. Simply brush the deposits away with a wire brush or a piece of old sacking. Do not use water as this will bring new salts to the surface, aggravating the problem.

❀ Efflorescence will generally be a problem only for a couple of years on a new, freestanding wall, but the moisture behind a soil-retaining wall may cause a recurrence of the salts over many years. If you want to paint a wall that has been efflorescing with oil-based products, wait until the wall has dried out completely, and treat with an alkaline-resistant primer to neutralise the effects of the soluble salts before painting.

❀ Alternatively, use a paint specially formulated for this purpose, and which includes a primer. Water-based products are not adversely affected by alkaline salts, so the priming step can be omitted if such products are being used.

BELOW: *Always leave a newly constructed wall for at least three months before applying any treatment and brush any efflorescence off with a brush for a perfect finish.*

BUILDING HARD SURFACES

The garden floor can be a very dominant element in a garden design, yet its planning is all too often neglected in favour of perhaps the more exciting part of gardening –planting. Although most gardeners take great pride in their lawns, which are, essentially, living, green garden floors, the same attention is not lavished on hard-floored areas. An expanse of grey concrete, interrupted only by the odd weed, is not going to enhance any garden. The visual impact of hard flooring, particularly in large-scale applications such as driveways and patios, is often not considered until installation is complete, by which time it is too late to change your mind.

The planning stage

❀ Take home as many samples of hard flooring as you need, and view them *in situ* for several days before making a decision. Since hard surfaces are a critical part of the permanent structure of a garden design, highly visible even when most of the plants are dormant, you need to choose the material according to the style of your garden and house, as well as for practical and economical reasons.

❀ A path of modern grey slabs will clearly do nothing to enhance a 17th-century red-brick house. Equally, a herringbone path of weathered old paving bricks would look wildly uncomfortable in an austere urban setting.

❀ As well as being a prominent visual feature, hard surfaces are important practical components within the garden. They work hard for their keep, yet are often ignored until problems occur, such as frozen puddles in a pathway which trip up the unwary

ABOVE: *Plan your terracing carefully to maximise sunlight and create different flooring patterns and levels to add interest to the area.*

ABOVE: *Cobbles are uncomfortable to walk on, so stepping stones provide a welcome contrasting surface.*

ABOVE: *Gravel is an inexpensive yet elegant garden flooring material.*

pedestrian. Proper planning at the outset, choosing materials appropriate to the situation and purpose, and simple routine maintenance, will give you a garden floor to be proud of.

❀ The type of material you choose for a path or drive will largely depend on its primary function. For example, a path intended chiefly for decoration, which will barely be walked on, will have quite different demands placed on it than the walkway that leads to your front door.

Practical matters

❀ Consider whether your preferred material is suitable for the design of your path, drive or other hard surfaced area. For example, gravel or crazy paving can easily be used to make an intricately winding path, but to produce an undulating narrow shape in large paving slabs would involve a lot of tedious calculation and cutting, and would not necessarily look natural or comfortable on completion.

❀ It may sound obvious, but make sure that your hard surfaces are adequately sized for their function. As a rough guide, paths need to be at least 1 m (3 ft) wide to allow comfortable access. Do not assume, if you are replacing an existing hard surface, that you automatically lay a new surface the same size as the old one. It is all too easy to have a driveway or parking space professionally, and expensively, laid only to find that it is too small for your car, or too cramped to allow room for your vehicle and pedestrian access around it.

❀ Mark out your proposed design with rope or a hose, or by dropping dry sand through a funnel to leave a trail. Check out the area from every angle, preferably over a period of a few days. This is especially important in areas like patios, which are garden rooms as well as hard surfaces.

❀ You will want to make sure that the area you are planning to use for entertaining receives the kind of light you want, at the time of day the patio will most commonly be used. For example, if you are installing a patio chiefly for early evening dining, there is no point placing it next to the house if the sunlight is at the other end of your garden at that time.

TYPES OF HARD SURFACE

THERE are a number of options to choose from, when it comes to creating a hard floor in your garden.

Bricks

❀ It is tempting to economise on bricks for paving, but the shortcomings of using ordinary house bricks for this demanding function become clear all too quickly. Their porosity means that as water penetrates, freezes, then expands, it cracks away the layers of brick, creating an uneven, flaky, broken surface. This is unsightly and can also be dangerous to walk on, particularly when used as steps.

❀ Engineering bricks are often specified for paving instead, as they are much denser and impervious to water. However, they can become slippery when wet, so 'special' quality bricks are the recommended choice. These are also weather resistant, but are not so prone to weather damage.

❀ Second-hand bricks make a very attractive path, which tones in well with old buildings, but always check that you are buying proper pavers, not simply old house bricks sold as pavers. Insist on a written description if possible. Reliable architectural salvage companies are generally quite happy to provide such a guarantee, since they should be aware of the provenance of the salvaged material.

Stone

❀ Natural stone, once the first choice in path making, has been superseded in popularity by cast alternatives, due to the high cost of the real thing.

❀ Flagstones of slate, limestone, York stone or sandstone are exceptionally beautiful, as well as hard-wearing, and can be chosen to complement the local stone. Being of natural origin, they also harmonise wonderfully with plant, water and other organic garden elements. Their irregular surface and random patterning can never truly be mimicked by cast alternatives, but the difficulty of cutting them and their expense place them firmly in the luxury bracket.

Cobblestones

❀ The naturally rounded surface of cobblestones makes them uncomfortable to walk on, so their use is best restricted to ornamental applications. You could break up an expanse of paving slabs by interspersing the slabbed area with areas of cobblestones. They provide an interesting shift in texture, and complement planting well.

❀ Cobbles may be laid loose, or set in concrete or mortar for a more permanent, formal effect. Always ensure that the tops of the stones are level for an even finish for walking on.

Wood and bark

❀ Natural materials are particularly appropriate and attractive in a woodland, or semi-wild setting, which would look uncomfortable paved with a harsh, non-organic surface such as concrete. Sawn rounds of timber are surprisingly hard-wearing as pavers if they are well treated by soaking in preservative prior to installation, then laid on a bed of sand on top of perforated polythene sheeting.

❀ Fill the gaps between the circles with a sand and gravel mix or chipped bark. Bark needs topping up every few years as it slowly degrades. Wooden decking is increasingly popular as exterior flooring, and looks equally good in urban or country locations. Wooden rounds are also often used as stepping stones across a lawn.

ABOVE: *Decking is a decidedly contemporary flooring material, ideally suited to modern urban gardens.*

Concrete

❀ Concrete may not be the most attractive hard garden surface, but it is probably the most durable, relatively inexpensive, maintenance free if properly installed and suitable for awkward shapes such as winding paths and driveways.

❀ Essentially, concrete consists of cement combined with an aggregate (fine particles of stone). These dry ingredients are mixed with water, which reacts chemically with the cement and binds the stone particles into a firm, compacted material capable of withstanding tough treatment.

❀ Various mixtures of concrete are used, incorporating, for example, PVA to enhance frost resistance, and/or pigments to produce colours other than the usual grey.

❀ For small jobs, concrete can be mixed by hand, but for more extensive areas, it is well worth hiring a concrete mixer, or having ready-mixed concrete delivered direct to the site. Careful preparation of the site is critical. All too often, concrete is seen as the easy paving option, but if added to an unstable, inadequately prepared surface, the results will be unsatisfactory.

❀ Concrete is also available formed into cast slabs, which can mimic real stone. These provide a popular, affordable alternative to real stone paving.

Gravel

❀ Gravel is another popular, affordable and versatile material. It can withstand heavy use on a driveway, yet is equally suited to small-scale settings such as walkways through a herb garden. Gravel is easy to install, even in curved situations, but for best effect needs to be placed on a proper bed of consolidated coarse gravel.

brick patterns

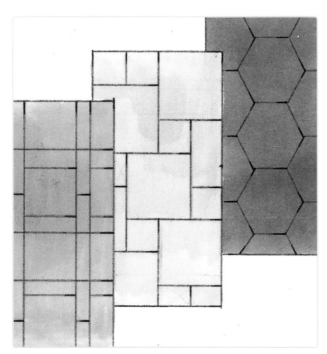

paving slab patterns

decking patterns

PATIOS

ALTHOUGH, technically, a patio is an area paved with flagstones, enclosed by walls, it has come to be used as a generic term for a hard-surfaced area, usually, but not always, adjoining a house, which is used for relaxing and entertaining. Installing a patio is quite a major undertaking, and needs extremely careful planning and preparation. Mistakes are costly, and permanent.

Customising an existing patio

❀ You may have inherited a patio that is technically sound, and performs its practical function perfectly, but which is bland and uninspiring. Sympathetic planting can do much to improve matters, without extensive structural work.

❀ Container plants look thoroughly at home on patios, and can be changed seasonally. Choose the style and materials of the containers to link the patio with the house.

❀ Removing some of the slabs and replacing them with planting, and/or other surfaces, such as cobbles, broken slate, gravel or coloured aggregate, will also enliven the overall scheme. You could also introduce vertical elements to break up an overlarge expanse of paving, for example trellis, a pergola, raised beds that incorporate seating, or simply a stunning table, chairs and parasol.

ABOVE: *Although patios were originally made up of stone flags, nowadays more and more people are opting for wooden decking.*

PLANNING A PATIO

THERE is a surprising amount to think about when planning a patio, if you want to create a feature that will be as visually attractive as it is practical. It is easy to be swayed into buying a load of paving because it appealed on one sunny afternoon in the garden centre, or was on special offer, only to find that it is quite unsuitable when installed.

Site

❀ Of course, a patio adjoining the house is ideal. Food, drinks, books and cushions may be easily transported between house and garden, particularly if you are fortunate enough to have French doors that lead directly on to the patio.

❀ However, if the area that initially suggests itself as the patio site is very shaded at the time of day that you plan to use it most, you may want to think about having an additional hard-surfaced area elsewhere in the garden. If the problem is one of light shade, caused by overhanging foliage, then the answer may be as simple as pruning back unwanted growth.

❀ If wind is a problem, but the site is otherwise perfect, then consider installing some form of windbreak, for

ABOVE: *This colourful patio appears at first glance to be stone, but it is decking interwoven with blue strips of wood and small clumps of herbs.*

ABOVE: *The word patio is now a generic term for a hard-surfaced area that is used for relaxing and entertaining.*

example a semi-permeable natural screen such as hurdle fencing, bamboo or an interwoven fence. Privacy may also be an important issue, particularly if you plan to sunbathe and relax on your patio, yet your garden is exposed. Again, natural or artificial screens can come into their own here.

Size

❀ It may sound obvious, but check that the size of patio you are planning is adequate for your needs. If you just want to sit outside and read occasionally, then technically you will need only a quite limited space, but if you enjoy container gardening, you may want to increase the patio to accommodate significant numbers of sizeable plants.

❀ If you plan to cook outside frequently – perhaps on a large gas-fired barbecue or outdoor stove – and entertain on a regular basis, your requirements will be quite different. You will need space for a table and chairs that will comfortably accommodate your guests, together with space for food cooking and preparation.

Patio surfaces

❀ Once you have established what the patio is mostly going to be used for, where it is going to be, and how big it needs to be, you can at last turn your attention to how it is going to look. The general guidelines on the previous pages on choosing materials still apply.

❀ Choose a surface to suit your home. Patios are a dominant visual feature, and can just as easily detract from the beauty and value of your home as they can add to it. Do not be tempted to mix too many types of surface in an effort to add interest. By the time a patio has dining seats, sun loungers, perhaps more than one table, possibly lighting, screening, maybe a water feature, together with a barbecue and all the other paraphernalia that tends to accumulate on a patio, it will quickly become very busy looking and is unlikely to need much in the way of added interest underfoot.

❀ Two surfaces are probably the most you will need to create a dynamic, but balanced and restrained patio, for example slabs interspersed with pebbles and planting, or wooden decking bordered by gravel.

PATHS

PATHS are hard-working surfaces. They carry not only foot traffic, but often wheelbarrows, heavily loaded sack trolleys and bicycles, too. They may also be required to permit the regular use of wheelchairs or a pram. If planning a garden from scratch, these individual needs can be catered for.

Choosing a path

❀ Always make the path sufficiently wide for its purpose. Ideally, two people should be able to walk along a path, side by side, without any sense of being cramped.

❀ Choose materials suited to the surroundings, as well as to the practical requirements placed on them. For example, a tarmac path may be inexpensive and hard-wearing, but will be an unforgiving feature leading up to your front door. It may be worth investing in a more attractive surface for such a prominent position.

Gravel paths

❀ Washed gravel is an attractive and inexpensive paving material. The ideal size of stone is approximately 2 cm ($^3/_4$ in) in diameter. This generally presents the least problems in terms of stones being brought into the house via shoes.

ABOVE: *Paths should always be planned according to individual requirements; consider what your needs are before deciding on the style of walkway that would suit you best.*

ABOVE: *Here the blue of the sea and gentle pink of the flowers in the background are reflected in the soft colours of the paving on the terrace.*

Brick paths

❀ Brick paths are particularly attractive and, if created using bricks sympathetic to those used for the house, provide a strong yet unobtrusive visual link between the house and garden. They may be laid in a variety of patterns, including straight or angled herringbone, basket weave and stretcher bond.

Concrete paving

❀ Concrete is an enduringly popular choice for paving. It is relatively inexpensive, yet very durable. Concrete is only hard-wearing if it is installed properly, so careful planning is essential before starting to prepare the path.

❀ Concrete is a much maligned surface, decried for its bland grey appearance. However, a well-laid concrete path can, in some cases, be more attractive than a more showy surface of ill-proportioned, poorly installed, over-bright imitation stone slabs, which may have cost much more.

Textural possibilities

❀ You can vary the surface texture of a finished concrete path for added visual interest. The natural surface that results from the tamping process, which completes the path laying, is practical and non-slip, with a slightly rough texture.

❀ The setting concrete may be dragged with a broom to create a subtly striped, rippled finish, or swept with a wooden float for a smooth finish that works well in stark, modern settings. Another option is to mimic the effects of crazy paving by marking the surface of the concrete with a stick to resemble irregularly shaped slabs.

❦ Embedding a decorative aggregate in the surface of the concrete is another option. Scatter dampened pebbles on to the newly laid concrete and tamp with timber until flush with the surface. When all surface water has evaporated, gently wash away cement from around the pebbles until they protrude. An alternative textural finish is achieved by simply washing away the fine surface of the setting concrete to reveal the gravel below.

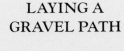

LAYING A BRICK PATH

Brick paths need to be laid on a 7.5 cm (3 in) thick, compacted hard core base, topped with a 5-cm (2-in) thick layer of sharp sand.

1 *Support the bricks with a permanent edging such as timber or a row of bricks set on end into concrete.*

2 *Set the bricks with fine sand and water well. Ensure that the sand packs down between the bricks. Repeat until the cracks are packed.*

LAYING A GRAVEL PATH

Prepare a site for gravel well. Edging, to contain the gravel, is very important. Bricks laid on their edge and set in concrete are popular edgings.

1 *Thoroughly compact the hard core surface for the path, then top it with a 5-cm (2-in) deep layer of coarse gravel.*

2 *Follow this with a layer of hoggin (clay binder), spread it to fill any cracks, then roll it. Finally, add a 2.5–4 cm (1–1½ in) layer of washed gravel and roll this, too.*

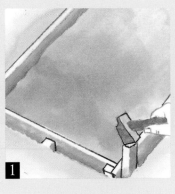

LAYING CONCRETE PAVING SLABS

Paving slabs are widely available. Choose a finish sympathetic to your garden style for best results. Laying heavy slabs is simple but hard work.

1 *Take care to set out the slabs and lay them properly for best results. Try to use only whole slabs to avoid the need for cutting slabs.*

2 *Lay paving slabs on a firm, level base of hard-core topped with sharp sand and tamp them down. A slight, even slope will be needed to allow water to run off the surface. Paint with mortar after a couple of days*

DRIVEWAYS

DRIVEWAYS have the toughest hard-surface job of all. They need to be able to withstand heavy, continual traffic. Gravel is an attractive, relatively inexpensive material for driveways and makes a satisfying crunch as you park. Concrete is a popular alternative. Commercial contractors can install concrete drives imprinted with patterns. These can be more attractive than flat concrete drives, yet less expensive than specialist individual bricks or slabs.

Planning driveways

❀ It may sound obvious that the first step in planning a driveway or car parking pad is to ascertain how big the area needs to be, yet it is alarmingly easy to underestimate the amount of space that a vehicle occupies. As a general rule, a minimum width of 3 m (10 ft) is required, but this will vary according to your individual needs – you may regularly need to park a much larger vehicle in your garden. Consider, too, the turning circle of your vehicle.

❀ You may not have unlimited space for a drive, but if you do have a little more than the bare minimum available to give over to a drive, life will be very much more convenient for you. Imagine not having to shout at your children about banging the car doors against the wall or fence on a daily basis, and you might resent less having to give over a little of your garden to the car.

❀ A very easy mistake to make is to forget to allow for opening the car doors, which becomes a real problem if the driveway is close to a wall. Ideally, also allow plenty of space for pedestrian access around parked cars. If you know that prams and bikes are going to be wheeled past your parked car regularly, it is well worth incorporating a little extra space into your driveway to avoid frayed tempers

ABOVE: *Be prepared to cut back on your borders to allow space for your parking area.*

as the paint gets repeatedly scraped away from the side of the car by an exuberant young cyclist.

❀ It is tempting to make driveways as small as possible, since they are not generally things of inherent loveliness. However, if you refuse to move your flowerbed a single inch to accommodate a reasonably sized driveway, you may find your precious perennials destroyed anyway, as people scramble out of the car and across the ornamental borders.

RIGHT: *A hard-working driveway is softened visually by a curved edge and planted border.*

The importance of slope

❀ Parking areas and driveways must have a sufficient slope to allow water to fall away, so that the surface retains enough traction for vehicles in icy conditions. You do not want puddles forming in the drive, so the surface needs to be absolutely even. When a concrete parking area is laid next to a house, it must slope away markedly from the building, and must be at least 15 cm (6 in) below the damp course.

❀ As a general guide to the degree of fall-off required, a drive needs a 1-in-40 gradient – 2.5 cm per metre (1 in per yard) to be effective. A hard surface such as a parking area or patio installed next to a house needs a 1-in-60 gradient – 1.6 cm per metre ($^5/_8$ in per yard).

PREVENTING CONCRETE FROM CRACKING

TEMPERATURE changes cause concrete to expand and contract. If this motion is allowed to continue randomly, the surface will crack open at its weakest point. Control joints, also known as expansion joints, made of compressible material such as wooden planks, are added at regular intervals to concentrate or absorb the force of the contraction and expansion.

Pathways need control joints at approximately 2-m (7-ft) intervals, while driveways need such joints every 4 m (13 ft). If a parking area is more than twice as long as its width, or its length is more than 40 times its thickness, you will need to divide the concrete into equal sections with control joints. Control joints are also always needed between concrete that adjoins a wall, and where concrete surrounds inspection chambers.

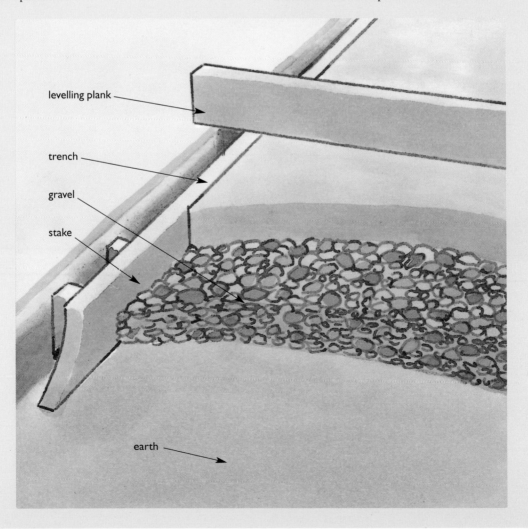

levelling plank

trench

gravel

stake

earth

BUILDING PONDS

Water, contained or moving, is a fabulous addition to any garden.
Even the smallest plot can accommodate a water feature, even if it is as
simple as a wall-mounted spout trickling water into a small ornamental
trough. The sound of moving water is incredibly tranquil, and gazing
into the reflections of a pond is also very calming. Do not be put off
by the technical aspects of water gardening. There are ways of
incorporating water into a garden design that need no complex
wiring or plumbing arrangements. For example, simply adding
a bird-bath and keeping it topped up with a watering can
is a feature that will attract birds to your garden.

Water and wildlife

❀ Many gardeners introduce water features because they
want to encourage wildlife to come into the garden. This
has many significant benefits beyond the immediate
pleasures of watching frogs leaping around the pond, or
birds enjoying a morning bath.

BELOW: *A fountain adds interest to a geometric pond.*

❀ Introducing wildlife to your garden moves you closer to
an organic gardening style – that is, gardening using all
the forces of nature to optimum effect. Birds, animals
and insects will be attracted by a ready supply of water,
and will repay you by assisting in pest control and by
improving soil fertility.

❀ Birds will not only amuse you with their antics in your
bird-bath, but also devour pests such as wireworms and
leatherjackets and improve soil fertility by adding their
droppings, and eventually their bodies when they die, to
produce humus. Birds with good access to water will also
eat less of your berries and fruits.

CONTAINER PONDS

CONTAINER ponds are a brilliant introduction to water
gardening, and are wonderfully adaptable to individual
needs. Even if you are gardening outside a fifth-floor
apartment, on an area little bigger than a fire escape, you can
still have a pond. Another great attribute of self-contained
ponds is that they are portable. You can move one around to
change the look of the garden, in the same way that you
dress it differently throughout the seasons with container
plants. You can also take it with you when you move house.

Choosing containers

❀ A wide variety of containers are suitable, such as glazed
pots in aquatic tones of cobalt blue or viridian, or half-
barrels, which look very comfortable in cottage-style
settings. Plants can include miniature water lilies, which
prefer still water, combined with marginal and
oxygenating plants, while goldfish can dart prettily in

ABOVE: *There is a pond style to suit every gardening taste – this Oriental-looking pond is full of koi carp.*

and out of the foliage. If you are using a metal container, make sure that it is not of a type that will leach rust into the water, as this can harm plants and fish. Painting a galvanised container with black bituminous paint will render it safe.

❀ It may sound obvious, but always choose a container that is leakproof. Ask to have the container filled with water if you are in any doubt as to its watertightness. Risking momentary embarrassment will save a lot of aggravation later. Small containers look unattractive if you need to line them with something. Although you can drain a leaking container and seal it internally with a proprietary sealant before painting it with bituminous paint, this is not a job most gardeners would actively seek to undertake.

Winter care

❀ Ideally, bring a ceramic container pond under cover for winter, as it may crack if the water in it freezes and then expands. Alternatively, drain and store it upside down if keeping it outside, so that it does not fill with rainwater, which may also freeze and cause cracking.

❀ Barrel ponds are made of wood, which is a natural insulator, so can be left out of doors in sheltered conditions. However, pay attention to the individual needs of the fish and plants in all types of container pond. Even if the wood does not crack in freezing conditions, the fish may not be so resilient.

BELOW: *Here water is piped in steps from a spouting fountain in one ceramic container to a second and on into a third.*

PERMANENT PONDS

SINCE permanent ponds are designed to be just that, it is well worth taking a really careful look at all the factors that need to be considered before starting work. It can be all too easy to be swayed into buying a liner that has been made into an attractively landscaped pond in a garden centre, but which may be quite unsuitable in the site available in your own garden, so do plan thoroughly before purchasing.

Size

❀ To keep the water clear, and to sustain a reasonable amount of wildlife such as several different types of fish, you will need a pond with a minimum depth of 60 cm (24 in), with a water surface of at least 3.7 sq m (40 sq ft).

Site

❀ Ideally, site a pond in an area that receives at least six hours of sunlight each day, is sheltered from easterly winds, and not close to deciduous trees, which will shower it with leaves every autumn. Decayed leaves produce gases and salts that are hazardous to fish, and encourage green algae.

❀ Ponds can obviously be positioned in shady sites, and the reflections on the surface of the water can light up a dull corner, but most pond plants need good light in order to thrive. A water feature without organic elements, for example a fountain or waterspout, is a better choice in a shady spot.

BELOW: *Blue ceramic pots and blue paving that surround the pond are matched by blue flowers.*

❀ If you are planning to incorporate moving water within your pond, you will need access to electricity. Although you can have an electricity supply installed where it is needed, you may find the cost precludes this option.

❀ Rather than surrender your dream of a cascading fountain entirely, you may reach a compromise by siting your pond close to a mains power source, such as an outbuilding or the house itself. Solar-powered pumps are another option. At the time of writing, they are in their infancy, expensive and with power that diminishes as light levels drop. However, they are an ecologically

BELOW: *Ponds can be as big or small as the space in a garden dictates.*

sound development, and of particular interest to gardeners without access to external power supplies.

Shape and style

❀ Choose a shape that harmonises with the rest of your garden. A pond that mimics a natural pool, complete with rocky outcrops and alpine planting, is all too often the automatic choice of the novice water gardener; yet it may look hopelessly incongruous in an austere, modern setting. Conversely, a small, higgledy-piggledy cottage-style garden would look very uncomfortable with a ferociously geometric formal pool at its centre.

Safety

❀ Any amount of standing water poses a potential drowning hazard, especially to a small child. The only truly child-friendly water features are those with no standing water, such as pebble fountains.

❀ However, it is possible to render a conventional pond childproof by covering the water with a strong metal grid, which may be concealed by growing plants through it. The grid can be removed when your children have grown up, but remember that your uncovered pond is also dangerous to any visiting children, who will be particularly attracted by the novelty of unfamiliarity.

MAKING A LINED POND

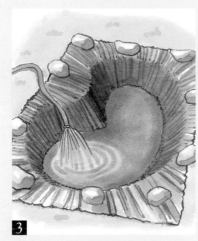

1

2

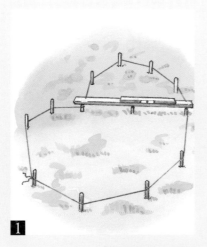

3

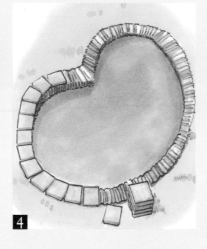

4

2 Excavate the hole, initially working around the edge to a depth of approximately 30 cm (12 in) to produce a planting shelf for marginal plants. Continue by digging out the central part of the pond, leaving the planting shelf the same width as its depth. Remove any roots, rocks and debris from the base of the pond, since these may puncture the liner.

3 Place the liner across the hole and leave it to settle for an hour or so. Making sure that the liner is centred over the hole, place stones around its edges to weigh it down. Fill the pond with slow-running water, allowing the liner to settle evenly into the hole. Gradually remove the stones from the edge of the liner as the pond fills. Fold the liner neatly, if necessary, to incorporate any corners.

4 Remove the stones and trim the liner with scissors, leaving a 15-cm (6-in) 'fringe' all the way around. Lay edging stones on a mortar base around the perimeter of the pond to conceal the excess liner.

1 Mark out the required pond shape on the ground, using a hose or string and pegs. Measure the area of the pond to calculate the amount of flexible pond liner required (see over).

CHOOSING POND LINERS

TRADITIONALLY, puddled clay was used to retain water in ponds, but it is not a reliable or convenient lining method. Concrete is still used in some commercial applications, but is costly and laborious to install. Most modern water gardeners choose between rigid and flexible liners when installing a pond.

❀ Preformed liners can be expensive, and their 'ready-made' look is deceptive. They are actually more difficult to install than flexible liners, which are brilliantly versatile.

❀ Always buy the best-quality liner you can afford, so that you don't need to replace it in a hurry. This is particularly important if you are planning a large, complex water garden, full of fish and plants, which would be time-consuming and tedious to dismantle for liner repair or replacement.

RIGID LINERS

PREFORMED liners are an extremely popular choice, but the cheaper, more commonly used semi-rigid preformed liners actually move about as you are trying to fit them, making installation very difficult. Any inaccuracy in fitting is soon cruelly revealed as water gathers at one end or, worse still, the liner cracks as it is forced to try and hold a great weight of water at a point that is not sufficiently supported beneath the liner. They are also short-lived, lasting only five to 10 years. They are generally too shallow for overwintering fish, unless you use a pond heater. They are also too shallow for many plants. Truly rigid liners are much more expensive, and do last for 25 years or more if installed properly; but for most situations, a good-quality flexible liner is a better choice.

ABOVE: A well-maintained pond brings a whole new dimension to gardening.

FLEXIBLE LINERS

WITH a flexible liner you can create a truly customised pond, shaped as you wish, with appropriate depth for all the plants and fish that you want. Mark out the shape on the ground using a line of sand, a hose or rope to get a feel for your design before you commit to it. To calculate the amount of flexible liner needed, measure the length and width of the desired pond. Add double the maximum depth of the pond to each measurement. For an irregularly shaped pond, follow the same process, first fitting the irregular shape into an imaginary rectangle to determine its rough size.

Butyl rubber

❀ This is wonderfully forgiving and tolerant, easy to install, flexible, and will even adapt over time as the soil beneath it settles. As long as it is not punctured by careless handling or animal attack, it will last for at least 25 years, a major plus if you are installing a complicated water feature.

Long-life PVC

❀ Not as expensive as butyl rubber, this material has been chemically treated to enhance its flexibility so that it will resist cracking in sunlight. Some liners classified as long-life PVC have been nylon reinforced, which does strengthen them, but does not necessarily make them less brittle. Both types should last up to 25 years.

PVC

❀ PVC is really suitable only for lining a bog garden, where the liner will be totally concealed from the sun, since PVC becomes brittle after repeated sun exposure, and will start to crack around the edges where it is not covered with water.

❀ Although punctures in flexible liners beneath the water can be repaired, it is not possible to repair cracks around the pond's rim satisfactorily. PVC is inexpensive and may be an option if you are installing a water feature destined to be very short-lived. The average life expectancy of a PVC liner is between five and 10 years.

Black polythene

❀ Do not be tempted to use cheap black polythene as a pond liner, not even for a bog garden. It is simply not substantial enough, and will last for only two or three years at the most.

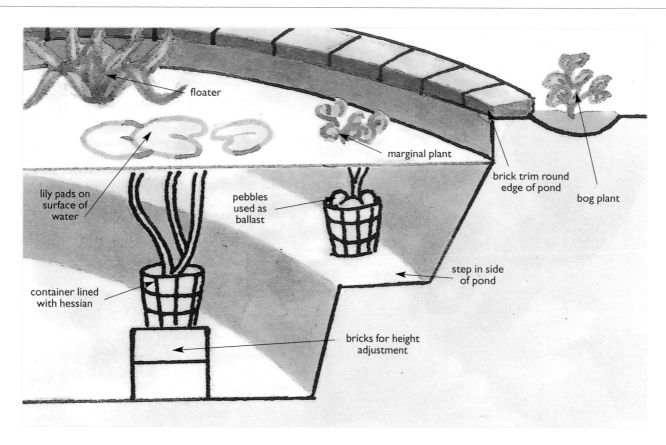

ABOVE: *Cross-section of a stepped and lined permanent pond, showing planting features.*

PLANTING UP A POND BASKET

1 Use a container of adequate size for the root system of the fully grown plant. Unless it is of very fine mesh, line the container with hessian. Add moist aquatic soil to the container and place the plant on top. Backfill with more aquatic soil, firming it in.

2 To weight down the container and prevent soil dispersing into the water, add a top dressing of gravel.

3 Cut away any excess hessian and fix string handles to the rim of the container to help you lower it into position in the pond. If the plant is too immature and light to stay anchored below the surface of the water, add more gravel or large pebbles as ballast until the plant grows bigger.

MAINTAINING A POND

Your pond will require various maintenance tasks, depending on the season.

Spring

❀ Feed fish according to their individual needs when you notice that they have become active.

❀ Check that all electrical components of your water feature are in good working order.

❀ Remove, clean and store your pond heater.

❀ Reconnect the submersible pump on your fountain or waterfall.

❀ Lift, divide and replant new portions of congested water lilies and other overcrowded plants.

❀ Start to plant new aquatics.

❀ Fertilise established aquatic plants, following the manufacturer's directions explicitly so that you do not inadvertently feed the algae rather than the cultivated plants.

Autumn

❀ As long as fish appear active, continue feeding.

❀ Continue planting until the weather begins to grow cooler.

❀ Continue lifting, dividing and replanting new portions of overcrowded plants until the colder weather arrives.

❀ Cut down and remove the foliage and flower stems of plants as they fade, having first checked the individual needs of each plant. For example, marginal plants should not be cut down below the water level.

❀ Remove debris from the pond regularly.

❀ Screen the pond by placing mesh netting over the surface, if necessary, to keep out leaves until neighbouring trees are bare.

❀ Remove tender plants and overwinter them in water in a cool, but frost-free environment.

❀ Remove, clean and store the submersible pump.

❀ Install the pond heater.

Summer

❀ Continue feeding the fish, following the food manufacturer's directions precisely.

❀ Continue planting.

❀ Monitor the water level and top up as necessary. In hot conditions, the level can drop 2.5–5 cm (1–2 in) in a week, which can make a real difference in a small pond, and is obviously hazardous to plants, fish and the pond liner. If you are going away for a long period, have a friend keep an eye on the water level in your absence and top it up if necessary.

❀ Remove blanket weed from the surface of the water using a rake or by winding it on to a stick.

❀ Deadhead faded flower heads before they set seed.

Winter

❀ Stop feeding the fish.

❀ Stop planting.

❀ Take precautionary measures against the worst of the winter weather. Float a ball on the surface of the water if you do not have a pond heater to prevent ice forming. In a small pool, the whole pond can become frozen, which is lethal for fish and many plants. In larger ponds, the ice itself is not a killer, but if the surface of the water is covered with ice for more than a day or so, the toxic methane gas released from submerged, decaying vegetation is allowed to build up and can be lethal to fish. Keeping a small area of the pond free of ice permits the gas to disperse into the air.

Treating leaks

❀ If a pond is losing more water than you would expect from normal levels of evaporation, you will need to investigate further. Temporarily house fish and plants elsewhere during your explorations.

❀ If you have a fountain or other water course fitted, turn off the pump and see if the water level drops, since most leaks occur around the cascade part. If no leak is visible here, or if you do not have a water course fitted, top up the pond and allow the water level to drop naturally until you see the leak. The planting shelf is another common site of leaks.

❀ Sudden, dramatic water loss indicates a major hole, which will need to be fixed in a similar way to repairing a puncture on a bicycle tyre. Use a kit appropriate to the type of liner you have.

❀ If all efforts to find the leak prove fruitless, you may need to put a replacement liner over the old one.

Leaks in newly installed ponds

❀ Check that the edges of the pond are level. The problem may simply be caused by gravity – the water flowing out of the pond at its lowest point. Another potential problem, which is easily rectified, is that a fold in a flexible liner may be forming a lip, over which water is running, away from the pond. A quick adjustment will stop the leak instantly.

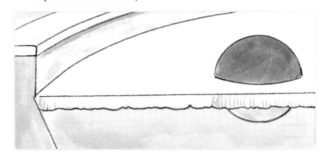

ABOVE: *Float a ball in a newly made pond to ensure that the edges are level – if they are not the ball will naturally drift to the lower edge.*

MENDING A MAJOR HOLE IN A POND

If water is lost suddenly from a pond, this indicates a major hole has formed in the liner.

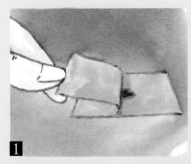

1 *Locate the hole and find a repair kit to suit the lining of the pond. Place glue over and around the hole in the pond liner. Smear the glue on the patch. Allow to firm up.*

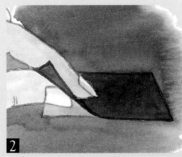

2 *Place the patch firmly on the glue over the hole in the liner, press down and seal. Allow to harden.*

MAINTENANCE

Planted ponds need maintenance to remain healthy and attractive.

1 *Cut away yellowing leaves with a sharp knife.*

2 *Remove blanketweed by revolving a stick in the water.*

3 *Skim off duckweed by drawing a plank across the water's surface.*

INSTALLATION

WATER and electricity are always a combination to be taken seriously where safety is concerned. Low-voltage pumps are available, but are suitable only for small-scale features as they have limited power. Solar-powered pumps are also an option, but are not yet realistic alternatives to mains-powered systems because of their high initial cost and intermittent power in changing weather conditions.

❋ If you are in any doubt at all about installing an electrically powered water feature, use a qualified electrician familiar with this type of work.

❋ A mains cable needs to be run through a conduit pipe to protect it from damage. The conduit is concealed beneath the soil, decking or paving. Always fit a residual current device (RCD), which will cause the power to cut out immediately should there be an interruption to the supply.

❋ Alternatively, have armoured cable and a weatherproof outdoor box with permanently wired-in cables professionally installed.

BELOW: *Water features can incorporate seemingly humble household materials with style and wit.*

TYPES OF MOVING WATER FEATURE

MOVING water can be incorporated within a pond or pool, or can be a self-contained fountain. Fountains are a particularly useful way of introducing water in difficult situations. Confined spaces that cannot house ponds can almost always offer a vertical surface for a self-contained wall-mounted fountain. In addition, many types of fountains and streams run off over pebbles or slates, so that there is no standing water, which might pose a drowning hazard for small children.

Fountains

❋ There are many different types of jet available, which fit on the outlet on the top of a submersible pump, to produce a variety of effects. Even a pump with no jet fitted will produce an attractive ripple of water. Choose a jet pattern that is suited your chosen water feature and its surroundings.

CHOOSING A PUMP

SUBMERSIBLE pumps are suitable for most applications. They are installed at the lowest part of the system, but not on the bottom of the pond where they would draw in the sediment that collects there and quickly become blocked. An upturned pond basket makes a good support.

Buy the best-quality pump you can afford. The pump included as part of an inexpensive fountain kit may be of such low power that the water cascade turns out to be no more than a dispiriting dribble. If the fountain or water feature itself appeals, and it is reasonably priced, consider buying a better pump to replace the one sold with the kit.

If you are creating your own moving water feature, it is worth buying your pump from a reputable specialist water garden supplier, who is dealing with pumps all the time and will be able to advise you as to the most appropriate pump for your needs. Pumps have differing outputs, and these should be clearly marked on the packaging. The output determines how high the pump can propel the water. Clearly, a small bubble fountain does not need a powerful pump, but if you are planning a large fountain that incorporates a gusher jet, you will need more power.

ABOVE: An ingenious cobble fountain, using large slabs of stone to give a generous flow of water over the cobbles and a lovely splashing sound.

❀ For example, a bell-jet fountain may look very appealing in the quiet shelter of an enclosed garden centre display, but the neat, bell-shaped fall of water will not be consistent in an exposed, windy position. A foam jet would be a better choice in this situation. All jets are prone to blockage to some degree, so site your fountain where you can easily access the jets for routine maintenance.

Waterfalls

❀ Waterfalls are not as popular as fountains, largely because they are not generally self-contained and they are more difficult to incorporate within a garden scheme in a convincing way. Ideally, a waterfall should appear totally natural and in harmony with its environment. A good way of introducing a waterfall is to have it linking two streams together. Be especially careful about landscaping a waterfall. Think about how it will look when the water is turned off. It is all too easy to create a concrete edifice that looks like a miniature quarry rather than an idyllic alpine vista.

CHOOSING THE TYPE OF JET

ALTHOUGH narrow jets of water can sometimes be effective spouting from an informal pool, fountains tend to be more suited to formal layouts. Stone fountains suit symmetrical balance, paved paths, clipped hedges and straight edges. Small, enclosed medieval gardens often had paved paths leading to a fountain in the centre.

However, a fountain jet in an informal pond or a terrace pool will help to oxygenate the water. A few hours of fountain operation in a small pool on a hot summer's day will greatly enhance the oxygen level for fish and plants.

You can diminish turbulence on the water surface by using certain types of jet. For example, a bell jet confines the spray to a very small area of a pool's surface, and will not disturb the leaves of water lilies.

WATERING SYSTEMS

ALL gardens need watering in hot, dry weather. In very tiny gardens, a watering can may be adequate, but most gardens need something more.

Watering by hand

❀ Some people are content to water by hand, using a simple hose on a reel. The reel can be mobile or fixed to a wall, in which case it should ideally be concealed by shrubs or climbers where it will be unobtrusive.

Using sprinklers

❀ Rather than watering by hand, you may prefer to leave a sprinkler on and move it around the garden from time to time. Oscillating sprinklers are the most versatile option for large gardens. Static sprinklers are the simplest and are good for small, confined areas. Pulse jet sprinklers are the most costly but will cover the largest area. Before using a sprinkler, check how far the spray reaches. It can be very annoying for neighbours if they get sprayed unexpectedly!

Using perforated hoses

❀ These are laid among the flowerbeds or around the perimeter wall, which often gets particularly dry. Rather than simply laying them on the soil, you can bury them about 5 cm (2 in) below the surface so that the water will not evaporate so quickly.

Automatic watering systems

❀ These range from simple devices that fit on to a tap and cut off after a measured volume of water has passed through, to sophisticated programmable timers.

ABOVE: *Careful positioning of a wooden barrel in an inconspicuous corner of the garden will look decorative and provide a constant supply of rainwater to water the plants.*

ABOVE: *A sturdy metal watering can will suffice for the watering needs of container gardens.*

ABOVE: *Sprinklers can be an invaluable aid to watering. This one is watering a herbaceous border in the early evening, when the water is less likely to evaporate before it gets to the plants' roots.*

EARLY ENGLISH GARDENS

DURING the dangerous and war-torn Middle Ages, monasteries played an important role in preserving the art of gardening. Sadly, there are no remnants of medieval gardens today so we have to rely on pictures and writings.

These describe enclosed gardens, similar in shape to the ancient Persian ones. Right up to Tudor and Stuart times, small enclosed gardens were scattered higgledy-piggledy encircling the house. Features included medicinal and herb gardens, trelliswork, fountains, turf seats and a meadow area planted with tulips, forget-me-nots and daisies. Mounts were also built, from which to view the garden. These might be as high as 9 m (30 ft), with a small shelter built on the top.

GARDEN LIGHTING

❦

In recent years the garden has increasingly come to be regarded as an additional living area, rather than an area purely for planting. Lighting may be purely functional or more atmospheric. It can extend the amount of time you are able to spend in the garden, as well as enhance your view of the garden from the house at night and when the weather is less kind. Garden centres and do-it-yourself (DIY) stores have increased the range of garden lighting available, so a beautifully lit garden is no longer the exclusive preserve of the garden designer.

Lighting for safety

❦ The first lighting consideration in most gardens is a practical one. At night you should be able to see your way clearly from the garden entrance to your front door. If there are any steps that are difficult to navigate safely in the dark, good lighting will greatly reduce the risk of accidents.

BELOW: *It is important to ensure that areas such as steps, which are difficult to navigate, are well-lit at night.*

❦ However, do not install intense, isolated lights, such as spotlights, at potential accident spots. As you move from an area of bright light into sudden darkness, your eyes cannot make the adjustment quickly enough to be safe, and you may have unwittingly increased your chances of a fall. Such areas need a broad spread of light so that the whole journey may be made in the same lighting condition. These lights are sometimes called spread lights.

Lighting for increased security

❀ Strong illumination around the home is a proven deterrent to intruders. Floodlights with in-built passive infra-red detectors (PIRs) are widely available. Activated by localised changes in heat, these are automatically switched on when a person or animal approaches.

❀ Think carefully about where you place these lights. Although they are undoubtedly effective close to the door, it can be very irritating for both you and your neighbours if the light is placed so that it is constantly being activated by passers-by. Moving the light just a few feet to one side may mean that you will still be able to see clearly to get your key in the door, and would-be intruders are effectively deterred.

❀ PIR lights are available in many styles, so choose one that fits in with the mood of your home. A high-tech light, for example, would look very incongruous outside a Victorian cottage, where a carriage lamp might sit very happily.

BELOW: *Lighting increases the amount of time you can comfortably spend in your garden.*

Lighting to extend garden use

❀ Al fresco cooking and eating have enjoyed a massive increase in popularity in recent years. Improvements in outdoor cooking methods, such as gas-fired barbecues and even outdoor Mexican-style ovens, have truly turned the garden into an additional room.

❀ When daylight hours grow shorter, there is no need to curtail the pleasures of patio living. Provide adequate light so that cooking and food preparation can continue comfortably, and you will find that outdoor entertaining can start earlier in the year and continue well into the autumn.

❀ Although a simple floodlight fitted to the wall of the house will illuminate a wide area, the light given is not intimate or attractive. More appropriate would be specific lighting of the cooking and eating area, together with lighting to highlight particular points of visual interest around the garden. This may be as simple as a spotlight above the barbecue and lanterns around the table, or a more sophisticated arrangement of permanent lighting throughout the garden.

BELOW: *Effective lighting extends the living space of your home out into the garden.*

Lighting for effect

❀ Anyone who has gazed out at the garden when it is illuminated for Christmas, even if the lighting is limited to a few fairy lights strung through a lone tree, will appreciate that lighting can increase your enjoyment of the garden, even when you are inside your home. This lighting for added mood is not the same as functional lighting.

❀ An even wash of light over the whole garden will add nothing in terms of charm or romance. Mood lighting, as in the home, comes from distinctly separate areas of light, positioned carefully so as to illuminate features of particular interest. Less attractive features can be left darkened to recede into the shadows.

❀ Just as too many decorative features in a garden can fight for attention and give an overbusy, cluttered look, care should be taken when planning accent lighting. Too many, different types of light can give a disjointed appearance – more appropriate in a large-scale municipal park than in the generally smaller domestic garden.

❀ A single, silhouetted tree or pond with submerged lights may be all that is required to make an impact. Clear white light is generally best for retaining a naturalistic feel. Reserve coloured lights for special occasions, or you may end up with a garden that looks uncomfortably like a fairy grotto instead of a sophisticated idyll.

BELOW: Mains lighting can be expensive and disruptive to install but the results will be worth the effort and expense involved.

The practicalities

❀ Most garden lighting will necessitate installation of electricity. There are two types of electric lighting used in the garden – low voltage and mains.

❀ Mains lighting is best considered at the planning stage of a garden, since the cables will need to be laid professionally, at least 46 cm (18 in) underground. This is obviously expensive and disruptive, but is necessary if you want powerful lighting around the garden, if long runs of cable and prolonged lamp life are required, or if you have a broad landscape to illuminate.

❀ Low-voltage lights use a transformer to reduce the voltage, effectively reducing the illumination power available, but also making the lights safer. The main advantage of a low-voltage system is that there is no need to submerge the cables.

❀ Heavy-duty low-voltage cable can even run along the soil surface if necessary, although it is better to submerge cable if possible, and house it in protective conduit to avoid damage while cultivating the garden.

BELOW: Subtle recessed lights are useful for unobtrusive illumination of areas such as walkways and steps.

Lighting patterns

❀ Generally, lighting falls into two categories – spotlighting and floodlighting. The difference is in the spread of light. Spotlighting is a narrow beam with sharp definition at the edges of the beam; floodlighting is a wide beam falling off softly at the edges. Either type may be used to create different effects, such as uplighting, backlighting and downlighting, although spotlighting is most often used because of its controlled, narrow beam.

❀ Backlighting is created by placing light behind a feature, for example a statue, so that it is thrown into dramatic silhouette. Uplighting entails placing light at ground level, pointing up at a plant or other feature. Mature trees look particularly striking lit in this way.

❀ Downlighting is self-explanatory – literally a light pointing downwards. This can be functional, such as wall lights pointing towards the patio, or used for dramatic effect, as in moonlighting, where lights are placed in a tree pointing downwards to imitate moonlight. Just as soft pools of downlight from table lamps create intimacy in the home, downlighting in the garden gives a cosy feel.

Types of external lights

❀ Most people will be familiar with wall-mounted external lights, such as those used to illuminate the front door or the area around garages and sheds. Post lights are also popular. In addition to the familiar carriage lamp-style post lights, there are shorter post lights available. These have a smaller spread of light and are a more subtle alternative.

❀ Spike lights may be less familiar, but are well worth exploring for their flexibility of use. This type of light is pushed into the lawn or soil, and is available both as a fixed position light, or one with an adjustable angle, so that specific lighting effects can be achieved.

❀ Recessed lights, such as those that replace bricks in walls bordering paths, can be very useful for lighting walkways safely yet unobtrusively. Whatever the choice, it is important not to get carried away with the exciting possibilities of garden lighting. The aim should be to enhance the garden with lighting, not dominate it.

RIGHT: *These garden steps are lit by an unusual and attractive lamp.*

GREENHOUSES AND FRAMES

❧

Greenhouses are often thought of as the exclusive preserve of the dedicated gardener. However, with greenhouses and frames to suit every pocket and size of garden, there is no need for even a novice gardener to feel daunted by the prospect of installing and running one. Although one normally associates greenhouses and frames with propagation, which may seem a little daunting and time consuming to a new gardener, there are other, more immediate benefits to owning a greenhouse or frame.

THE ADVANTAGES

THE most obvious benefit of having your own greenhouse or frame is that the growing season is extended beyond the first frosts of winter and the last frosts of spring. This is particularly useful if, like thousands of gardeners every year, you are tempted by the delights on display at the garden centre early in the year, which are too vulnerable to be put out in the garden until the risk of frost has passed.

Why choose a greenhouse?

❀ It is simply not practical to protect each individual bedding plant with fleece, yet if you wait until later in the season the best plants have sold out. Greenhouses and frames offer the perfect solution, providing an environment for hardening off, gradually acclimatising plants to the elements prior to planting out. Favourite tender plants may also be safely overwintered.

❀ For most gardeners propagation remains the impetus for buying a greenhouse. Although it will take time to repay the initial investment, great savings can be made by creating new stock in large numbers. The satisfaction in producing your own plants is immense and the techniques are essentially very simple.

ABOVE: *The benefits of having a greenhouse are many; young plants can be protected from frost and the warmer environment is useful for propagation.*

ABOVE: *Greenhouses should have good ventilation systems, with air vents at ground level, windows in the roof and doors that can be fixed open.*

GREENHOUSE MATERIALS

Y OU have a choice of structural and glazing materials when deciding on the type of greenhouse you would like.

Wood

❀ Wood is the traditional material for greenhouse structures and is undeniably very attractive, whether painted or stained, rendering the greenhouse not only a useful addition to the garden, but a striking visual feature in its own right.

❀ Hardwoods, for example oak, teak, or cedar, although expensive, are the optimum choices, as they require minimal attention. Softwoods should be pressure treated with preservative, and will need regular painting or re-treating with preservative.

❀ If an old wooden greenhouse is largely intact, it may well be worth renovating and may require only a little attention to the woodwork and glazing to restore it to its former glory.

Metal

❀ In recent years, aluminium has become the most popular structural material for greenhouses. It is less expensive than a hardwood greenhouse, easy to maintain, and its narrow glazing bars admit more light than wider wooden ones. It does not retain heat at night quite as well as a wooden greenhouse and is not generally considered as attractive, but for most gardeners, the advantages of cost and ease of maintenance more than compensate for these slight drawbacks.

❀ Both plastic-coated galvanised steel and galvanised iron houses will need checking regularly for rust. If rust develops they can require a certain amount of treatment and repainting.

Glass

❀ Glass is not only the most traditional glazing material for greenhouses, it is also the most effective. It is easier to clean and shade than plastic. It also retains heat well and conducts light better. However, it is not the most appropriate choice if the greenhouse is close to a play area or road, as it is obviously more prone to breaking than plastic.

Plastic

❀ Plastic glazing is not as durable as glass, yet is often more expensive. It discolours easily and tends to become scratched over time. This is not only unsightly, but dramatically reduces the amount of light passing through the glazing. Plastic will generally need replacing over time.

❀ Polycarbonate has better insulating properties and is almost unbreakable, making it a good choice for greenhouses close to roads and play areas. However it is expensive, easily scratched and prone to discolouring.

CIRCULATION OF ENERGY IN A GREENHOUSE

Energy from the sun is transmitted through the glass sides and roof of a greenhouse and warms the air inside as it travels round.

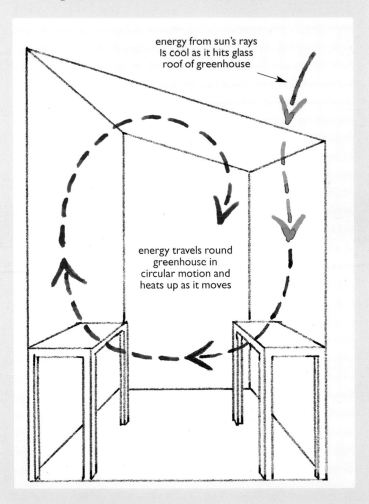

energy from sun's rays
Is cool as it hits glass
roof of greenhouse

energy travels round
greenhouse in
circular motion and
heats up as it moves

TYPES OF GREENHOUSE

THE greenhouse was originally the place in which the 'greens' (clipped evergreen shrubs) were housed over winter. It is is a functional building and should normally be integrated unobtrusively into the garden. When choosing your greenhouse you will find a variety of structural and glazing materials available as well as a wide choice of designs. Your choice will be dictated firstly by your budget and then by the space you have available in your garden. Avoid using climbers as screening for greenhouses, which will cut out much of the light from the roof and produce sickly plants within the greenhouse. A group of well-chosen decorative trees or shrubs placed to one side of the greenhouse will effectively provide an attractive visual barrier instead. Try to make sure that some of these are evergreens so that the hedge will disguise the greenhouse all year round.

The traditional greenhouse

❀ The traditional greenhouse has vertical sides, closed in the lower part, and an evenly spanned roof. It uses space well and the covered lower part conserves heat effectively, making it energy efficient. If you plan to grow a lot of low-growing border plants or use growing bags, a greenhouse without filled-in sides will be a better choice.

❀ A wide range of accessories such as shelves and staging is available to suit this type of greenhouse, making it a good all-round choice. Many sizes are available. Choose one to suit both your garden and the amount of time you plan to spend in the greenhouse. A keen propagator will quickly outgrow a small model.

BELOW: *A lean-to greenhouse can save a great deal of space and, as the wall acts as insulation, it retains its heat well.*

The lean-to greenhouse

❀ A lean-to greenhouse built against a wall is useful for those who do not want to give up precious garden space. You need a suitable wall, of course, so that the greenhouse can be tucked away at the side of the house.

❀ An alternative place would be a high wall at the far end of the garden, where the greenhouse can share an area with a vegetable plot and a compost heap or a propagating area for new plants, all screened off by a hedge or trellis. Because it is situated against a wall, it retains heat well, often benefiting not only from sunlight, but from a certain amount of heat emitted by the heating system of the home.

❀ Lean-to houses can be extremely attractive in their own right and can double up as garden rooms if there is a connecting door to the home. Their reduced glazed surface means that they are less expensive to heat than a conventional greenhouse, although, obviously, they receive less light than traditional models. Watering and heating systems are also comparatively simple to install, there being no need to lay cables to a more distant part of the garden.

❀ Another type of greenhouse attached to a wall, which shares the properties of the basic lean-to greenhouse, is the three-quarter span greenhouse. This is a traditional greenhouse with a quarter of one side removed. This is the side placed against a wall.

The mini greenhouse

❀ Mini greenhouses provide an excellent introduction to growing under glass, invaluable not only to the gardener with limited space, but also to the novice who does not wish to make a costly investment in a more substantial model. Both freestanding and lean-to mini greenhouses are available. The lean-to models are best situated against a south-west, west- or south-east facing wall or fence for maximum light.

Specialist greenhouses

❀ A range of greenhouses in unusual shapes and sizes is available. Some are designed primarily for their decorative properties, such as octagonal greenhouses, others for increased efficiency of heat retention or stability in high winds. A major drawback of a specialist greenhouse is that staging, shelving, glazing accessories and replacements are not standard items. The choice may therefore be both limited and expensive.

LEAN-TO GREENHOUSE

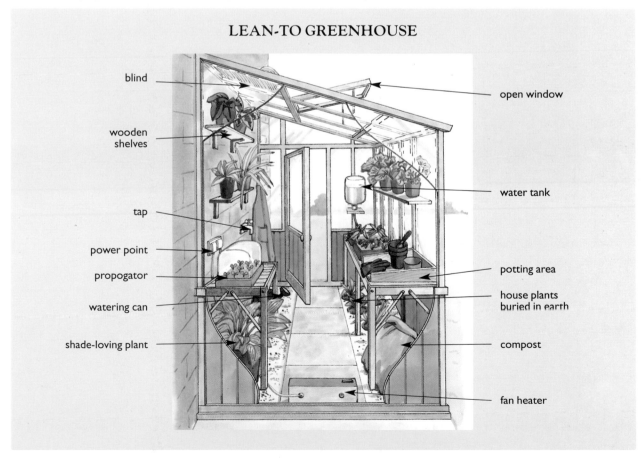

blind
wooden shelves
tap
power point
propogator
watering can
shade-loving plant

open window
water tank
potting area
house plants buried in earth
compost
fan heater

SITING THE GREENHOUSE

❀ Freestanding greenhouses need to be situated away from trees, in a bright but sheltered position, ideally placed so that the central walkway runs from east to west. The greenhouse must not be exposed to wind tunnels or frost pockets.

❀ In exposed areas it may be necessary to erect a wind-protective barrier, although you should take care not to make this fence or hedge so high and close that it blocks out light and makes it difficult to access any part of the greenhouse for maintenance. If possible, try to place the greenhouse near the shed or other utility structure to make a work area in scale with the other garden spaces. This will limit the number of paths required and will make it easier to supply water and electricity.

COLD FRAMES AND CLOCHES

❀ These provide many of the same benefits as greenhouses, extending the growing season, overwintering vulnerable plants and making it possible to grow an increased range of crops. They are obviously on a much smaller scale, making them an excellent choice for small gardens and novice gardeners unwilling to make bigger investments in terms of space and money.

❀ They also provide a useful adjunct to the greenhouse at busy times of the year when space is limited, for example when hardening off plants in the spring. For those gardeners who do not have a greenhouse, plants may be propagated in the home and then hardened off in frames or cold cloches.

ABOVE: *Greenhouses should be situated in a bright spot, with some shelter from wind tunnels or the danger of frost pockets.*

Cold frames

❀ The structure of cold frames can vary in the same way as greenhouse designs; some have filled in sides, some are glazed from top to bottom. The same guidelines on choosing structural and glazing materials apply. Since cold frames are generally at ground level, it is particularly important to install plastic glazing material if young children will be playing close to the frame.

❀ Cold frames are simple and inexpensive to make at home, using either wood treated with preservative or bricks if a supply of old bricks is easily to hand. Aluminium frames have a distinct advantage over these more permanent structures, since they can be moved around the garden to benefit from the maximum light available throughout the year.

❀ All cold frames should be sited in areas of good natural light, in a sheltered area, again following the same guidelines as for siting a greenhouse. Like greenhouses, cold frames may also need shading in summer and

ABOVE: *The structure of cold frames can vary; some are all glazed, others have only glazed sides.*

insulating in winter. They will certainly need adequate ventilation, so read the general care and maintenance guidelines for greenhouses when setting up a cold frame.

❀ Heating may be installed in these frames, although technically it then ceases to be called a cold frame.

Cloches

❀ Cloches are used chiefly in vegetable growing to protect young plants from the elements and predators. Cloches are available in many shapes such as tent-, tunnel- and dome-shaped, and come in a variety of materials. As with greenhouses, the recommended material for best light transmission and heat retention is glass, although the same safety caveats obviously apply and plastic is a better choice for gardeners with children.

❀ Plastic is inexpensive. Although it does not retain heat or allow such good light transmission, this is not of vital importance with all crops. Whatever the material, ensure that the cloche has well-fitting ends, or it has the potential to turn into a wind tunnel, which will quickly damage plants. Simple individual cloches may be made from cut-off plastic bottles. These may not be as attractive as traditional glass cloches, but they are infinitely cheaper and just as effective.

LEFT: *Cloches provide convenient, moveable protection for vulnerable plants.*

IN THE GREENHOUSE

CHOOSING the type of environment appropriate to the plants you wish to grow is at the heart of successful greenhouse gardening. Heat, humidity and ventilation will all need to be carefully considered at the planning stage, and controlled effectively throughout the year in all types of environment, from cold to tropical. Having selected your chosen environment, you will need to plan how it is to be installed and controlled.

The cold greenhouse

❀ A novice greenhouse gardener may be well advised to begin with an unheated greenhouse, while becoming accustomed to the basic principles of greenhouse gardening. These include ventilation, basic shading and insulation, as well as pest and disease control.

❀ Although the range of plants that may be grown in a cold greenhouse is obviously fairly narrow, the unheated greenhouse still has many uses, for example growing alpines, overwintering slightly tender plants and bringing plants on earlier than would otherwise be possible. A heated propagator could be used to increase the potential of this type of environment, although some propagation from cuttings may be possible without this.

The cool/frost-free greenhouse

❀ This type of house is heated just enough to keep frost at bay – a daytime temperature of 5–10°C (41–50°F) is required, with a night-time temperature that does not drop below 2°C (35°F).

❀ As well as providing all the same benefits as the cold greenhouse, frost-tender plants may be overwintered and flowering pot plants and summer crops grown in a cool/frost-free greenhouse. Again, a heated propagator will be useful, particularly for germinating seeds, as will a growing lamp to provide extra light for young seedlings.

ABOVE: *A greenhouse needs to be properly maintained in order to be both effective and attractive.*

The temperate greenhouse

❀ This environment is slightly warmer still, with a daytime temperature of 10–13°C (50–55°F) and a night-time temperature of no lower than 7°C (45°F). A good range of tender pot plants, vegetables and half-hardy plants will thrive in this type of house. Again, a propagator is needed for best results. Alternatively, boost the regular heating during the required period. A growing lamp is useful in either case.

The tropical/warm greenhouse

❀ The daytime temperature of this house is 13–18°C (55–64°F), falling to no less than 13°C (55°F) at night. An exciting range of plants may be grown in this environment, including ornamental and edible tropical and subtropical plants.

❀ This type of house is also sufficiently warm to propagate seedlings without a propagator, although the additional light provided by a growing lamp would still be useful.

Heating

❀ There are various methods of heating your greenhouse. Electric heaters are convenient, reliable and clean to use; they are also generally energy efficient since most are thermostatically controlled. However, you will need an electricity supply to the greenhouse, which could prove expensive.

❀ Fan, convector and tubular heaters are all possibilities. Fan heaters are particularly versatile; they are portable and can be used as a fan only in summer to cool the greenhouse. Independent gas and paraffin heaters release both fumes and water vapour, which can result in a stagnant, moist atmosphere that encourages disease, so good ventilation is particularly important with these.

❀ Whatever the choice, every greenhouse needs a thermometer to check that the desired temperature is being maintained. A frost alarm is useful in unheated greenhouses, and also in heated ones where a sudden temperature drop due to a power cut, for example, would spell disaster.

Insulation

❀ Effective insulation will conserve heat, reducing heating costs considerably. Double-glazing is too expensive for most gardeners. Plastic bubble wrap, fixed with pins, clips or suction pads, is an affordable and efficient alternative. It also allows a good amount of light transmission. Plain plastic sheeting is cheaper, but does not provide such efficient insulation.

INSULATING AND SHADING

A greenhouse must be protected from heat in the summer and from sudden drops in temperature and frost in the winter.

1 *Plastic bubble wrap is an effective insulator, while allowing good light transmission into the greenhouse.*

2 *Applying a shading wash prevents your greenhouse from overheating in summer.*

3 *Alternatively, fit blinds to keep the greenhouse cool in hot weather.*

Ventilation

❀ Good ventilation is critical to healthy plants. It prevents a build-up of stagnant air, which fosters pests and diseases, and maintains the desired greenhouse temperature. Even the cool greenhouse needs adequate ventilation to keep damp, stale conditions at bay in winter.

❀ Besides the ventilation systems fitted in the greenhouse on purchase, many ancillary options are available, some very sophisticated, such as thermostatically controlled vent openers and extractor fans. If you leave the greenhouse door open in summer, fix netting across the opening to keep out animal intruders.

Shading

❀ Shading also controls the temperature of the greenhouse. Shading washes are inexpensive, effective and simple to apply to the exterior of the greenhouse, although the finished result is not particularly glamorous. The wash allows through enough light for good plant growth and can be rubbed away at the end of the summer. Blinds are effective and smart but need constant attention. Thermostatically controlled automatic ones are convenient but expensive.

BELOW: *Attractive to look at, this little greenhouse is made of extruded aluminium and can be glazed in tempered safety glass. The finish is polyester, so it requires very little maintenance.*

Watering

❀ In the rain-free environment of a greenhouse, effective watering is critical. A watering can is an option in a small greenhouse but you will probably need to consider other watering methods. Systems where water is drawn up into the plants using capillary action are widely used; these involve placing plants on capillary matting, a part of which is trailed into a water reservoir.

❀ Trickle irrigation is another option. These automated watering systems need careful monitoring to ensure plants are being watered according to their individual needs and the time of year.

Humidity

❀ Humidity is the amount of water vapour in the air. Excess humidity can be reduced by ventilation, or increased by adding water to the air – be it simply spray misting by hand, sloshing down the floor and staging with water during the summer or sophisticated automated spray systems.

❀ Hygrometers measure humidity and are useful in greenhouses. A relative humidity level between 40 and 75 per cent is desirable for most greenhouse plants. Above this, mildew and grey mould may develop.

Greenhouse pests and diseases

❀ The protected environment of the greenhouse provides an ideal breeding ground for pests and diseases. Adequate attention to ventilation and humidity control, plus scrupulous hygiene, will go a long way to maintaining a healthy greenhouse.

❀ Throughout the year, take care to use only sterile compost and clean pots. Regularly sweep the floor to remove leaves and debris, which may contain harmful spores. Clean the greenhouse thoroughly each autumn. Remove the plants to a suitable place and disinfect and rinse the greenhouse well, both inside and out.

Pest and disease control

❀ Check the undersides of leaves regularly, as pest infestations can quickly build up here unnoticed. Treat pests and diseases promptly – fumigation is effective against both. Biological controls are another option, and involve introducing parasites and predators that feed on particular pests. Chemical sprays are another, although less environmentally friendly solution.

FRENCH FORMALITY

THE FRENCH took the Italian Renaissance garden and gave it their own brand of formality. French gardens were larger and the terrain flatter. They reflected the absolute power of the king and were strictly regimented and controlled. Versailles, built for Louis XIV, the 'Sun King', is the epitome of such gardens. The enormous palace was an extension of a modest hunting lodge that belonged to Louis's father. The garden stretches away in formal avenues wide enough to take an army and disappears into the distance. Louis's gardener, André le Nôtre, designed the gardens to the glory of his king and as a vast theatre for outdoor fêtes in which His Highness could make graceful and noticeable entrances and exits. Enormous parterres were planted as intricate garden 'embroideries' whose patterns were best seen from the first-floor windows.

RIGHT: *The Basin d'Apollo at Versailles, France, in all its glory, making use of the flatness of the land and the enormous amount of space to display huge stretches of water, golden sculptures and long, wide avenues stretching back towards the palace.*

GROWING FRUIT AND VEGETABLES

Growing your own fresh produce can be one of the most rewarding tasks for a gardener. Whatever the size and shape of your plot, everyone can manage to incorporate a fruit or vegetable garden of some kind.

✿

Take time to assess the potential of your garden for growing fruit and vegetables.

✿

Be prepared for some hard work – fresh produce needs year-round attention to get the best results.

✿

You can even go one step further and try raising your fruit and vegetables organically.

VEGETABLE GARDENS

One of the great joys of gardening is undoubtedly producing your own edible crops. Tomatoes picked fresh from your own plot, still warm from the sun that ripened them, are an incomparable treat. Shop-bought vegetables have often had all the flavour bred out of them in a rush to cultivate the highest possible yield, as well as having possibly been treated with pesticides and fertilisers that you would prefer not to eat. With home-grown produce, you have the security of knowing exactly what has gone into the production of your own crops.

HOME-GROWN IS BEST

WHEN you grow your own vegetables, you can choose varieties that may not be commercially available, because you are growing them for their culinary attributes, rather than for profitability. Vitamin content and taste are also optimised, because you can cook and eat your crops immediately after harvest, unlike the shop-bought equivalents, where the vitamin content has been slowly oxidising away as the produce sits on the shelf.

❀ Although growing your own vegetables can have economic benefits, for most gardeners it is the unique satisfaction of producing food from seed to table that provides the motivation.

ABOVE: *Mixing edible crops with ornamental plants is an increasingly popular way of growing vegetables, especially in a limited space.*

CHOOSING A VEGETABLE GARDEN TO SUIT YOU

THE type of vegetable gardening you do will depend on the size of your plot and the amount of time and energy you intend to devote to growing vegetables. You also need to decide whether you are wanting just a few choice crops that are expensive to buy in the shops and taste so much better home-grown, or enough vegetables to feed your family all year round.

❀ A well-organised plot, approximately 7 x 4 m (23 x 13 ft), should yield enough crops for this. Don't be dismayed, however, if you have a much smaller area. It is possible to grow a considerable quantity of vegetables in even a restricted space, and growing vegetables in containers has become increasingly popular in recent years.

ABOVE: *Maintaining a productive vegetable garden is hard work, but the results are definitely well worth the effort.*

VEGETABLE CROPS

Legumes and pod crops:

Okra
Scarlet runner beans
Lima beans
French beans
Peas
Broad beans

Alliums:

Bulb onions
Pickling onions
Spring onions
Shallots
European Welsh onions
Oriental bunching onions
Leeks
Garlic

Solanaceous, root and tuberous crops:

Sweet peppers
Tomatoes
Aubergines
Celery
Celeriac
Beetroot
Carrots
Sweet potatoes
Parsnips
Scorzonera
Salsify
Potatoes

Brassicas:

Kales
Cauliflowers
Cabbages
Brussels sprouts
Purple sprouting broccoli
Calabrese
Oriental mustards
Chinese broccoli
Pak choi
Mizuna greens
Chinese cabbages
Kohlrabi
Swedes
Turnips
Radishes

THE TRADITIONAL VEGETABLE GARDEN

KEEN vegetable gardeners like to set aside an area of the garden exclusively for vegetables. The entire area can be cultivated, and the primary purpose of the plot is to provide optimum growing conditions for vegetables, rather than gardening for any particular decorative merit. That said, there is something inherently beautiful about a well-maintained vegetable garden. It has natural geometry, because the crops are grown in rows so that you can move freely between them to tend them.

❀ A vegetable plot should not be undertaken lightly, since maintaining one is truly a labour of love. It will need to be dug over every autumn, weeded regularly, and the vegetables nurtured tenderly and protected against marauding pests and the elements.

❀ There is also considerable work in planning the plot effectively, in order to maximise the space, prevent gluts and to keep pests and diseases at bay by careful crop rotation. Intercropping is a good way of saving space in a traditional plot, but does need careful planning. For example, sow fast-maturing crops such as saladings, between slow-maturing vegetables like carrots. The fast-growing crop will have matured and been harvested before the other crop needs the space.

Crop rotation

❀ Vegetables should not be grown in the same place each year. Soil-dwelling pests and diseases endemic to a particular crop would steadily increase if repeatedly given their favourite host. Also, continually cropping the same vegetable in the same place can lead to an imbalance in soil nutrients.

❀ Crop rotation can seem so dauntingly complex that some gardeners abandon it altogether. It is far better for the novice vegetable gardener to practise a very simple three-year plan – dividing crops into three types: roots, brassicas and others – than to embark on a complicated regime that may be impossible to follow long term.

❀ A very simple rule is that if a vegetable from one group does particularly badly one year, never follow it the next year with a crop from the same group, unless you are willing to risk having the same poor result.

ABOVE: *Raised beds ease the work of the vegetable gardener and look neat and attractive.*

VEGETABLES IN CONTAINERS

GROWING vegetables in containers has developed from the ubiquitous commercial growing bag of tomatoes that starts many gardeners on the path towards more ambitious vegetable gardening. Even gardeners with extremely limited space to devote to vegetables are able to produce edible crops, which not only taste great, are chemical free, vitamin rich and super fresh, but also attractive plants in their own right. Cabbages, for example, are increasingly grown not only as food crops, but for their ornamental properties. There are breeds of tomato that have a delightful tumbling growth habit, perfectly suited to containers such as hanging baskets and the multi-holed terracotta pots, more usually seen housing strawberries.

❀ Growing vegetables in containers has many other benefits besides maximising space. The soil pest problems, weeding and digging that make vegetable growing in open soil hard work are eradicated. Since container-grown vegetables are portable, you can grow plants that need particular local environments, moving them as necessary to suit the changing climate and their individual needs.

❀ For example, you may be able to grow tender vegetables, which need a sheltered spot, against a sunny wall, far away from the main, exposed vegetable plot where they would perish. Choose containers sufficiently sized to suit the crop. For example,

long-rooted vegetables such as carrots need a depth of at least 46 cm (18 in) to flourish, while a lettuce can thrive in a window box.

DRAWBACKS

A DISADVANTAGE of container growing vegetables is that you will need to pay particular attention to watering and feeding. Another issue to consider is that plastic growing bags are not attractive, and can be quite unsightly if you have a lot of them, undisguised, surrounding your house.

THE ORNAMENTAL POTAGER

PLANNING a vegetable garden that is ornamental as well as productive has become very fashionable. Potager is the French word for kitchen garden, but is now used internationally to describe a garden where edible plants are grown with an emphasis on their decorative potential. Other elements are included to produce an area that is as pretty as it is productive – for example neat pathways of brick or gravel passing between geometric beds enclosed by formal dwarf box hedging, sometimes embellished further with vines, roses and grapes draped over arches traversing the walkways.

❀ Many of the vegetables in the potager are chosen for their visual appeal, for example leaf beet and red lettuces, although even ordinary varieties appear more attractive when displayed in such a charming setting.

VEGETABLES IN THE BORDER

INCORPORATING vegetables within the herbaceous border has also become increasingly acceptable and fashionable. Many gardeners do not have the space to devote a whole area to vegetables, along with the attendant demands on time and the potential production of crop gluts, which can be difficult to handle without wastage.

❀ Gardeners have mixed flowers with edible crops for many years, although historically, cottage gardeners would have been concerned with having herbs to hand for practical reasons, and any decorative effect would have been fairly incidental.

❀ Today, ornamental crops, as in the potager, are often selected in preference to more workaday species.

For example, ruby chard, a variety of leaf beet, has stunning red stalks, worthy of inclusion in the border in their own right. There are also prettily coloured, flowering runner beans, which can add height at the back of the border, and courgettes, with their spectacular exotic-looking, edible yellow flowers, in addition to their stripy fruits.

❀ Although growing vegetables in the border is convenient and attractive, as well as producing useful edible crops, the work and thought involved should not be underestimated. The vegetables will compete with the ornamentals for food, light and water, so never overcrowd when planting. Ideally, consider the ornamentals as the adjuncts to the edibles, not the other way around, so that the vegetables are given the best possible growing conditions.

COMPANION PLANTING

FASCINATING work has been done on companion planting, which means growing plants side by side for their positive effects on each other, whether directly or indirectly. It is worth researching this subject further, particularly if you are planning to grow edibles and ornamentals together.

❀ Combining certain flowers and edible crops often has significant benefits, particularly in assisting pest and disease control. For example, garlic is an excellent

friend to roses, since it is reputed to deter aphids as well as improving the roses' perfume. Equally importantly, research on companion planting reveals that some combinations have a detrimental effect on each other, for example garlic planted alongside peas and beans.

ABOVE: *A well-tended vegetable plot can yield a wonderful array of crops that will sustain you throughout the year.*

BELOW: *A neatly planted allotment growing strawberries, chives and shallots to ripen in the early summer.*

ABOVE: *Neat rows of vegetables have a pleasing symmetry, which bears testimony to the care with which they are tended.*

ABOVE: *A garden planted with vegetables can be as attractive as one packed with purely ornamental plants.*

GROWING VEGETABLES

VEGETABLES grow best in a sunny, sheltered spot, on a loamy, humus-rich soil with a pH between 6.5 and 7.0. Other soils can be improved by incorporating plenty of well-rotted organic matter and by thorough cultivation.

Sowing vegetables and early care

 Read seed packets carefully to determine the recommended sowing depth and method, together with anticipated germination and harvesting time, so that you can plan your planting accordingly. General propagation guidelines apply when sowing vegetables. Seed may be sown directly into the soil where it is to mature, into a seedbed, or into pots and trays.

Preparing the soil

❀ The soil needs to be in optimum condition to give vegetables the best possible chance of growing success. Tedious as it may be, digging the vegetable plot is of prime importance. It introduces air into the soil; it raises clods of earth, which can be broken down by

frost, thereby improving soil texture; and it encourages the biological activity that is necessary for soil fertility.

❀ In some cases, notably on light soils where digging would disturb rather than improve the soil structure, the no-dig method is used. Generous layers of well-rotted organic matter are spread over the soil as a mulch, and resident worms obligingly incorporate this into the soil, improving soil fertility. Young plants are inserted through the mulch, and new crops are grown between the roots of previous crops, which are allowed to decompose in the soil.

❀ Seeds need good overall contact with the soil in order to germinate so, if you are preparing a seedbed, it is necessary to rake the soil to a fine tilth in the sowing season that follows the autumn digging.

Feeding the soil

❀ Intensively cultivated soil needs to be well nourished for best results. This can be achieved with organic or inorganic fertilisers. Many gardeners prefer organic fertilisers, since a desire to eat produce that is uncontaminated by chemicals is the motivation for many gardeners to grow their own vegetables.

❦ Organic manures and fertilisers encourage worm activity, which benefits soil fertility. Higher yields may be possible with chemical fertilisers, but in the domestic setting, as opposed to a large-scale agricultural environment, quality and flavour are generally considered to be of more importance than maximum yields.

❦ The amount of fertiliser required is governed partly by soil type. For example, heavy clay soil retains nutrients for longer than a fast-draining sandy soil. Another factor is the kind of crop grown. Leafy crops like cabbages need lots of nitrogen — approximately one-third supplied on planting, followed by the remaining two-thirds as the plant grows.

❦ An enthusiasm to keep plants well fed needs to be tempered with common sense. Overwintering vegetable crops that have been fed with too much nitrogen in autumn are vulnerable to frost damage, as soft growth would be encouraged at a harsh time of year. Respect the individual requirements of each crop. Fruiting crops like tomatoes will need regular feeding with appropriate fertilisers as the plants come into flower, to ensure optimum flowering and fruiting.

Watering

❦ Vegetables have water requirements in line with most other plants. They need particular watering care during germination and at the seedling stage until their roots are established. After transplanting, again take special care with watering until the plants are re-established. Root crops need steady watering from sowing until cropping. Fruiting and flowering crops need most water when they are in flower and as the fruits develop. Foliage crops need thorough watering 12–15 days prior to harvesting.

BELOW: *Regularly incorporating compost with the soil is an important part of successful vegetable gardening, as in this well-tended plot featuring sweet peas, asparagus, broad beans and onions.*

VEGETABLE GAZETTEER

Vegetables are extremely rewarding to grow, and do well on most soils. Pay attention to the individual needs of your crops and the yields will be higher, and your chances of success more consistent. Crop successively to avoid a glut of vegetables that is hard to cope with.

Vegetable	Sow	Plant/Plant out	Harvest	Yeild per m²
Asparagus	Apr	Apr	May–Jun	1.5 kg (3¼ lb)
Aubergine	Feb	Apr	Aug–Sep	5 kg (11 lb)
Bean, broad	Feb–Apr	–	Jul–Aug	4 kg (8¾ lb)
Bean, runner	Apr (UG)	May–Jun	May–Jun Aug–Oct	4 kg (8¾ lb)
Beetroot	Apr–Jun	–	Jun–Oct	2 kg (4½ lb)
Broccoli	Apr–May	Jun–Jul	Feb–May	2 kg (4½ lb)
Brussels sprout	Mar–Apr	May–Jun	Oct–Feb	1.5 kg (3¼ lb)
Cabbage	Apr	May–Jun	Aug–Sep	4 kg (8¾ lb)
Calabrese	Apr–May	Jun–Jul	Aug–Oct	2 kg (4½ lb)
Capsicum	Feb (UG)	Apr (UG)	Aug–Sep	1.5 kg (3¼ lb)
Carrot	Apr–Jun	–	Sep–Oct	2 kg (4½ lb)
Cauliflower	Apr	Jun	Aug–Sep	4.5 kg (10 lb)
Celeriac	Mar (UG)	May–Jun	Oct–Nov	3 kg (6½ lb)
Celery	Mar–Apr (UG)	Jun	Aug–Oct	4 kg (8¾ lb)
Chard	Apr	–	Aug–Nov	1 kg (2 lb)
Chicory	May	–	Dec–Mar	0.4 kg (13 oz)
Courgette	May–Jun	–	Jul–Sep	2 kg (4½ lb)
Cucumber	May–Jun	–	Aug–Sep	3 kg (6½ lb)
Endive	Apr–Aug	–	Sep–Feb	1.5 kg (3¼ lb)
Kale	May	Jul	Dec–Mar	1.5 kg (3¼ lb)
Kohlrabi	Apr–Jun	–	Aug–Oct	2.5 kg (5½ lb)
Leek	Mar–Apr	Jun	Nov–Mar	1.5 kg (3¼ lb)
Lettuce	Mar–Jul	–	Jun–Oct	1 kg (2 lb)
Marrow	May–Jun	–	Aug–Oct	2 kg (4½ lb)
Onion	Mar–Apr	–	Aug–Sep	1.5 kg (3¼ lb)
Parsnip	Mar	–	Nov–Feb	1.5 kg (3¼ lb)
Pea	Mar–Jul	–	May–Oct	3 kg (6½ lb)
Potato	Apr	–	Sep–Oct	3 kg (6½ lb)
Radish	Mar–Jun	–	May–Sep	0.4 kg (13 oz)
Salsify	Apr	–	Nov–Jan	1.5 kg (3¼ lb)
Shallot	Feb–Mar	Aug		2 kg (4½ lb)
Spinach	Mar–May	–	Jun–Oct	1.5 kg (3¼ lb)
Squash	May (UG)	Jun–Jul	Oct–Nov	2 kg (4½ lb)
Swede	May–Jun	–	Nov–Feb	2 kg (4½ lb)
Sweetcorn	May	–	Aug–Sep	0.5 kg (1 lb)
Tomato	Mar–Apr (UG)	Jun	Aug–Sep	2.5 kg (5½ lb)
Turnip	Jul–Aug	–	Oct–Dec	1.5 kg (3¼ lb)

Frost tolerant	Cultivation	Suitable for freezing
yes	difficult	yes
no	difficult	yes
yes	average	yes
no	simple	yes
yes	average	yes
yes	average	yes
yes	simple	yes
yes	simple	yes
no	average	yes
no	average	yes
yes	average	yes
yes	difficult	yes
yes	average	yes
yes	difficult	yes
yes	simple	no
yes	difficult	no
no	average	yes
no	average	no
yes	average	no
yes	average	yes
yes	average	yes
yes	average	yes
no	simple	no
no	average	yes
no	average	yes
yes	average	yes
no	simple	yes
no	simple	yes
yes	simple	no
yes	average	no
no	average	no
yes	average	yes
no	average	no
yes	simple	yes
no	difficult	yes
no	average	yes
no	simple	yes

THE ENGLISH LANDSCAPE GARDEN

EARLY English gardens had been places of refuge from a terrifying world outside where both nature and men were hostile and aggressive. By the early eighteenth century nature had been greatly tamed and, in addition, many wealthy young Englishmen had travelled to Italy on the 'Grand Tour', taking in the wonders of Renaissance architecture and gardens and the fashionable landscape paintings that idealised natural scenery. They wanted to turn their lands literally into paintings. Rich and powerful landowners were able to get acts through Parliament, allowing them to enclose large areas of common land and even to move whole villages so they would not spoil the view. Lancelot 'Capability' Brown became famous for his designs of landscape gardens, damming up rivers to create lakes, moving earth to create rolling hills and planting clumps of natural-looking trees. Dotted about in the landscape were follies and temples designed to catch the eye.

Earlier gardens had their hedges razed and parterres dug up. Green grass came right up to the house and a combined ditch and sunken wall, known as a ha ha, meant that the eye could gaze right out into the countryside with no apparent hindrance. Perhaps as an antidote to the lack of colour and flowers, the *ferme ornée*, or ornamental farm, was invented. This retained the idea of the landscape, but took the form of a sort of landscape walk in which the verges and hedges would be planted with flowering shrubs. Plenty of seats were provided along the route at strategic points for a good view. Small groups of sheep or cows were encouraged to graze picturesquely nearby.

Humphrey Repton, who followed Capability Brown, was largely responsible for turning landscape back into a garden. He produced watercolour sketches for his clients with sliding 'before' and 'after' pictures to demonstrate what he proposed. He created flowerbeds near the house and would often add a new low fence or wall to divide the more colourful part of the garden from the landscape beyond.

RIGHT: *The Gothic temple at Painshill in Surrey, England, one of the most popular and visited gardens of the eighteenth century, was built between 1738 and 1773. It consisted of a garden walk centred around a lake, with a series of 'set pieces' such as a Roman mausoleum, a rustic hermitage and a grotto.*

ABOVE: *A mature holy basil (labiatae) has grown bushy and in a wooden half barrel.*

GROWING HERBS

Herbs are enjoying a major resurgence in popularity – both as attractive plants and for everyday use in cooking. Of course, herbs have also been used for centuries to decorate and perfume the home, as well as for their medicinal attributes.

✿ Since harvesting herbs regularly actually helps the plants, by keeping them compact and bushy, and encouraging new, fresh, tasty young growth, herb gardens are best placed within reasonable range of the kitchen. You will feel less like tramping down the garden path in the pouring rain for a handful of fresh herbs, than simply reaching out to a window box or herb garden close to the kitchen door.

✿ Herbs make great container plants, since many of them enjoy the well-drained conditions that containers can provide. At one end of the spectrum, a perfectly useful and decorative herb garden can be planted into small pots which, when placed on a sunny windowsill, will provide you with a an easily accessible supply of herbs all year round.

✿ By contrast, twinned tubs flanking your front door and containing elegant standard bay trees with plaited stems are major herb investments that may need winter protection – and even protection against theft. Whatever size of garden you have, you will always be able to find room for a few herbs.

✿ Concentrate on growing a few varieties well, rather than a diversity of species that can quickly grow untidy. Where possible, separate each herb – perhaps by growing each one in an individual container or, as in a traditional herb garden, in distinct compartments.

✿ Many herbs can be quite invasive and vigorous growing. Separating them helps to prevent one herb overwhelming another, looks neat, and enables you to harvest and cultivate one herb without disturbing its neighbour. Divided containers are available specifically for this purpose, or you may have space to plant a knot garden, or herb garden in a wheel formation, with each spoke delineated by bricks or path edging, to create separate sections.

DIVIDING HERBS AND OTHER SMALL PLANTS

Dividing small plants is an excellent way of adding to your stocks at zero expense and with minimal effort. In addition, many perennial plants benefit from being lifted and divided every few years. Left undivided, their middles may start to die out, and the remaining growth can become straggly.

Ease the plant into sections, teasing out the roots gently, rather than tearing them apart. Replant each section and water well. When dividing old plants, discard the weak, old, central section and replant only the fresh young growth around the edges of the plant.

RESTRICTING THE SPREAD OF MINT

Invasive and fast growing, mint is best grown in a container in the ground, which will restrict its root spread yet provide adequate moisture. Use a standard pot or bottomless bucket; some gardeners use slate embedded in the ground to restrict the root run.

1 *Dig a hole large enough for the rim of a generously sized pot to be buried just below ground level.*

2 *Place the pot in the ground and bed it firmly into the soil with your hands. Make sure the rim is level with the soil surface.*

3 *Add a small amount of potting compost to the bottom of the pot.*

4 *Place the mint in the pot and then backfill the pot with compost and firm it around the plant. Water well. Lift, divide and repot the plant each spring.*

STARTING OUT

MANY herb gardens begin with an impulse buy of a healthy, container-grown perennial herb from the wide range of herbs on display at the garden centre, and this can be an excellent start. Although many herbs can be grown from seed, if you need only one example of a herb, such as rosemary, it is cheaper, as well as easier, to buy a single plant. Herbs such as chives, which you may want in larger quantities, for example, to use as a decorative edging or as a companion plant elsewhere in the garden, are easily propagated by division; so just a few plants from the garden centre will quickly yield many more. Some annual herbs, such as nasturtiums and basil, are quick and easy to grow from seed.

Cultivation requirements

❀ Many herbs are sun lovers, needing at least six hours of sunlight a day in order to thrive. Without good light, they can become thin and straggly, with a poor aroma. Most herbs also dislike being waterlogged, so plant them in well-drained soil. Some, such as thyme, sage and dwarf lavender, are very drought tolerant and actively enjoy sunny, dry conditions. Most herbs prefer warm conditions. Although they can tolerate temperatures of 7°C (45°F), herbs do not thrive in the cold.

❀ Protect cherished perennial herbs such as bay and rosemary against extremely cold or windy weather conditions. A simple way to care for tender herbs is to plant them in containers, plunged into the ground during the milder months and removed for overwintering in a protected environment. Some herbs, such as mint, are very invasive, and are always best planted in containers within the soil so that they do not colonise the garden.

HARVESTING HERBS

Pick leaves at any time during the growing season. Evergreens such as thyme may be harvested at any time, but allow new growth to harden off before winter.

PLANTING A CONTAINER HERB GARDEN

1 *Strawberry pots allow many different herbs to be grown in a small space. Place a layer of crocks at the bottom of the pot. Fill up to the first planting hole with compost mixed with water-retaining gel.*

2 *Taking care not to disturb the root ball, push the roots of the first herb through the lowest planting hole into the pot.*

3 *Work up the pot, adding more compost and plants until you reach the top. Plant more herbs in the top of the pot. Water slowly and carefully so that the water reaches into every planting pocket.*

4 *Each spring, lift and divide any herbs that are growing too large or straggly for the pot.*

❀ Harvest leaves in the morning, after the dew has evaporated from the foliage. Leaves are at their most flavoursome and tender just before the herb comes into flower. If harvesting the flowers, you should collect these at midday in dry weather, just as the flower is beginning to open fully.

❀ Take care to keep your harvested herbs loose, and with plenty of air circulating freely around them to prevent bruising, crushing or other deterioration prior to use. Traditional trugs are perfect for collecting herbs.

❀ Herb seed may be collected when it is fully hardened and ripe, on a warm, dry day. Roots are generally harvested in autumn when the parts of the plant above the ground are starting to die back.

❀ The active components sought by herbalists for medicinal uses will have developed in the root systems of perennials in the second or third year after planting. Annual roots may be harvested at the end of each year. If you are not planning on using the herbs immediately after picking, then prepare them for preservation as soon as possible after harvesting, for optimum results.

STORING HERBS

How you handle herbs after harvesting will depend on the type of herb, and its intended use. Some herbs lose a lot of their flavour if dried. The taste and aroma of such herbs is better retained by freezing or by preserving in oil or vinegar.

Freezing herbs

❀ Freezing is a simple and effective way of preserving much of the flavour, colour and nutritional content of herbs. Some of the more delicate herbs produce fresher tasting results when frozen rather than dried. Freeze them in labelled plastic bags or rigid containers. Alternatively, freeze small quantities of finely chopped herbs in individual ice cube trays and top up with water for convenient cooking quantities.

Herb oils and vinegars

❀ Herbs may be infused in oil or vinegar. These are simple to make; they liven up salads and marinades and make lovely gifts, too. Herb vinegars are also popular in cooking and as hair or skin rinses.

DRYING YOUR HERBS

Herbs need to be dried as quickly as possible after harvesting, in order to retain maximum colour and scent. It is important that any moisture is removed before the plant material begins to deteriorate – rotting or becoming mouldy.

1 *Pick several stems or leaves of your herb, in this case rosemary. Remove any leaves that would crowd together and hold too much moisture so that they would rot rather than dry out. Make small bunches for quick drying. Hang them upside down in a dry, warm, dark or shaded place is needed, such as an airing cupboard. Allow plenty of air to circulate around the drying herbs.*

2 *When drying is complete, after one to four weeks, the herbs may be rubbed through a sieve to remove the stalks, or shredded by hand, and bottled. Keep the bottled herbs in a dark, dry place until needed.*

GROWING AND USING HERBS

This chart identifies some of the most regularly used herbs. In addition it shows their various uses in cooking and, in some cases, medical treatments and explains how to grow them most effectively.

Herb	Use	Cultivation
Basil	Used in many popular Italian dishes; natural partner to tomatoes. Roughly tear the leaves, rather than chop	Tender annual; cannot withstand frost
Bay	Prime ingredient of bouquet garni; goes well with fish, stews and rice dishes. Tear the edges of the leaf before adding to a dish, and remove before serving the meal	Evergreen shrub; can withstand cold, but benefits from frost and wind protection
Borage	Delicately flavoured and pretty addition to long summer drinks	Hardy annual; grow in a sunny position, in any soil type
Chives	Mild onion flavour; partners cheese, potatoes, eggs and butter particularly well. Not as rich in sulphur as onions, thus do not have the same tendency to cause digestive disturbance	Hardy perennial. Chives left to flower are pretty perennial plants, easily propagated by division. For the tastiest flavour, do not allow the plant to flower
Coriander	Young leaves are deliciously perfumed and widely used in curries, as are the aromatic seeds	Hardy annual; prefers a sunny, well-drained position
Dill	Partners salmon and other types of fish especially well	Hardy annual; grow in a sheltered, cool position in rich, deep soil
Feverfew	Mainly ornamental; medicinal use as a cure for headache – note, herbal remedies should only ever be taken on the advice of an experienced practitioner	Hardy perennial; self-seeds readily. Prefers dry, well-drained soil in a sunny position

Herb		Use	Cultivation
Lavender		Popular culinary ingredient; adds delicate perfumed flavour to honey, and to savoury dishes. Popular in pot pourri, sleep pillows and as decorative flower – fresh and dried	Hardy evergreen; grow in a dry, sunny position; clip after flowering
Marjoram		Partners eggs, cheese and tomatoes particularly well	Hardy perennial; grow in moist, sunny position
Mint		Used in mint sauce as essential accompaniment to roast lamb	Hardy perennial; grow in moist soil in partial shade or sun. Very invasive, therefore best grown in a container
Oregano		Widely used in bouquet garni, stuffings and for sprinkling over meat before roasting	Hardy perennial; grow in a well-drained, sunny position
Parsley		Popular garnish; goes particularly well with fish and potatoes	Hardy biennial; grow in slightly sheltered, rich moist soil
Rosemary		Traditional accompaniment to lamb and pork	Evergreen; grow in a sunny position in sandy, well-drained soil, preferably in sheltered position
Sage		Natural partner to onions; popular as a stuffing to counteract the richness of roast meats	Evergreen; grow in sunny site on light, well-drained soil
Thyme		Used in widely in soups and stews, omelettes and salads	Evergreen; grow in light, stony soil in full sun

FRUIT GARDENING

Compared with vegetables, fruit gardening is very straightforward and relatively undemanding. While a vegetable patch needs consistent work and management to be at all productive – digging, feeding, weeding, planning successional sowing, intercropping and crop rotation – most fruits simply need to be planted in appropriate surroundings and will thrive with very rudimentary care. Some fruit trees will crop successfully for years with almost no attention, provided they have been planted properly and cared for early on.

THE ADVANTAGES OF GROWING YOUR OWN

GROWING your own fruit guarantees a chemical-free crop and offers the delicious taste and beneficial vitamins of fruit fresh from the plant. Some commercially grown fruits, for example grapes, are particularly likely to have been drenched in chemicals during cultivation.

❀ It is very easy to grow fruit organically, without recourse to pesticides and fertilisers, since perennial fruit plants do well on quite poor soil, and have a chance to benefit from the full ecological support that builds up in an established area. Companion planting can assist even further, attracting increased populations of predators and pollinators once a plant has settled in.

❀ Fruit can also be an extremely decorative element of garden design. Fruit trees are attractive all year round,

ABOVE: *Strawberries are simple and satisfying to grow.*

LEFT: *Fruit trees such as apples thrive in open orchards.*

even in winter when bare. Fruits can be trained to divide the garden vertically, and enliven or conceal walls and fences. Vines can scramble across arches, trellis, sheds and pergolas.

CHOOSING FRUITS TO SUIT YOU

THE TYPES of fruit you grow will depend on the size of your garden and the amount of time and energy you intend to devote to fruit growing, among other factors.

❀ Some fruit trees can grow to 7 m (23 ft) tall and are clearly unsuitable for a tiny garden, whereas those produced on dwarf rootstock may be suitable for

ABOVE: *Fruit can be grown successfully even where space is extremely limited, by using vertical surfaces to support plants.*

container growing. Think carefully about the species and where to grow it, before visiting the nursery or garden centre.

❀ Consider your site carefully, too. Although many fruit trees will do well with very little attention, they will do best if planted with consideration for their growing needs. Most fruits prefer a sheltered, sunny position. The sun encourages ripening and the production of good flavour and colour. Shelter helps keep the plants warm and reduces the risk of wind damage. In addition, the insect activity so important for pollination is reduced on windy sites, which will restrict cropping.

❀ Although an entire orchard is obviously the optimum area for growing fruit trees, and a large fruit cage, big enough for an adult to stand in, is great for growing soft fruits, it is possible to grow a reasonable fruit crop even in a restricted space.

❀ Growing fruits in containers, as with vegetables, has become increasingly popular, allowing every gardener – even those who can devote no more than a patio or a couple of large planters flanking the front door to fruit growing – to have the satisfaction of eating fruit fresh from the plant.

GROWING STRAWBERRIES

Simple to grow, strawberries are an ideal introduction to fruit growing. Although they will thrive with little attention, some basic care will improve the amount and quality of the crop considerably.

1 Plant strawberry plants in well-drained, humus-rich soil, spaced approximately 46 cm (18 in) apart.

2 As the ripening strawberries dangle towards the soil, a mulch of clean straw or a rubber strawberry mat will protect the fruit from mud splashes and from rotting. Mulching also retains moisture within the soil in hot weather and suppresses competitive weed growth.

3 To ensure the best crop possible, remove runners from the plants as soon as they appear. These runners can then be grown on to produce new plants.

4 When the strawberry plants have fruted, cut back the old foliage to within approximately 10 cm (4 in) of the leaf stems and remove debris and old straw from around the plants.

espaliered tree   standard tree   cordon vine   fan-shaped tree

GENERAL CARE FOR FRUIT GROWING

BUY only sound, sturdy plants, especially when selecting trees and bushes, which will be long-term garden residents. Plants of certified 'A' grade stock are guaranteed to be healthy and free of disease. This is a particularly useful guideline for buying good-quality soft fruits, which can be prone to diseases such as mosaic virus, which may not be detectable on a young plant.

❀ Choose cultivars suited to your site, and according to the effect you want – perhaps a tree you can train to an espalier shape to cover a warm wall, or a standard to take pride of place in a lawn. Make sure that you buy a rootstock appropriate to the scale of your plot. Rootstocks range from very vigorous to dwarf, so choose carefully. Remember that most tree fruits need cross pollinating, unless you choose a 'family' tree with several varieties on it, which fertilise each other.

Planting

❀ Fruit bushes and trees are generally planted in late autumn or early winter, although container-grown plants can be planted out at any time, weather permitting. Most fruit thrives on well-drained, slightly acidic soil with good water reserves in the subsoil.

❀ To avoid the risk of disease, plant at the correct spacing. Many fruits are susceptible to rot caused by the fungal diseases that thrive in humid, overcrowded conditions. Where plants have sufficient air and light, fungal diseases rarely occur, and do not spread very easily if they do appear at all.

Supporting

❀ Apart from strawberries, bush currants and gooseberries, all fruits need supporting, either by staking or training against a surface. To stake a bare-rooted plant, drive a vertical stake into the planting hole before adding the plant.

❀ Container-grown plants need an angled stake added after planting. Soft fruits such as raspberries and some types of redcurrants and gooseberries need support systems of wires and posts, or wires fixed to walls or fences. Whatever support you choose, it must be well secured.

Feeding

❀ Some plant food will have been added at planting time, and leaf fall will return some more fertility to the soil, but harvesting fruit means that nutrients are being removed permanently from the soil, which will need replacing for best results.

❀ Regular mulching with well-rotted organic matter will aid soil fertility, and adding an organic fertiliser in late winter is beneficial. Although this may seem early, tree roots will just be starting into life again and organic fertilisers take time to be absorbed into the soil and become available to plant roots.

❀ Some fruits have particular feeding needs, so read labels carefully when buying and note any special requirements. For example, redcurrants and gooseberries need potash; stone fruits need calcium.

Watating

❀ The shallow, fibrous roots of soft fruits are especially vulnerable to drought, so be vigilant in attending to their watering needs. Top fruit will generally need watering only if grown against a fence or wall.

Protecting

❀ Most fruiting plants need some form of protection against frost, birds and other pests, and diseases. Barrier protection such as netting, fleece or cages is simple and effective. Try to avoid using chemical sprays as these can kill or deter pollinating insects, and are undesirable products to have in contact with edible crops. Remember to remove coverings used to protect against late spring frosts during the day, so as to allow insects to pollinate the flowers.

COMPANION PLANTING

AS WITH vegetables, growing fruit in tandem with other plants often has substantial benefits, especially in relation to pest and disease control. For example, alliums – particularly chives – are useful to apple trees, as they help prevent apple scab. Planting nasturtiums around the base of an apple tree and encouraging them to scramble up the trunk will deter woolly aphids. Conversely, some planting combinations are actively harmful, for example innocently pretty anemones harbouring plum rust and planted near plum trees.

HARVESTING AND STORING APPLES

When to harvest depends on whether the apples are to be eaten immediately or stored long term. For the former, choose apples at their pinnacle of ripeness. Assess this visually, by watching the developing colour, and also by twisting the fruit gently on the branch. If the stalk snaps easily under this light pressure and the apple comes away cleanly, it is fully ripe.

1 *Pick apples for storing just before they are completely ripe. They should be top quality, unblemished and free of any bruising or pest damage, which could contaminate the entire store.*

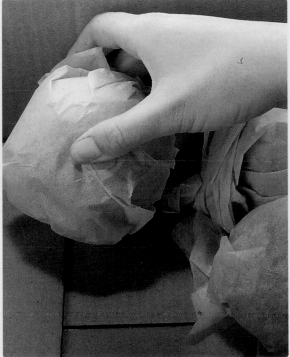

2 *Wrap each apple carefully in greaseproof paper and place in a shallow box. Store in a cool dark place. These harvesting and storage guidelines can be applied equally to pears.*

ABOVE: *Some fruit trees make attractive and productive container plants.*

GROWING FRUIT IN CONTAINERS

GROWING fruit in containers has grown in popularity in recent years. Even gardeners with diminutive plots can produce fruit crops that taste wonderful, are free of chemicals, rich in nutrients and absolutely fresh. Most fruiting plants are also extremely decorative as well as productive. For example, apple trees are often grown as much for their ornamental virtues as for their edible fruits. Strawberries possess a convenient tumbling growth habit, ideally suited to hanging baskets as well as the multi-holed terracotta pots that are more familiar as strawberry planters.

❀ Choose your species carefully when planting fruit in containers, especially if growing fruit trees. The plant should be clearly labelled in the garden centre or nursery, with full details of its rootstock, how much space it requires, and whether it is self-fertilising or will

RIGHT: *Strawberries reward even minimal care with generous crops of juicy, ripe fruit.*

need other trees around it for pollination. For example, if you have the space and inclination for only a single apple tree in a container, you will need a dwarf rootstock, such as M27 or M9, with a 'family' of three or four compatible varieties grafted on to it so that no further trees are needed for pollination.

Suitable containers

❀ Choose your container with due consideration to the needs of the plant you are growing. Fruit trees prefer a free root run, so will need generously proportioned containers. Cherries, plums, pears, apples and the like need containers that are at least 38 cm (15 in) deep, preferably much deeper.

❀ Dustbins, although not the most attractive of containers, make perfect homes for container-grown fruit trees. You could choose a galvanised metal one for industrial chic, or wrap bamboo or other natural screening around an inexpensive plastic bin. The latter option has the added advantage that you could easily conceal a layer of plastic bubble wrap beneath the decorative natural wrapping for added winter insulation.

❀ There are also very attractive large containers that once served quite different purposes, for example old washing tubs, which look like giant Chinese lanterns made of silvery metal that has softened in tone over the years.

Caring for container-grown fruit

❀ The container fruit gardener needs to pay special attention to planting, watering, feeding and potting on, particularly if growing trees in containers.
One useful way of reducing the effort involved in potting on every two years or so is to plant in a container that is initially oversized, lifting up the plant when necessary and adding further layers of compost beneath the first until the plant eventually outgrows the container. Plant with a good organic potting compost.

❀ Ideally, arrange some sort of permanent watering system for containers, to save work and ensure that the compost doesn't dry out. To give an idea of the watering needs of a container-grown fruit tree, you may find that in hot weather it needs a drink three or four times a day! Clearly, it is worth investing in a system that makes this an achievable proposition. Watering is not generally needed during winter.

Fruits for container growing

❀ For the best chance of success, always choose fruits with a good track record as container-grown plants. Strawberries are a perennial favourite and can be grown in all sorts of containers. Even individual small pots of strawberries on a windowsill will produce a good yield. Growing strawberries in containers has the additional

ABOVE: *Figs thrive in containers, since they like having their roots restricted.*

benefit of reducing the risk of slug attack and removing the need for the laborious mulching and weeding that is required when growing strawberries in the ground.

❀ Figs make good container plants, since they like having their roots restricted. Conversely, grapes hate root restriction and never do well in containers. Apples are a better choice than pears, since pears are not available on dwarf rootstocks at the time of writing, and even the smallest grows to at least 2.4 m (8 ft) tall.

❀ Some fruits are perfectly happy in containers, but their growth habit makes them too untidy a choice for decorative planting, for example raspberries, which grow tall and need staking and netting. Chosen well, watered well and placed in a spot sympathetic to their needs, container-grown fruits will be an attractive and rewarding addition to your garden.

LEFT: *Pear trees do not thrive in containers because they are not available in dwarf rootstocks.*

FRUIT GAZETTEER

Many fruits are remarkably tolerant to neglect. Even a fruit tree untended for several years will produce a reasonable crop, but all fruits will benefit from some appropriate care and attention. This will keep the plants healthy, cropping with a good yield and producing well-sized fruits.

FRUIT	Apple	Apricot	Blueberry	Blackcurrent	Fig
NEEDS FULL SUN	yes	yes	yes	yes	yes
HARDY BELOW -8°C (18°F)	yes	yes	yes	yes	no
HEIGHT x SPREAD	controlled by rootstock	controlled by rootstock	1.5 x 1.5 m (5 x 5 ft)	1.2 x 1.2 m (4 x 4 ft)	2.4 x 3 m (8 x 10 ft)
SOIL REQUIREMENTS	deep, well drained	slightly alkaline	acidic	rich, moist, heavy	slightly alkaline
COMPANION PLANT	chives	garlic	no	nettles	rue
CULTIVATION	simple	average	simple	simple	average

FRUIT	Gooseberry	Grape	Kiwi	Peach	Pear
NEEDS FULL SUN	yes	yes	yes	yes	yes
HARDY BELOW -8°C (18°F)	yes	no	yes	yes	yes
HEIGHT X SPREAD	1.2 x 1.2 m (4 x 4 ft)	Height 6 m (20 ft)	Height 9 m (30 ft)	controlled by rootstock	controlled by rootstock
SOIL REQUIREMENTS	rich, moist	average	average	acidic/neutral	rich, moist
COMPANION PLANT	Limnanthes douglasii	blackberries	no	garlic	no
CULTIVATION	simple	simple	average	simple	difficult

FRUIT	Plum	Raspberry	Redcurrant	Strawberry	Whitecurrant
NEEDS FULL SUN	yes	yes	no	yes	no
HARDY BELOW -8°C (18°F)	yes	yes	yes	yes	yes
HEIGHT x SPREAD	controlled by rootstock	Height 1.8 m (6 ft)	1.2 x 1.2 m (4 x 4 ft)	15 x 30 cm (6 x 12 in)	1.2 x 1.2 m (4 x 4 ft)
SOIL REQUIREMENTS	heavy, moist	acidic/neutral	cool, average	rich	cool, average
COMPANION PLANT	garlic	garlic	nettles	onion	nettles
CULTIVATION	average	simple	simple	simple	average

THE JEKYLL/LUTYENS PARTNERSHIP

GERTRUDE JEKYLL was a friend of William Robinson's and the most influential garden designer in England before the Second World War. In 1889 she met a young architect called Edwin Lutyens and they collaborated on many gardens. He worked on the architectural aspects and hard landscaping and she on the planting. She had trained as a painter and was influenced by the sophisticated colour theories of the day. She developed single-colour and graded colour schemes, quite different from the earlier brash bedding colours. Her naturalistic approach was particularly successful within the formal framework of Lutyens' bricks, steps and paving.

ABOVE: *Les Bois des Moutiers in France. The house was designed by Lutyens for the family that still own it today and the planting was very much in line with Gertrude Jekyll's philosophy, with graduated colour schemes in the formal section and a grand informality at the back of the house.*

ORGANIC PRACTICES

In recent years, there has been a noticeable swing away from some of the advice previously issued almost automatically by gardening experts. Nowadays, the advice on pest and weed control is not necessarily limited to a directive to buy the strongest chemicals available and apply them routinely. Providing an alternative approach in addition to, or instead of, a chemical solution has increasingly become the gardening norm. This naturalistic approach is not new. It is merely a return to the centuries of gardening wisdom that preceded the onslaught of garden chemicals, which came to be seen as essential horticultural kit in the last hundred years.

THE PRINCIPLES

ORGANIC gardening is not just about reducing a reliance on chemical support. Choosing a 'natural' pest killer is not necessarily much more ecologically sound than using a chemical variant. Organic practice is about considering the garden in a much more holistic way.

❀ Rather than automatically dismissing all garden creatures as pests and all plants other than crops as weeds, an organic approach considers, values and utilises the complex interplay between plants and creatures, the elements and the soil – a series of relationships that can be turned to a gardener's advantage. The organic approach is not a single rule or dictate. It is a way of gardening that is ecologically sound, sustainable, naturalistic and environmentally friendly.

The benefits

❀ Most people have a creeping awareness of the ecological issues that have become of increasing concern in recent years – namely, a desire not to pollute the environment or our bodies with chemicals, and a wish to encourage nature back into our lives on a daily basis, by encouraging birds, butterflies and other creatures to visit our gardens.

BELOW: *Respecting a plant's natural habitat and replicating it in a garden setting is the simplest way to encourage healthy growth.*

❀ These are not just cosmetic concerns or matters of gardening fashion. People have become increasingly concerned about what they are eating – aware, for example, that there is little point in washing fruit in order to remove pesticides and fertilisers from the skin if, as is the case with some commercially grown fruit, the flesh is contaminated with chemicals throughout. Organic produce has therefore become increasingly popular, and many gardeners have started to grow their own.

Valuing the soil

❀ Besides enhancing the quality of food production, an organic approach has much to offer the garden as a whole. Organic gardening centres around protecting and increasing the life blood of the garden – the soil.

❀ For the past hundred years or so, farmers and domestic gardeners have been using artificial fertilisers to encourage plant growth and chemicals to control pests in the soil. Safety issues with regard to the often dangerous chemicals involved seem obvious now, as do concerns over potentially poisoning not only our own bodies directly, but also harming life around us, since chemicals wash out into water supplies and find their way into the diet of wildlife.

ABOVE: *Plant according to the conditions prevalent in your garden, such as the dappled shade of this woodland path, and the plants will grow vigorously with few additional requirements.*

❀ Another, less immediately visible layer of damage has slowly occurred as commercial and domestic gardeners have become reliant on chemicals. Soil, abused and neglected, ceases to live, and without living soil beneath our feet we cannot hope to sustain life above the soil. Healthy soil is vibrantly alive with organisms, which convert inert minerals and water into materials that plants need in order to grow.

❀ Overuse of chemical fertilisers and overintensive cultivation are short-sighted gardening methods, and strip the soil of humus-making organisms. Since soil without humus is essentially finely ground rock on which nothing will flourish, the aim of organic gardening is to introduce and sustain the natural life within garden soil. This raises soil fertility, improves moisture retention and encourages plant health, as well as gradually building up and supporting a wider natural environment. For example, by encouraging worms, which feed blackbirds, not only do you add the sweet sound of bird-song to your garden, but the birds will repay your soil by adding their droppings, feathers, eggshells and eventually their own bodies to further enrich your soil.

ABOVE: *Producing your own compost is probably the single most important step you can take towards gardening organically; a compost heap does not need to be elaborate or expensive.*

GOING ORGANIC: WHERE TO BEGIN

CHANGING the habits of a gardening lifetime to 'go organic' can seem overwhelming, but there are some simple immediate steps, which will have a positive impact on your garden.

✿ Stop using chemical insecticides, fertilisers, fungicides and herbicides. Buy only ecofriendly products; for example, choose not to buy peat from non-sustainable sources, or bulbs gathered from wild sites. Incorporate as many natural control/encouragement techniques as possible – for example companion planting and creating habitats to attract helpful wildlife into your garden.

✿ Since respecting and nurturing the soil is at the heart of organic gardening, producing your own compost is the most important first step in becoming an organic gardener. Organisms are essentially any items that have once lived. Converting

these items back into compost is not only ecologically sound on the grounds of recycling and avoiding waste, but also marvellously helpful to the soil.

✿ Well-balanced, well-matured compost is a perfect plant food, which does not carry the risks of overfeeding or even active damage associated with chemical fertilisers. Importantly, the humus-making organisms present in compost not only convert plant food into substances accessible to the plants, but also gradually help return the soil to its naturally balanced, healthy state. This encourages plants to grow more easily and be more resistant to disease.

Compost making

✿ Garden compost is preferable to farmyard manure, since it contains a wider range of nutrients and micro-organisms. There are many different methods for making compost, but all share the same basic principles.

✿ Generally, good composting comes from using a variety of different substances rather than one material only, and it must be well mixed, aerated and moistened. Getting this balance of materials, air and moisture right is the key to successful composting, together with efficient mixing and effective insulation to retain heat well. The bigger your compost heap, the more efficiently it will heat up and 'cook' to produce compost reasonably quickly.

RIGHT: *Throw all your degradable rubbish into the compost holder to provide rich mulch for the plants.*

❁ An expensive compost container is not essential.
A simple home-made compost heap, an area
approximately 1 sq m (1¼ sq yd) contained within a
construction of wood, wire or brick will be very
effective, if not as elegant as a commercial equivalent.
Protect the heap against rainfall and insulate it –
although unsightly, an effective lid is a piece of old

ABOVE: *Organic vegetables, like these lettuces, chives and spring onions,
are full of vitamins and natural goodness.*

carpet covered with plastic sheeting. A conventional
lid, insulated by plastic bags filled with crumpled
newspaper placed inside it out of sight, is a more
attractive solution.

WHAT TO COMPOST

❁ A good composting mixture contains moist green
matter that will rot fairly quickly, such as grass
clippings, together with more brackish materials
such as straw and twiggy stems, which break down
more slowly but add useful bulk.

❁ Do not squash down huge heaps of grass clippings,
which will inhibit a good flow of air. Intersperse
thin, uncompressed layers, approximately 15 cm
(6 in) thick, with other materials.

❁ Fibrous matter will compost more readily if shredded
or cut into small pieces before being added to the
heap. Ideally, add a layer of manure every 30 cm (12
in). The nitrogen in the manure will speed up the
composting process and contribute beneficial soil
organisms.

❁ Kitchen waste, such as crushed eggshells, vegetable
peelings, tea leaves and coffee grounds are all
suitable, but avoid meat, fish and cooked food,
which encourage vermin. Never use the compost
area as an extra rubbish bin.

❁ Nappies, pet litter and general household debris will
produce a stinking mess, not the sweet-smelling
friable brown compost that is your aim. Also, do not
create problems for yourself by adding perennial
weeds, diseased plant matter and seeding flower
heads to the heap.

❁ Compost generally takes about three weeks to reach
its maximum temperature, then goes on to mature in
around three to six months. The compost will benefit
from turning during this time.

ABOVE: *An organic environment need not be wild and undisciplined. A pond of any kind will attract beneficial wildlife to the garden.*

THE VALUE OF A
POSITIVE ECOSYSTEM

THIS sounds terrifyingly technical, yet simply describes a garden environment that becomes increasingly self-supporting. By encouraging wildlife into the garden, you can share all the benefits of the natural cycle, which may have been thrown destructively off kilter by contemporary gardening methods. For example, aim to attract predators that live on pests, which live on other pests and so on.

❧ Predators generally breed more slowly than pests, which can create a major problem if you are using chemical pest controls, which can unwittingly destroy useful predators along with the pests. The self-regulating system of pests and predators is thus thrown off-balance and can take years to rebuild. It is important to rethink the way that you regard what you may previously have considered purely as pests. For example, a butterfly, beautiful in its own right, as well as helping to produce more flowers in your garden by pollination, was once a caterpillar, munching its way through leaves.

❧ Aim to control the wildlife in your garden and make it work for you, rather than destroying it unilaterally. A pest by another name can also be seen as wildlife, a pollinator, a predator and ultimately, fertiliser. Not all pests are as lethal to plants as gardeners have

BELOW: *Leaving the seed heads on plants provide valuable seed heads for birds.*

been led to believe over the past century, and there are pest control options available to the organic gardener, that do not involve saturating your garden with hazardous chemicals.

CREATING A POSITIVE ECOSYSTEM

BUTTERFLIES, beetles, wasps, bees and hoverflies are pollinators. They all transfer pollen, which encourages more flowers in your garden, for as long a season as possible. Of course, as the pollinators die, their decomposing bodies make a further contribution to soil fertility.

Attracting pollinators

❀ Some plants are particularly attractive to pollinators. It is important to provide as long a season of nectar for them as possible, so plant a range of plants popular to pollinators – from early spring flowers like bluebells and *aubrieta* through to summer flowers such as buddleja, valerian and lavender.

❀ Hoverflies are superb aphid eaters, and should be encouraged by planting their favourite, the poached egg flower (*Limnanthes douglasii*), a pretty, easy-to-grow annual.

❀ Other plants attractive to hoverflies include broom, marigolds, golden rod and Michaelmas daisies, as well as most other flowers. Lacewings and ladybirds take nectar from the same flowers as hoverflies, but also like dill, yarrow and alliums, which are spectacular ornamental plants to grow in any case.

BELOW: *A predatory ground beetle on a plant stem.*

ABOVE: *Frogs and toads are very beneficial garden creatures, eating the slugs and snails that can cause untold plant damage.*

Encouraging frogs and toads

❀ Toads, frogs and newts eat many pests, notably slugs, and a wise organic gardener provides water and moist areas for these garden friends to inhabit. A pond is the obvious environment, but any moist, sheltered corner may be home to these useful creatures.

❀ Some organic gardeners deliberately create a temptingly moist, overgrown area in the greenhouse, where frogs and toads congregate, so helping to control greenhouse pests such as earwigs, and numerous other insects and grubs. Do allow the creatures access to a pond for mating and breeding.

Beneficial beetles

❀ Beetles comprise a huge group of insects – at least 250,000 species. Although there are exceptions, such as wood-boring beetles, most are garden helpers, eating slugs and soil pests, as well as pollinating in inclement conditions when other pollinators do not fly.

❀ Some beetles are ground dwellers, while others can fly. It is a good idea to help protect useful ground-dwelling beetles from larger predators by providing them with dense-foliaged, dew-collecting plants such as lady's mantle to hide beneath. Propping up some slates and adding pieces of wood, stones, old tiles or brassica collars to the vegetable plot will encourage beetles to dwell there and see off aphids.

ABOVE: *A garden spider on a dewy web formed on a seed head in the early morning.*

Spiders

✿ Spiders are beneficial in two ways. They prey on pests, and also provide food for wrens, robins and other garden friends. Encourage spiders by allowing the natural debris that builds up under hedges to accumulate. Dead twigs and leaves make a perfect habitat for spiders and other useful insects and small mammals.

Birds

✿ Although birds can damage crops, the benefits of attracting them into your garden far outweigh the disadvantages. Thus the organic gardener prefers to protect vulnerable plants against bird attack, while actively encouraging particularly useful birds to visit and live in the garden.

✿ Providing nesting places in which young birds can be safely reared, along with feeding the birds to help them survive the winter and providing an adequate water supply, will all repay you many times over.

✿ Most birds are berry or seed eaters, so growing fruit and other berrying plants will obviously attract them. Leaving the seed heads on plants will also help. Keen organic gardeners often plant sacrificial crops, so

valuable are some birds to the garden as a whole. Stop feeding in summer, in order to encourage the birds to devour unwanted pests.

✿ Some birds are especially useful, and it is well worth providing conditions that are likely to attract them by supplying birdboxes designed to replicate their natural preferences, and favoured foodstuffs. For example, blue tits, which devour caterpillars, aphids and leaf miners, nest in small holes in trees, so prefer nesting boxes with a small round hole on the front which mimics this environment; while robins will settle in boxes with wider, open fronts.

✿ However you feed the birds in your garden, be consistent. In winter, a wasted journey to an empty bird table can exhaust what may already be a weak bird. Ideally, feed twice a day during winter.

✿ Site nesting boxes carefully, away from feeding tables, as the feeding birds would disturb the nesting birds. Position nesting boxes approximately 2 m (7 ft) up a tree trunk, pole or wall, facing away from prevailing winds and strong sun. Open-fronted boxes should be placed in thick cover.

RIGHT: *Birds are great insect eaters and are well worth attracting into your garden.*

Hedgehogs

❀ Hedgehogs are popular garden creatures, eating slugs, caterpillars, beetles and other insects. Contrary to popular opinion, hedgehogs should not be fed on milk. They fare much better on cat or dog food, which may help encourage them into the garden if put out in the autumn when they are laying down fat stores for their winter hibernation.

❀ Purpose-built hedgehog houses can be bought or made and installed under hedges or shrubs. Always check a bonfire for hibernating hedgehogs before lighting it. Many hedgehogs perish in this way each year. If you have a pond, supply a rough piece of wood on one side as a ladder, as hedgehogs can drown in steep-sided ponds.

ABOVE: *Hedgehogs are marvellous mobile slug controls.*

ABOVE: *A common long-eared bat hanging asleep from a tree branch.*

Worms

❀ The humble worm is a vital garden creature. The casts that they excrete are a wonderful soil texturiser and fertiliser, and worm burrows assist soil drainage and aeration. Of course, if you are going to encourage birds, you also need worms. Encourage worms by keeping the soil moist and mulched, with plenty of organic matter incorporated. Liming also encourages worms, since they prefer slightly alkaline soil.

Bats

❀ Although unpopular with many people, bats perform useful functions, which make it well worth encouraging them to take up residence in your garden. They eat vast numbers of flying pests, for example aphids and mosquitoes. Many bat species are declining, so providing favourable roosting and hibernating sites for them in your garden is a very worthy undertaking.

❀ Bats are not easy to attract and have very specific requirements, but you could try putting up a bat box in a suitable place and seeing if any roost. Ideally, have two bat boxes – one facing south for summer, one facing north for winter hibernation – both at least 1.5 m (5 ft), but preferably 5 m (16 ft), off the ground, placed on a tree trunk or under the house eaves.

THE ORGANIC APPROACH TO PESTS AND DISEASES

ABOVE: *Use shears rather than a chemical weedkiller to get rid of unwanted growth in your garden.*

As already described, the organic gardener takes a wider view of garden wildlife than simply eradicating every living creature with hazardous chemicals. By encouraging predators into the garden, some pests are kept under natural control, while taking care of the soil and general good plant husbandry encourages plants to grow healthily and with improved disease resistance.

❀ A very exciting recent development in gardening has been the growing acceptance of companion planting as a valuable horticultural tool. Although this practice has been undertaken for centuries, it has only recently been brought to centre stage as a useful gardening technique, rather than being viewed as a quaint mixture of folklore and myth.

Companion planting

❀ Growing particular combinations of plants for specific beneficial effect has long been practised, and a developing trend away from treating pests and diseases with chemicals has provoked a resurgence of interest in this intriguing area of garden science.

❀ The organic approach in general takes a holistic view of the garden, accepting, utilising and maximising all the complex beneficial interconnections of nature, while minimising negative interplay. Companion planting springs from this viewpoint, and works in a number of ways.

❀ Some plants repel undesirable insects, or lure them away from other specific plants. For example, marigolds deter whitefly, so are often grown near plants susceptible to whitefly attack, such as tomatoes grown in greenhouses. Marigolds are particularly well known nowadays as a companion plant, valued for their long-flowering attractiveness, as well as for their ability to kill eelworms and fend off pests.

❀ Some plants help each other directly, by providing shelter from the elements or by less immediately obvious means, such as by positive secretions from roots and leaves. For example, some roots exude substances that render them distasteful to pests, and this useful property can be transmitted through the soil to neighbouring plants. Some plants can help the soil, for example legumes, which render nitrogen available to other plants.

❀ While some plants are good neighbours, others are enemy combinations. This may be down to one plant shading another, preventing germination, or to one plant starving its neighbours of soil nutrients, or producing root secretions which inhibit growth. Companion planting notes these undesirable relationships and minimises them.

Organic pest and disease control

❀ You might expect this section to be a list of home-made concoctions for alternatives to chemical pest- and weedkillers, but the organic approach is more wide ranging than simply replacing chemicals with 'natural' recipes.

❀ Organic gardening focuses on a broadly healthy, long-term approach, rather than the quick-fix to gardening problems that we have been taught by manufacturers to regard as the norm. The organic gardener takes care to provide optimum growing conditions for plants, thereby encouraging natural plant health and disease resistance. Good hygiene practices also help keep disease at bay, as does choosing to plant varieties resistant to disease.

❀ Crop rotation is a well-accepted way of protecting plants from pests and diseases. Mechanical methods are also part of the organic pest control lexicon. These include erecting physical barriers to pests, for example protecting food crops with netting to exclude birds, or simply picking off offending creatures, such as plucking caterpillars off brassicas.

RIGHT: *Pulling up weeds by hand is laborious but effective, especially on perennial weeds that hoeing does not remove.*

MAKING EARWIG POTS

The traditional earwig trap is not a thing of great beauty but it is very effective at attracting and trapping earwigs that would otherwise attack particularly susceptible plants such as dahlias. In a cottage garden border the straw-filled pots can even appear prettily rustic. A more unobtrusive option is to leave pieces of rolled-up newspaper on the soil around the base of vulnerable plants. Any kind of trap will need daily checking and emptying.

1 *To make a traditional trap, stuff a flowerpot with straw.*

2 *Invert it and place it on a garden cane in the border. Each morning, check the trap and dispose of any earwigs that have taken up residence overnight.*

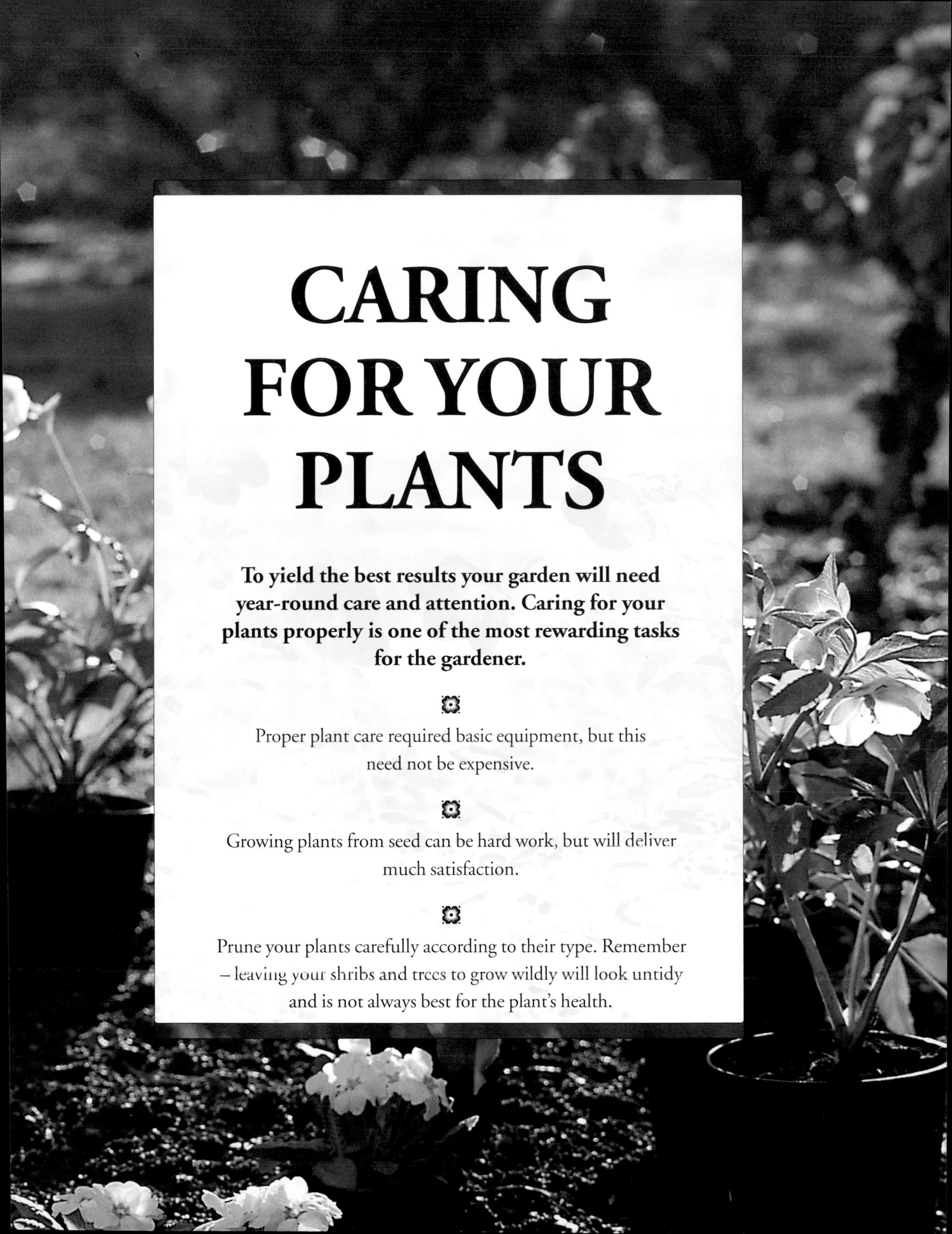

CARING FOR YOUR PLANTS

To yield the best results your garden will need year-round care and attention. Caring for your plants properly is one of the most rewarding tasks for the gardener.

❂

Proper plant care required basic equipment, but this need not be expensive.

❂

Growing plants from seed can be hard work, but will deliver much satisfaction.

❂

Prune your plants carefully according to their type. Remember – leaving your shribs and trees to grow wildly will look untidy and is not always best for the plant's health.

PROPAGATING YOUR PLANTS

Growing your own plants from seed or increasing your stocks from existing plants is undoubtedly one of the most satisfying areas of gardening. It is not only an economical way of filling the garden, but the thrill of stocking your garden with plants that you have produced yourself is incomparable. You can regenerate old, tired-looking plants, and also produce back-up stocks of plants that may be vulnerable to frost damage or disease. Propagation is also a very sociable occupation, since you will often find that you produce many more new plants than you have room for, and so gardening friendships develop as cuttings and seedlings are exchanged.

THE BASICS

THE word propagation somehow conjures up quite off-putting connotations of science laboratories, specialist equipment and in-depth botanical knowledge. However, it simply means 'to breed, to multiply', and applies to every method of increasing plant stocks – from broadcast sowing of annual seeds directly into the soil, to taking and rooting cuttings.

❀ Specialist equipment such as greenhouses and mist benches are useful but by no means essential to many forms of propagation. A bright (but not sunny windowsill), a cold frame and, if possible, a small heated propagator will enable you to grow a very wide range of plants.

ABOVE: *Always use perfectly clean pots and trays for healthy, disease-free propagation and cover them with mesh-wire or netting if there is a danger of something falling on the delicate new plants.*

PROPAGATION EQUIPMENT

THE very simplest form of propagation – sowing seed directly into the soil – needs no special equipment, as every child who has ever grown an abundance of nasturtiums from an inexpertly cast handful of seeds will testify.

❀ However, many gardeners, thrilled by early triumphs from sowing direct into the soil, quickly become more adventurous, and keen to extend the range of plants grown. Just a few simple pieces of equipment will dramatically increase your chances of consistent success.

ABOVE: *Seed can be sown directly into the soil, but the success rate may not be as great as if the plants had been transplanted from pots.*

Pots and trays

❀ There is a wide range of pots and trays available, and the choice can seem quite overwhelming. Since hygiene is a critical concern when propagating, it may be advisable to start your propagating experience with new, single-use modular seed trays, since these will not hold any old, potentially lethal bacteria or fungi.

❀ These trays consist of individual plastic cells, which make it easy to sow seeds singly and avoid any damage when thinning out the seedlings. The trays are flimsy and are held securely in a more rigid tray. This type of tray is generally intended only for a single season's use.

❀ More lasting and expensive trays are available in rigid plastics. These will need to be thoroughly disinfected after each use, and stored out of the sunlight. Novice propagators with limited space and time will probably prefer the inexpensive, labour- and storage-space saving flexible tray option. These trays are usually sold with a useful clear plastic lid, which assists in providing the warm, humid environment necessary for successful germination.

❀ Larger pots are useful for sowing larger seeds, such as climbers or shrubs and, of course, are also needed for potting on all plants. Fibre-based pots are especially good for plants that resent root disturbance. The young plant is simply planted out still in its pot, which will eventually break down into the soil. Home-made biodegradable pots can also be made from simple cones of newspaper.

water vapour falls on to plant

ABOVE: *A rigid-topped propagator offers an excellent start to young plants. Water vapour condenses on the inside of the lid and falls onto the plants, so the general atmosphere within the unit is moist. This combination helps the plants to replace the water lost through their leaves.*

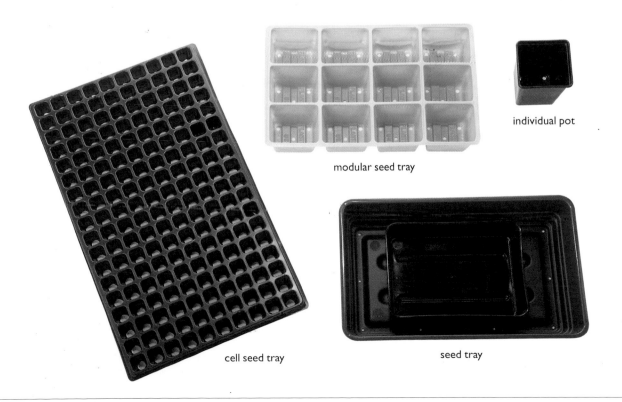

cell seed tray

modular seed tray

individual pot

seed tray

HOME-MADE PROPAGATION EQUIPMENT

POLYTHENE bags, simply suspended above pots or trays with canes or with wire twisted into hoops, are a popular and inexpensive way of providing a warm, humid atmosphere that will encourage rapid germination and healthy growth.

❀ Cut-off clear plastic bottles, upended over pots, are another effective, low-cost idea. It is important in each case to keep the leaves of the young plants away from the plastic itself, as they will rot if they come into direct contact with the moisture that collects there.

Heated propagators

❀ A little heat from underneath assists germination generally, and is essential for the germination of some plants. Small, self-contained domestic heated propagators are available, which sit on the windowsill. These are an ideal next step up from the plastic bag propagation technique. Heated bases that fit under seed trays are also available.

RIGHT: Any size or shape of plant pot can be used for making home-made propagation equipment.

ABOVE: *Cold frames provide an excellent introduction to growing under glass. They can easily overheat in summer because of their diminutive size. Propping the lid of the frame open in hot weather allows the rising warm air to escape, as well as keeping the plants inside well ventilated and at a reasonable temperature.*

❀ Many gardeners, encouraged by early successes with propagation, quickly run out of windowsills, and spill over into the greenhouse. If propagating in a greenhouse early in the year when temperatures are still low, you will need to invest in a more sophisticated propagator with a thermostat and a powerful heating element. You will probably also need larger units than the domestic models, which house only two or three seed trays.

LEFT: *Growing cuttings under plastic is an inexpensive way to increase your plant stocks.*

Mist propagators

❀ Enthusiastic propagating gardeners will enjoy the benefits of mist propagators. These incorporate all that plants need for their best possible chance of successful, easy germination and early, healthy growth.

❀ The simplest mist propagators to use are the self-contained enclosed units that include a heating element, thermostat, transparent lid and a misting head.

❀ A constant film of water is maintained on the plant material and, when the misting head operates, the risk of fungal disease is reduced, as spores are effectively washed out of the air and from foliage before they can infect plant tissue. This is a more sophisticated version of what happens in the plastic bag propagator – just on a larger, more convenient scale and with the added benefit of consistent heat from underneath and controlled humidity. The misting head is activated automatically when the plants become too dry. Open misting units are also available.

Cold frame

❀ A cold frame is extremely useful for hardening off plants. The air and soil temperatures in cold frames are warmer than in open soil, making it possible to acclimatise plants gradually to the conditions outdoors after their cosseted start in the home or greenhouse.

❀ The lid should be removed on warmer days to air the plants, and covered at night with additional insulation if extremely cold weather is expected. If transparent insulation, such as plastic bubble wrap or layers of clear plastic, is used there is no need to remove this during the day, as it still transmits light to the plants.

Soil-warming cables

❀ These are designed to warm the compost in unheated propagators, or to heat the soil and air in a cold frame or a mist bench in a greenhouse. They are fitted in an S-shape pattern, with the cable not touching at any point, buried approximately 7.5 cm (3 in) below the surface of moist sand.

❀ The cables are sold with instructions as to what size area they are capable of warming effectively, and it is obviously important to follow strictly all directions concerning their installation and use.

❀ The best cables have a wired-in thermostat. All should be used in conjunction with a residual current device (RCD) in case they are accidentally cut through during cultivation. Most novice propagators will find self-contained propagation units more convenient to install and use than cable systems.

BELOW: *A cold frame propped open to increase ventilation.*

warm air
circulates within
the cold frame

SOWING INDOORS

FINE and medium seeds may be sown by the method shown here. Large or pelleted seeds (seeds specially prepared in a coating to make a pellet for easier sowing) should be sown individually in compartments, degradable containers, or evenly spaced in pans (shallow pots).

❀ Mixing very fine seeds with an equal quantity of fine sand before sowing makes even distribution much easier. Always check the individual germination requirements of your seeds. Some germinate in darkness, others in light. The directions given here are necessarily generalised but apply to most fine seeds, such as many half-hardy annuals, which are popular plants to grow indoors from seed.

PROPAGATION COMPOST

Plants have a much better chance of germination if sown into the correct sort of compost. Fine seeds, in particular, need to be in good overall contact with the soil.

❀ Purpose-made seed compost is finely textured to meet this requirement. It is also moisture retentive and low in nutrients, since salts can damage seedlings. As the seedlings grow, they will need to be transplanted to a soil that can feed them adequately.

Seed compost

❀ A general-purpose seed compost consists of two parts sterilised loam, one part peat or peat substitute and one part sand, plus a small amount of lime. It is advisable to buy a pre-mixed seed compost, as you can then be sure that the proportions are accurate.

Cuttings compost

❀ Cuttings composts are free draining, as they are designed for use in high-humidity environments. A general-purpose cuttings compost comprises roughly one part peat or peat substitute and one part sand (or other free-draining substance such as perlite), plus a small percentage of lime, dried blood, calcium carbonate, potassium nitrate and potassium sulphate.

❀ As with seed compost, buying a pre-mixed cuttings compost will ensure you have the correct proportions of each component.

RIGHT: Overcrowding and a lack of ventilation can cause 'damping off', a catastrophic scourge, wreaking havoc on plants by damaging and distorting new leaves and shoots, as well as weakening the plant as a whole.

HYGIENE

Hygiene is critically important in propagation. The moist, humid conditions within a propagator are as perfect for the development of fungal diseases as they are for developing healthy plants.

❀ It is therefore essential to use sterilised containers, compost and tools to reduce this risk. Fungicidal solutions are available, which may be applied to protect seedlings further. Ensure that you follow the manufacturer's directions strictly.

❀ Taking cuttings inevitably exposes bare plant tissue, which is an increased risk of infection. Good hygiene practices will decrease the risk. Clean tools with a methylated spirit solution between cuttings to avoid cross contamination, and keep benches spotlessly clean.

Preventing damping off

❀ Overcrowding causes an overly moist, stagnant atmosphere in which fungi can flourish. These air- or soil-borne fungi can cause the condition known as 'damping-off', whereby roots become diseased, darken and then die. The seedling collapses, and a fluffy growth may be seen on the compost as well as on the seedlings.

❀ There is no cure for damping off, so attention to cleanliness, pricking out seedlings to avoid overcrowding (see below), not overwatering and providing adequate air flow above and around the plants are essential requisites. Keep the surface of the compost clear of any fallen leaves or other debris, which could foster disease.

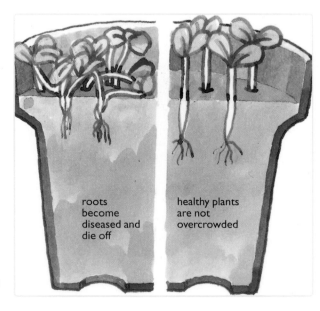

roots become diseased and die off

healthy plants are not overcrowded

SOWING SEEDS IN A TRAY

1 *Fill a seed tray with good-quality seed compost and firm it to within 1.5 cm (3/4 in) of the top, using a presser board. Water the compost and leave to stand for approximately 30 minutes.*

2 *Scatter the seed or the seed and sand mixture evenly across the surface.*

3 *Sieve over a layer of moist compost to produce a covering approximately the same depth as the size of the seeds that you have planted.*

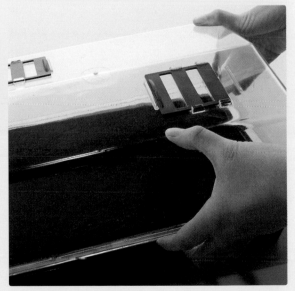

4 *Cover the tray with glass or clear plastic, not allowing it to touch the seeds, and place the tray somewhere warm and bright. If the tray is placed in direct sunlight, shade it with fine netting.*

CARE OF PROPAGATED PLANTS

As well as taking good care of hygiene when preparing compost, containers and cuttings or seeds for propagation, care must be taken of the young plants as they germinate and grow.

Firming in

❀ It is essential that seeds are in good contact with the compost since water is drawn up by capillary action. If air pockets form around the seeds water cannot be transmitted to where it is needed, so it is important to firm the compost gently when planting seed. However, do not compress the soil heavily.

Watering

❀ Propagated plants need a consistently moist, but not wet, environment. An overly saturated compost will reduce the oxygen available to the plants and potentially encourage disease.

Caring for new seedlings

❀ Seedlings must have sufficient room around them to breathe. As soon as shoots appear, remove the propagator lid. Protect the seedlings from draughts and harsh sunlight, but keep them in bright light. Continue to water, ensuring that the roots do not dry out.

ABOVE: *Ensure that your new plants have enough water, but make sure that they are not over-watered, as this may encourage disease.*

Pricking out

❀ When seedlings appear, the plants are still very vulnerable. As well as the risk of damping off, overcrowded seedlings will be competing for light and nutrients. If they do not succumb to disease, they will probably become underfed, weak, spindly plants that will never achieve their full, healthy potential. They therefore need to be thinned out. This planting-on process is known as pricking out.

❀ The initial leaves you see after germination are seed leaves, or cotyledons, which swell on germination, forcing the seed coat open. These provide the initial food reserves for the plant. The next pair of leaves to appear will be the first 'true' leaves, and seedlings may be pricked out when the true leaves are well developed. Discard weak, unhealthy-looking seedlings.

❀ Fill the next appropriate size up of container with good-quality potting compost – a 7.5 cm (3 in) diameter pot or planting compartment will suit a single seedling, while a larger pot may hold three growing plants comfortably.

❀ Knock the container of seedlings gently to loosen the compost. Carefully separate the seedlings, handling them only by the seed leaves to avoid damaging the seedlings. Carefully lift each healthy seedling from the soil, trying to maintain a little compost around its roots if possible. Plant them at the same depth in the soil as they were in the first tray and gently firm the compost around them. Tap the container to settle the compost, and water the seedlings to settle the compost around their roots.

❀ To give the plants a good chance of recovery from the pricking-out process, increase the humidity as for germinating, by covering the container with clear plastic, just for a few days. Ensure that the plastic does not touch the leaves.

Hardening off

❀ Gradually acclimatising plants to the very different conditions outside the protected environment of the propagator should be taken every bit as seriously as the initial, exciting part of the propagation procedure.

❀ Hardening off takes time. The natural waxes coating the leaves of the young plants need to adapt their form and thickness in order to reduce water loss – a process that takes place over several days and cannot be hurried. The pores on the leaves, which control water loss and through which oxygen and carbon dioxide pass in and out of the leaves, also need time to adapt to the harsher conditions outside.

❀ As a rule, hardening off takes about two weeks. When the young plants have become well established inside, they can be moved to an unheated cold frame, where they are still protected by polythene or glass. Gradually increase the amount of ventilation by opening or removing the cover for increasingly long periods until the plants are fully acclimatised. Close the frame at night to begin with, graduating to leaving it open at night, except when frost is anticipated. Insulate the cold frame if the weather is very harsh.

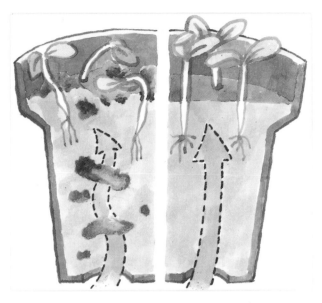

ABOVE: *It is important to press down compost evenly before planting seeds, so that water can be drawn up towards the roots of the seedlings by capillary action. Air pockets in the soil will break this action and the seedlings will therefore not flourish as they should.*

PRICKING OUT

All young seedlings are vulnerable so handle them with care as you are replanting them.

1 *Make a hole in the soil with a dibber or pencil roughly to the same depth as the seedlings were planted in their old pot or seed tray.*

2 *Place the seedling carefully into the hole, leaving a little of the old compost around the roots to prevent damage, and gently firm the earth around the plant to prevent air pockets.*

Potting on

❀ As the plants grow, they will need more space for the roots to grow uncramped, and will need more nutrients from the soil. The subsequent container needs to be big enough to allow a generous layer of new compost to be placed around the existing rootball, but it should not be too oversized, as this will not encourage good root formation.

❀ Allow the plant to dry out slightly before transplanting, so that it may be easily removed from its container with minimal root disturbance. Fill the new pot with a layer of drainage material and new potting compost. Tap it to remove air pockets and plant at the same depth as before, filling in with compost carefully and firming in gently. Water well and leave to drain.

SOWING OUTDOORS

❀ Hardy perennials and annuals are generally sown directly into the soil in their desired final positions, avoiding any need for transplanting later. This is a particularly useful technique for growing deep tap-rooted plants such as poppies, which do not transplant well. Sowing usually takes place in spring, after the risk of frost has passed and when the soil has warmed, so that the seeds do not rot.

❀ However, precise sowing times will depend on when and where the plants are to flower, and the temperatures they need for germination. For example, some hardy biennials, which are also sown outside, grow quickly and should not be sown until midsummer, while others are slow starters and need to be sown in late spring. Always read seed packets carefully before sowing, and be sympathetic to the requirements of particular seed types best growing success.

❀ There are two methods for sowing outdoors – broadcast and drill sowing. In drill sowing, the seeds are sown in rows. Broadcast sowing is literally casting the seeds broadly on the seedbed where they are to grow. Both types of sowing need to be on properly prepared soil for the best possible chance of success.

The seedbed

❀ Ideally, you will be sowing into a bed that has been dug over the previous autumn, and which benefited from the addition of some mature organic matter at the same time – roughly 1 cu m ($1^1/_3$ cu yd) of organic matter to every 4 cu m ($5^1/_4$ cu yd) of soil. You do not want to sow seed into an overly rich soil, as this will encourage the production of foliage rather than flowers.

❀ If, however, you know that you are sowing into very poor soil, you may fork in a fertiliser dressing at the rate of approximately 60 g per sq m (2 oz per sq yd). If your soil is particularly heavy, you may wish to incorporate grit or coarse sand to open it up and improve drainage.

WATERING PROPAGATED PLANTS

Seedlings need careful watering to encourage growth after sowing outdoors.

1 *To water a large area, connect up a hosepipe to the mains water supply. Choose a pipe with a very fine rose.*

2 *Begin to water the area, preventing the soil from becoming waterlogged and rinsing out all the nutrients. Move on to the next area and repeat.*

BROADCAST SOWING

1 *Tread the soil evenly to produce a firm, even surface. Rake the soil to remove stones and retain a level surface with a fine, crumbly texture, so that the seeds have a good opportunity to gain direct overall contact with the soil.*

2 *Sow the seeds finely and evenly over the prepared area. Very fine seeds may be mixed with sand to produce a more consistent spread.*

3 *Rake in the seeds very lightly, working at right angles, first one way, then the other, so that they suffer minimal disturbance.*

4 *Label the area, and water the seed using a watering can with a fine rose.*

Drill sowing

❀ In drill sowing, shallow drills, or rows, are marked out with the corner of a hoe or a trowel tip. The seeds are sown equally spaced along these rows, beneath a fine layer of soil, and are gently watered in and labelled.

❀ Drill sowing has the advantage that, since the seedlings grow in recognisable rows, it is easier to distinguish desirable plants from emerging weed seedlings. Generally, both drill-sown and broadcast-sown seeds will need thinning out.

Thinning out

❀ To prevent overcrowding, and the attendant problems as plants fight for air, light and nutrients, most seedlings will need to be thinned out as they grow.

Working when the soil is moist and the weather is mild, remove surplus seedlings, particularly the weaker, less healthy-looking specimens.

❀ Take care to press gently on to the soil around the seedlings as you work, to minimise root disturbance to those seedlings that are remaining in place.

❀ If the seedlings have grown very densely, you may need to dig up entire clumps and gently separate out healthy seedlings before replanting.

❀ Surplus seedlings can be used to bulk out sparse areas where germination was poor or sowing was patchy. They can also be planted elsewhere in the garden, as well as making wonderful offerings to gardening friends. Firm in transplanted seedlings gently, and lightly water in to settle their roots.

GROWING FROM CUTTINGS

TAKING cuttings from plant stems to produce new plants is a popular way of adding to your stocks at minimal cost. It is a good way of producing additional plants from a parent plant that is of dubious hardiness, and is an economical way of introducing a plant to your own garden that you may have admired in a friend's plot. Many gardening friendships grow alongside the developing cuttings.

❀ Stem cuttings are loosely divided into three groups, according to the season the cutting is taken, and the maturity of the parent plant. Individual plants respond to different cutting techniques, and it is wise to research the needs of a particular plant before attempting its propagation by taking cuttings. As a rough guide, perennials and small shrubs are propagated by softwood cuttings, while trees, roses and many shrubs are propagated by semi-ripe and hardwood cuttings. Once you know which technique a plant prefers, the basic techniques of taking and rooting cuttings are very straightforward.

❀ There are some general rules that apply to all cuttings. Cut only from healthy plants, and take cuttings from non-flowering side shoots, as these generally root more easily than cuttings taken from the main stem. Always use a clean, sharp knife to avoid damaging plant tissue.

TAKING A STEM-TIP CUTTING

1 *Take the cutting from the parent plant then cut straight across the stem, just below a node, so that the cutting is approximately 7.5 cm (3 in) long.*

2 *Gently remove the leaves from the lower half of the cutting. Dip the base of the cutting in hormone rooting powder.*

3 *Make a hole in a container of cuttings compost, using a dibber or pencil, and insert the cutting. Gently firm and water it in.*

4 *Create a warm, humid environment by supporting a clear plastic bag above the cutting, not allowing it to touch the leaves, or place the cutting in a propagator. Keep in bright light, but not direct sunlight. Inspect daily for signs of disease or dryness and act accordingly. Pot on when the cuttings has rooted – roughly two to three weeks.*

TAKING A SOFTWOOD CUTTING

1 *From the parent plant, cut a young, vigorous side shoot approximately 10 cm (4 in) long, trimming it straight across, just below a leaf joint.*

2 *Gently remove the leaves from the lower half of the cutting. Dip the base of the cutting into hormone rooting powder.*

3 *Make a hole in the cuttings compost with a dibber or pencil and insert the cutting, firming it in gently with the dibber and ensuring that there are no air pockets around it.*

4 *Gently water in the cutting and cover with a clear plastic bag suspended above the plant on canes or wires so that it does not touch the foliage and cause it to rot.*

❀ Plant the cutting as soon as possible after taking it, and ensure that it has excellent all-round contact with the compost when planted. As with all propagation techniques, use compost, containers and utensils that are scrupulously clean to avoid the risk of plant infection. You may wish to water in with sterilised water mixed with fungi cide for added protection. Do not check that plants have rooted by tugging at the cuttings impatiently. Look out for new growth instead.

Stem-tip cuttings

❀ Herbaceous perennials that do not divide well are often grown by the stem-tip method. Cuttings may be taken at any time during the growing season, assuming that suitable shoots are available. These need to be healthy and sturdy, with no flower buds. Plant the cuttings as soon as possible after collection.

Softwood cuttings

❀ Softwood cuttings are cuttings of the current season's growth, taken from early spring through to midsummer. Generally, they are literally soft, immature tissue, green from tip to base and, as such, wilt quickly after cutting. If propagating by this method, speed and care when collecting are of the essence. Collect the cuttings in a closed plastic bag, kept away from sunlight.

❀ Prepare the cuttings as soon as possible after collection for the best chance of success. Some softwood cuttings root readily in water, while others need to be put into compost. Research the particular requirements of the plant you are propagating. Some will need the heat from beneath, provided by a propagator or heated mat, for rooting. Some may be placed in a cold frame. As when germinating seeds, keep the cuttings in a well-lit but not directly sunny position.

❀ Once you have planted the cuttings, check the pot or propagator on alternate days to see if water is needed. Most softwood cuttings root in approximately six to eight weeks. When new growth appears, the plant may be gradually hardened off.

Semi-ripe cuttings

❀ Semi-ripe cuttings are also taken from the current season's growth, but are cut later in the year – from midsummer through to early autumn. Again, choose non-flowering, healthy side shoots. These should be soft at the top and just hard at the base.

❀ Because they are slightly harder than softwood cuttings, semi-ripe cuttings are not so susceptible to wilt. However, they do take longer to root, and for this reason they are often propagated from heel cuttings, which means they have the base of the stem 'wounded' to encourage rooting.

❀ Wounding involves making a shallow cut, approximately 2.5–3.5 cm (1–1¹⁄₂ in) up from the base of the cutting, and stripping away the bark from this point to the base, using a sharp knife, not tearing away the bark. Root production is then stimulated from the wounded edge as well as the base of the cutting. Heel cuttings expose the swollen base of the season's growth, which contains a concentration of growth hormones, thereby assisting rooting.

TAKING A HEEL CUTTING

1 *Pull off a strong, non-flowering side shoot from the parent plant, pulling outwards and downwards so that you bring away a small heel of bark. Tug sharply, rather than peeling the heel cutting away. Take care not to strip away bark from the parent plant, as this could encourage infection.*

2 *Using a clean, sharp knife, cut off the leaves from the lower half of the cutting's stem. Trim away any excess, damaged plant tissue and any long tails of bark.*

3 *Dip the bottom 2.5 cm (1 in) of the cutting into hormone rooting powder. This helps prevent fungicidal attack, as well as assisting rooting.*

4 *Dib a planting hole in a small pot of cuttings compost. Gently firm in and water in the cutting. Cover the pot with a clear plastic bag, suspended*

away from the foliage on canes or wire, or place in a propagator. Situate the cutting in bright light, but not direct sunlight.

Hardwood cuttings

❀ Many shrubs can be raised from hardwood cuttings. These are taken from ripe, vigorous, current season's growth – from mid-autumn to early winter. Hardwood cuttings from deciduous shrubs are taken just after the leaves have fallen.

❀ Cuttings propagated in this way are slow to root but, well cared for, will produce strong, resilient plants in about a year. Propagate hardwood cuttings in containers, in a cold frame, or even in open ground.

❀ To grow cuttings on, dip the end of the cutting into hormone rooting powder. Dib a planting hole and plant in cuttings compost in a container. Firm and water in gently. Label and place pots in a cold frame. Water well during the growing season. Harden off before planting out.

TAKING A HARDWOOD CUTTING

1 *Take pencil-thick cuttings at the junction of the current, and last season's growth.*

2 *Trim the cuttings to approximately 15 cm (6 in) lengths. At the top, cut just above buds or leaves, and at the base, cut just below buds or leaves. Make an angled cut at the top, cut straight across at the bottom – you will then know which way up to plant the cutting.*

3 *Remove any remaining deciduous leaves On evergreen cuttings, remove leaves from the lower two-thirds of the stem and cut large leaves in half across.*

4 *If propagating outside, plant cuttings 15 cm (6 in) apart, in a trench 15 cm (6 in) deep filled with compost and sharp sand. Back fill with soil, and water in. Firm the soil after heavy frosts and water during periods of drought.*

DIVIDING PLANTS

DIVIDING plants not only regenerates what might have become quite a sad-looking plant, but is also an incredibly easy and cost-effective way of increasing your plant stocks. Many perennials will deteriorate over time, slowly dying out in the centre, unless they are lifted and divided every three or four years.

❀ Division entails literally splitting the old plant into lots of smaller sections, the most healthy of which are replanted. Large divisions made in spring may even flower later in the season – albeit initially with shorter stems than the original, established plants.

❀ If the size difference between the young plants and their neighbours in the border bothers you, plant the new sections in pots or nursery beds until they are of a suitable size to put in their new positions.

Where to begin

❀ Left to their own devices, most plants reproduce themselves anyway. Propagation by division, complex as it may sound, simply involves the gardener taking a more active part in a natural process.

❀ Most gardeners start by dividing perennials since it is usually a reproachfully sad-looking border plant, dying out in the middle and straggly around the edges, that

DIVIDING RHIZOMES

1 *Carefully remove the clump from the ground with a fork, taking care to insert the fork well away from the rhizomes as you do not damage them. Shake away any excess soil.*

2 *Roughly break up the clump with your hands or a fork. Large clumps may need the back-to-back fork technique used on large perennials. Detach fresh new rhizomes using a clean, sharp knife. Each piece should have buds or leaves above it and roots below it. Discard diseased or old rhizomes.*

3 *Trim back long roots by one-third. On irises, cut the leaves into a mitred shape, approximately 15 cm (6 in) long to avoid damage by wind rock. Dust the cut edges of the rhizome with hormone rooting powder to help prevent disease and to encourage new growth.*

4 *Plant the new rhizomes at the same depth at which they were originally growing, their leaves and buds upright. Water and firm in.*

provokes some activity. Rather than simply discarding the whole plant, it is well worth taking some healthy sections from the outside of the plant, and producing many healthy, young plants from the single old specimen.

When to divide

❀ Be aware that some plants resent disturbance, so always check the needs of a particular plant before dividing it. Division usually takes place in the semi-dormant seasons – early spring or autumn – on a day when the soil is moist but not waterlogged.

❀ Some plants have a marked preference for the time of year that they are moved, however, so again, research carefully before moving plants. Rhizomes (plants with fleshy, almost horizontal underground stems), such as bergenias, rhizomatous lilies and rhizomatous irises, are very easy to divide and are generally divided in the late summer.

DIVIDING PERENNIALS

1 *Dig up the overcrowded clump with a fork, disturbing the roots as little as possible. Shake off excess soil locate the best points for division. Discard diseased parts, as well as the central part of the plant. Divisions from the outer section of the clump will grow into new, healthy plants. Wash away excess soil with water if you cannot see the roots and shoots clearly enough for accurate division.*

2 *Divide the plant into sections that have healthy roots and shoots. You divide some plants with your hands, but plants with fleshy, tough roots will need to be cut with a clean, sharp knife. Dust any cuts with fungicide, following the manufacturer's directions.*

3 *Very tough, fibrously rooted clumps may need to be divided using two forks placed back to back in the centre of the clump, to provide additional separation and leverage. Hand forks will suffice in some cases; full size garden forks may be needed in others. Always ease the forks apart gently, teasing out the roots to separate them, rather than wrenching them violently apart and breaking the roots.*

4 *Replant the new plant sections immediately after division, at the same depth at which they were already planted, with the roots spread well out. Firm in and water in well.*

Dividing bulbs

❀ After one or two seasons in the soil, most bulbs and corms produce offsets around their base. The offsets of bulbs are known as daughter bulbs; tiny ones are called bulblets. Corm offsets are known as cormels or cormlets. If these are allowed to develop unabated, they become overcrowded and compete for nutrients. The result, in most cases, is a dramatic reduction in flowering.

❀ It is therefore a good idea to lift and divide most clumps of bulbs and corms every three or four years, to sustain a really good show. Apart from preventing overcrowding, propagating bulbs also enables you to increase your flowering display at no cost, and with relatively little effort. Since the bulbs are increasing themselves naturally below the ground, it is simplicity itself to separate the developing bulbs from the parents and increase your stocks.

❀ Most popular bulbs and corms, for example narcissi, snowdrops, crocuses and lilies, will respond extremely well to division. Flowering will be increased and you will be able to plant over a wider area with your additional numbers of bulbs or corms. However, it is highly recommended that you check each plant's individual preference before planning division, as there are a few exceptions to these rules. For example, the Scarborough lily (*Vallota*) flowers well when overcrowded, while the autumn daffodil (*Sternbergia*) and cyclamens hate disturbance.

When to divide bulbs and corms

❀ Dividing is best done when the plant is dormant. However, it is obviously much easier to locate the bulbs when they have visible foliage, so division is usually undertaken when the leaves have almost entirely died down. Some bulbs have slightly different needs. For example, snowdrops are best divided when they are in full leaf, so again check each plant's individual requirements before you begin.

DIVIDING BULBS

1 *Gently lift the clump with a fork.*

2 *Shake off the excess soil and separate the clump into smaller, more manageable portions.*

3 *Pull away the individual bulbs with your hands. Discard soft, dried out, damaged or diseased bulbs.*

Clean the bulbs that you wish to replant, removing any loose tunics (the papery membrane enveloping bulbs).

4 *Plant the offset bulbs at the correct depth and spacing in prepared soil. This is generally between two and three times the size of the bulb, but check the requirements of the individual species before dividing.*

INCREASING BULBS BY SCORING

Towards the end of the dormant season, hyacinths may be increased by scoring.

1 *Use a sharp knife to make cuts through the basal plate of the bulb. Dust the cut areas with fungicide and store the bulb in damp perlite, mixed with fungicide, in a warm place. The injury caused by the cutting will encourage small bulbs (bulblets) to develop along the cuts.*

2 *When bulblets have formed, plant the bulb upside down in gritty compost. The bulblets will grow above the parent bulb and may be carefully separated from the old bulb for replanting. A simpler method is to score the parent bulb, plant it again immediately and wait for bulblets to form.*

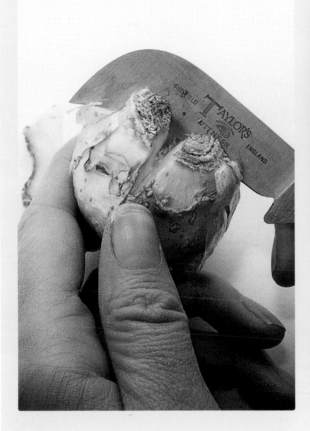

Scaling bulbs

❀ Scaling is a straightforward method for increasing the stocks of bulbs that consist of scales, most notably lilies, which are quite simple to propagate in this way. Propagating lilies is particularly satisfying since the bulbs are comparatively expensive to buy. A bonus is that, after scaling, the parent lily may be replanted to continue flowering as normal.

❀ Most lily bulbs comprise concentric rings of scales, joined at their bases to a basal plate. To scale lilies, work in early autumn, before root growth begins. Lift the bulbs, or scrape away soil from around the bulb and work *in situ*. Remove a few scales from the bulb, taking care to remove a little of the basal plate tissue when you detach the scales. This will greatly increase your chances of success.

❀ Coat the scales with fungicide and place them in a tray of two parts damp peat substitute and one part coarse sand. Keep them moist in a warm, shaded place for approximately two months. In spring, move them to a cold place for two months, to encourage good leaf development. Pot on the single bulblets and grow on for another year before planting out.

LAYERING

LAYERING offers the novice gardener a superb introduction to propagation, since the young plants are not separated from the parent plant until they have formed roots and are growing independently. This is obviously not as challenging as raising plants from seed or cuttings, where the new plants are very vulnerable until established and need particular care to ensure strong rooting and vigorous growth, and require vigilant attention to ensure disease is kept at bay.

❀ Layering is such a simple propagation method that some plants even layer themselves, for example strawberry plants and shrubs with low branches like the smoke bush (*Cotinus coggygria*). Others attempt to layer naturally (self-layering plants), and can be easily encouraged in their efforts by pegging or weighing down branches until they root.

❀ Many climbers, such as ivy, have trailing shoots that develop roots on contact with the soil. The propagation in this case has already taken place. All you need do is gently ease the new plant from the soil without damaging the roots, and cut it away from the main stem before replanting the new plant.

❀ Layering is also a very useful technique for increasing stocks of plants, such as some shrubs and climbers, that do not root easily from cuttings. Layering is not necessarily a rapid propagation method, but the plants produced are strong, already well adapted to the soil in which they are to grow to maturity, and the technique is not labour intensive.

❀ In addition, it needs no specialist equipment, can be done at any time of the year, and does not take up any space on your windowsill or in a greenhouse. Thus, every gardener could start their propagation experience with a little layering.

❀ There are essentially three types of layering: air layering, where the growing medium is brought up to the plant stem; a range of techniques where soil is mounded over a stem, for example French, trench and stool layering; and the basic range of techniques in which the stem is brought down into the soil, namely tip, serpentine, natural and simple layering.

❀ This is all easier than it sounds, and most amateur gardeners will find the last techniques mentioned, which capitalise on the plant's own desire to root when it reaches the soil, sufficient for their propagation needs.

Planting self-layered climbers

❀ You may spot several places along a trailing stem where the plant has taken root. It is easy to see where the stems have produced new root systems as there is abundant healthy young growth at these points.

❀ Gently ease these areas of the stem away from the ground, bringing the roots up carefully. Using sharp secateurs, cut away this section of stem from the parent plant. Cut the stem into sections, each with a good root system. Remove any leaves growing close to the rooted areas. Plant each portion of rooted stem in compost or directly in the garden, watering in well.

BELOW: *As the shoots of ivies (such as this* Hedera helix *'Goldheart') tend to produce roots naturally when they come into contact with the soil, the propagation is already done.*

INCREASING PLANTS BY LAYERING

1 *Although many plants layer themselves, some will benefit from a helping hand. Choose a healthy, flexible stem that may be easily bent to touch the soil. Cut off any side shoots.*

2 *Make a shallow hole in the ground at an appropriate point, and enrich the area with compost. For an increased chance of success, make a short slanting cut on the underside of the stem at the point where it is to be layered. The concentration off carbohydrates and hormones at the point of the wound, together with the plant being slightly stressed in the area, helps to promote root growth.*

3 *Twist the shoot to open the cut. Apply hormone rooting powder to the injured part, to discourage disease and further encourage rooting.*

4 *Place the injured part of the stem in the soil and secure it firmly with a metal peg or piece of bent wire, making sure that the cut remains open. Backfill with soil, firm and water in using a watering can fitted with a fine rose. Keep the area moist throughout the growing season. After about a year, scrape away the soil to check for new roots. If all is well, sever the new plant from the parent and leave it in situ to establish for another season before moving it to its final site*

PRUNING PLANTS

Pruning describes the act of cutting away unwanted growth – unwanted because it is diseased, old, or simply in the way. It is a subject that many gardeners find daunting. Individual plants have individual pruning needs, which means that any book covering pruning necessarily contains a large amount of information. Do not be put off by this. Once you understand the chief principles of pruning, together with the pruning requirements specific to the plants in your own garden, you will be equipped to enhance dramatically the look and health of many plants.

ABOVE: *Renovating a neglected plant by pruning is a simple yet very satisfying task.*

THE USES OF PRUNING

PRUNING can maintain a balance between growth and flowering. It can restrict growth, which may be necessary should a plant encroach on a walkway or into a neighbour's garden. It can train plants, encouraging a neat habit and profuse flowering or fruiting. Pruning can also help to maintain healthy plants, with good-quality stems, foliage, fruit and flowers.

❀ Pruning falls loosely into three categories – renovative, regenerative and formative pruning.

RENOVATIVE PRUNING

There are a number of specific conditions that can be treated or prevented by pruning.

Rubbing or crossing shoots

❀ Where shoots repeatedly rub against each other, they will eventually become damaged by friction, forming open wounds that expose the plant to disease spores. Crossing shoots also look untidy and prevent the plant from growing into a pleasing overall shape.

Removing dieback

❀ When young shoots die back towards the main stem, you need to cut them out. Otherwise dieback can continue unabated, affecting healthy tissue, too. To prevent this spread, prune back as far as the healthy part of the stem, cutting just above a bud.

Halting disease

❀ Cut out rot and disease before they spread and affect the rest of the plant. Remove dead shoots, as these not only harbour disease, but also look unattractive. Cut back as far as healthy wood.

Pruning to retain variegation

❀ Pruning is also used to prevent variegated plants from reverting – that is, becoming plain once more. If you see mature green leaves appearing on an otherwise variegated plant, cut them back to the point of origin, as

RENOVATIVE PRUNING

Renovative pruning is pruning to remove problems such as damaged and diseased parts of a plant. It is always preferable to prune to avoid problems in advance, rather than after they have occurred. Careful pruning can help stop plant troubles before they begin. For example, pruning to keep the plant uncongested, allows plenty of light and air to travel through the plant, keeping it growing well and discouraging pests and diseases.

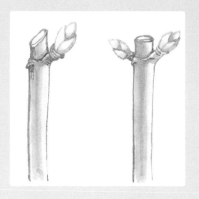

ABOVE: *Two examples of correct pruning; on the single shoot the cut is angled away from the bud; on the double shoot, the distance of the cut from the buds is just right.*

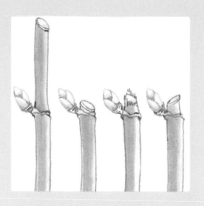

ABOVE: *Example of cutting incorrectly, from left to right: too far away, too close, with blunt secateurs, or sloping towards a bud. Bad techniques cause plant problems such as dieback, rotting and disease.*

they will tend to grow vigorously and gradually dominate the plant. Some plants develop variegated leaves only as the foliage matures, so check the individual characteristics of your plant and wait until you are certain before pruning.

REGENERATIVE PRUNING

Some plants benefit enormously from hard, yearly pruning. Plants such as dogwoods and willows require this heavy pruning so that they will produce strong, large leaves and healthy, colourful new stems. Other plants, notably shrub roses and fruit, grow much more vigorously and flower more profusely, with better-quality blooms, if pruned annually.

FORMATIVE PRUNING

Formative pruning is literally pruning so as to achieve and maintain a desirable form. It is always preferable to start creating the desired form early on in a plant's life, rather than trying to impose a shape on a plant once it has been allowed to grow unchecked for a long time.

PRUNING TECHNIQUES

ABOVE: *Removing badly crossing shoots encourages good air circulation throughout the plant.*

ABOVE: *Pruning variegated plants is vital to stop them reverting, in which case plain leaves will soon dominate the plant*

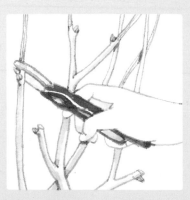

ABOVE: *Cut out dieback and damaged stems, which may otherwise cause infection and continue to die back.*

ABOVE: *Remove rotten stems, which could cause disease throughout the plant.*

PRUNING BASICS

CARELESS pruning can do more harm than good. It is critically important that you do not damage the plant when pruning. Use clean, sharp tools, and respect the natural growth pattern of the plant.

❀ For plants with leaves that grow alternately up the stem, cut at an angle, approximately 5 mm (1⁄4 in) above an outward-facing bud. Make sure that the cut slopes away from the bud so that moisture runs away from it, not towards it, which would encourage rot.

❀ For plants with leaves that grow in pairs, cut straight across, just above a pair of buds.

❀ In both cases, you need to cut quite close to the buds, as stem tissue heals much better close to growth buds. If the cut is too high, the stem will probably die back to the bud, which renders the plant susceptible to disease, and also looks unsightly. Conversely, do not cut right up against the bud, as you could damage the bud itself, or introduce infection.

❀ Always make a clean, sharp cut. A ragged cut or a bruised, torn stem is very prone to disease.

PRUNING TREES

THE individual requirements of a tree must be taken into account before pruning. Some trees will require minimal pruning or may even be harmed by pruning, for example the mulberry tree, while others, like tree of heaven (Ailanthus), will relish hard pruning in order to check growth and produce luxuriant foliage.

Evergreen trees

❀ Evergreens are generally pruned in late spring, but always check the individual needs of your particular evergreen before you prune.

❀ With young trees, train the main or leader stem upwards to establish a strong main stem and a good basic form for the tree. Prune out leader shoots that are competing with each other, as well as badly crossing or rubbing stems.

❀ Mature evergreens need little pruning, apart from removing any dead, damaged or diseased branches. Cut back to a healthy shoot or remove the offending branch altogether. Remove crossing lateral shoots and competing leader shoots. Do not be tempted to simply hack away at the top of a conifer that is too tall, as this can leave a very ugly shape. If possible, dig up the tree and start again.

Deciduous trees

❀ Most deciduous trees are pruned when dormant, in late autumn or winter. However, as always, check the individual requirements of your tree before pruning, since some trees need to be pruned in spring or summer.

❀ The aim of pruning and training a young tree is to produce an attractive and stable framework. The central stem should be straight, and the branches nicely spaced. It is particularly important to prune trees that bud in pairs, such as ash. If the central stem is allowed to develop into a fork, it may even split. Other trees, if allowed to fork too soon, will not have an attractive overall shape.

❀ To create a vertical stem on an ornamental tree remove competing shoots, as well as weak or crossing laterals. Remove all lateral shoots from the bottom third of the tree in the first spring after planting, and reduce the lateral shoots in the middle section of the tree by about half. In late autumn/early winter completely remove the lateral shoots on the middle section that you reduced in the spring. Continue this process over the next two years until you have produced a vertical stem reaching approximately 2 m (7 ft) in height.

Mature deciduous trees

❀ Established deciduous trees should need little pruning, other than to maintain the pleasing shape that has hopefully been created over the years. Remove congested branches from the centre of the tree, as these will block light and air flow. Retain the overall shape of the tree by removing any branches that have become too dominant and unsightly.

BELOW: *This elegant, sweeping avenue of trees should now only need pruning to keep the pleasing shape created by expert management over the years.*

PRUNING ORNAMENTAL TREES

There are basic rules for pruning young ornamental trees, but check on the individual requirements of each plant first.

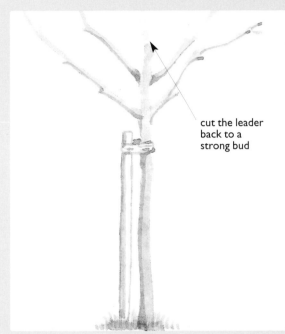

cut the leader
back to a
strong bud

1 *Three years after planting, cut the leader back to a strong lateral or bud, 30 cm (12 in) above the required length of clear stem.*

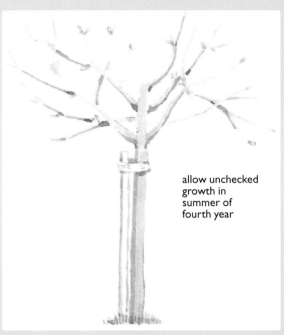

allow unchecked
growth in
summer of
fourth year

2 *During the summer of the fourth year, allow laterals and sublaterals to develop without pruning.*

prune out
crossing or
crowded laterals
and sublaterals

3 *In the autumn of the fourth year, prune out crossing or crowded laterals and sublaterals to leave between three and five evenly spaced laterals.*

remove branches
that spoil the
symmetry of
the tree

4 *In the fifth and subsequent years, remove young branches that spoil the tree's symmetry, as well as shoots that appear on the main stem.*

POLLARDING AND COPPICING

POLLARDING describes the act of pruning a tree back to its main stem, so as to produce new shoots at this point. Coppicing, similarly, involves the regular pruning of a tree close to the ground. Both techniques were traditionally employed to produce accessible and regular supplies of pliable wood for firewood, fence and basket making. Nowadays, coppicing and pollarding are generally done to produce colourful stems, or to restrict the size of a tree.

❀ Both pollarding and coppicing are generally done in late winter or early spring. When the trunk has reached the desired height, cut the branches back to approximately 5 cm (2 in) away from the main stem. This brutal-looking treatment will encourage a mass of new shoots to be produced during the summer. Ideally, repeat the process annually, and feed and mulch the tree after pruning.

HOW TO POLLARD AND COPPICE TREES

Pollarding and coppicing are generally done to provide colourful stems or to restrict the size of a tree. Both methods promote healthy regrowth.

ABOVE: *Pollarding means cutting stems hard back to the trunk to produce vigorous new shoots.*

ABOVE: Coppicing involves *pruning back almost to ground level to encourage basal shoots to develop.*

Cutting large branches

❀ The pruning of very large, mature trees is best dealt with by professional arborists. There may be judicial constraints on cutting certain trees in certain situations, so always check the legal position before planning major work on mature trees.

❀ Smaller trees, or overgrown old shrubs may have thickish branches that you are able to remove yourself safely. Use a pruning saw and cut in three stages, starting with an upward cut, so that the weight of the branch does not cause it to rip away from the plant in a ragged, uncontrolled way.

PRUNING SHRUBS

THE general rules and reasons for pruning trees apply equally to shrubs. Some shrubs require virtually no pruning other than a light 'haircut', but the majority will eventually deteriorate if left unpruned. For most shrubs, pruning encourages strong, healthy growth and vigorous flowering with well-sized, good-quality blooms.

❀ As a rule, flowering shrubs are pruned soon after the last of their flowers have died off. There are notable exceptions, however, such as some late summer-flowering shrubs like buddleja and hydrangea, which would be susceptible to frost damage if pruned at this time. Wait until spring before pruning these. As always, for best results, always check the individual requirements of a shrub before planning pruning.

Hard pruning

❀ Hard pruning on the right sort of shrub can produce really rewarding results. Tall, straggly flowering shrubs are a depressingly common sight in front gardens everywhere – mean, spindly stems topped with a few, small flowers that are so high they are not even at eye level where they can be enjoyed.

❀ Ideally, plan your shrub's pruning needs while the plant is still young, starting your pruning programme the first year after planting. It is always preferable to create and maintain a good pruning routine, rather than to attempt to resuscitate a shrub that may have become unhealthy, out of shape and congested as a result of having been left unpruned for many years.

❀ You can try cutting this sort of neglected shrub back to just above ground level, as it may produce basal shoots, but the results are not predictable. Most hard pruning is done in spring, to encourage vigorous growth, but always

HOW TO PRUNE SHRUBS

As with trees, it is important to understand the requirements of each indvidual shrub to avoid inflicting heavy damage or not getting the best out of a shrub by pruning too lightly.

ABOVE: *Hard pruning is advisable only for certain shrubs. It stimulates vigorous new growth and encourages a good floral display on appropriate plants.*

ABOVE: *Ungainly shrubs can be persuaded into more pleasing shapes by careful pruning, which provides a better framework of stems.*

ABOVE: *Some shrubs, like this dogwood (Cornus), are pruned hard in spring to produce colourful stems.*

check the individual requirements of any shrub before pruning, since pruning at the correct time of year is of crucial importance.

❀ Hard pruning seems very drastic, but on shrubs that flower on shoots produced in the current year, it is easy to see how, left unpruned, the stems would simply continue to grow, with the flowers appearing at the very ends only. You will need to cut back all the previous summer's growth to within approximately 5 cm (2 in) of last year's stem. Although the result looks brutal, the plant will generate healthy new shoots at this point.

❀ Cut back to a point just above a bud, outward facing if possible, to give the plant a good overall shape. In general, cut the plant back as far as new growth, but to regenerate a very bushy old shrub that has become crowded and out of shape, cut a few stems back almost to ground level to improve the overall shape.

Deadheading

❀ Many plants, such as heathers and lavenders, need deadheading as soon as the flowers have died back. Check if each plant needs deadheading before doing so automatically, as there are a few exceptions.

❀ Using shears, trim away the dead blooms to a point just below the flower spike. Take care not to cut into the old wood, as some shrubs do not flower well, or at all, on old wood, and you will be left with unattractive bare brown areas if you cut too enthusiastically.

BELOW: *Pruning shrubs at the right time will help to increase flower production next season.*

PRUNING CLIMBERS

CLIMBERS grow in several different ways. Clinging climbers such as ivy attach themselves to their supports by aerial roots or suckers, and do not require a supplementary support systems like trellis.

❀ Twining climbers, such as honeysuckle and clematis, entwine around a support by means of tendrils, stems or leaf stalks, and benefit from a support. Scrambling plants, for example some types of rose, hang on using hooked thorns. Scrambling, rambling plants will need tying on to a support. A guide to pruning scrambling climbers is given in the section on pruning roses that follows. For pruning twining climbers, see the section on pruning clematis.

Basic principles

❀ Climbers have different pruning needs, depending on their flowering season and the age of the wood on which they flower. As a guide, climbers that flower on the previous season's growth need pruning when flowering has finished. Climbers that flower on the current season's growth are pruned in early spring or at the end of winter, so that they have adequate time to produce new flowering shoots.

❀ Having checked that you are pruning at the right time of year for the plant concerned, there are general rules to follow for all pruning. Use sharp tools and make clean cuts, removing damaged or weak growth.

❀ Cut out branches that are rubbing, or that have become congested. Prune just above a bud or healthy shoot; on climbers that grow in an opposite-facing pattern, cut straight across above a pair of buds. On climbers that grow with an alternating pattern, make a cut that slopes away, just above a bud pointing in the direction that you want the new shoot to develop.

Pruning to control growth

❀ Although clinging climbers are easy to grow and establish, they can overwhelm a structure. Ivy, in particular, can inflict severe structural damage. Roots can penetrate mortar and, as plant stems thicken, guttering can be forced away from the building.

ABOVE: *Vigorous climbers, such as honeysuckle, need careful pruning to keep them in check.*

❀ Vigorous climbers like this can creep under and loosen roof tiles and wooden cladding. Once they have taken hold, removal is difficult, so it is important to keep a watchful annual pruning eye on these plants to ensure a balance between attractively cloaking growth and unwelcome invasion. Remove as much growth as you need, at the time of year appropriate to the plant.

RIGHT: *To retain a well-shaped, wall-trained climber, prune and train diligently from the start.*

Pruning for good coverage

❀ Pruning clinging climbers early in their life also promotes an even growth pattern with a well-spaced framework of new shoots. Although self-clinging climbers do not technically need tying in and supporting, they will grow to cover a surface more evenly if trained laterally while still young and pliable and pruned to encourage budding from side shoots.

❀ In order to do this successfully, you should either tie or peg down the young stems. In the second spring after planting, cut back the plant's side shoots to a point just above a bud near the main stem. As each new stem develops, cut back the tip the next year so that the shoots branch out and create better coverage of the support. Cut back other new shoots to within two buds of the nearest stem.

RENOVATING NEGLECTED CLIMBERS

A NEGLECTED climber is a rather depressing sight. Not only does the plant bulge unattractively from its support, but it may start to pull the support away from the wall or fence altogether.

❀ Neighbouring plants may be forced into deep shade, affecting their growth adversely, too. A tangled, congested mass of mostly dead or dying stems can be a daunting prospect. However, tackle it with confidence, since, in most cases, even severely overgrown climbers can be regenerated with appropriate pruning.

❀ Some climbers will grow again even if cut back almost to the base. As with all pruning, check the individual needs of your plant before picking up the secateurs. If the plant's ability to withstand drastic pruning is uncertain, tackle renovative pruning over a two-year period.

❀ Gradually, fresh, vigorous growth will replace what you have removed. Be methodical if you are undertaking renovative pruning over a protracted period; otherwise, new shoots will grow and become entwined with the old stems, which will make pruning extremely difficult.

❀ Although the plant will look unbalanced during this time, it is best to cut down one side of the plant only in the first year of renovation. A very neglected plant may take several years to recover from this treatment, so do not be hasty to dismiss the success of your work if the plant does not flower for two years or so, even after both sides have been pruned. Be patient.

prune any crossing or rubbing stems, which can cause plant weakness and disease

woody stems will need lopping, rather than trimming with secateurs

remove very tangled, matted growth for a neat, healthy climber

PRUNING ROSES

ROSE stems grow and produce flowers for only a few years before becoming exhausted and starting to develop flowers lower down the stem. Pruning is therefore needed to prevent the plant becoming an ungainly tangled mass of dying and living wood, with inferior blooms.

Rambling roses

❀ Rambling roses have diminished in popularity over the years. They bloom only once a year, albeit with a spectacular show of flowers, but are not generally disease resistant, and do need regular pruning.

❀ Flowers grow on new wood, so you will need to prune each year for a good show of flowers all over the plant. However, rambling roses are a good choice in some areas, where their natural talents can be exploited. Their long, flexible stems will clamber enthusiastically up dead trees that would otherwise be an eyesore, or scramble riotously along the soil to produce unusual ground cover.

Climbing roses

❀ Climbing roses have much less flexible stems than ramblers; many are more disease resistant, and some are repeat-flowering. Since flowers develop on a framework of established wood, pruning climbers is much less demanding than pruning ramblers. Essential pruning is restricted to removing dead, weak or diseased growth.

❀ Deadhead as much as is practical during the summer, and prune in the autumn, after flowering. If you also shorten the side shoots that have flowered, taking them back to approximately three buds, you will encourage a good coverage of flowers next year.

Regenerating an old climber

❀ If a climbing rose has been neglected, and lateral growth not encouraged by regular training and tying in, there may be many bare stems visible near ground level. You can encourage new, basal shoots to develop by cutting down some of the old bare stems almost to ground level.

SHRUB AND MINIATURE ROSES

The term 'shrub rose' covers many old varieties of rose, which predate the floribundas and hybrid teas roses so popular today. Shrub roses generally have a much shorter flowering period than their contemporary rivals, and often produce much bigger bushes, so are not as popular as they once were. However, there are notable exceptions to these rules. Some shrub roses are repeat-flowering; some do grow in smaller bush sizes and some, although they do flower only once in a season, flower spectacularly and over such a long period that they are still excellent choices. Shrub roses do not generally have very demanding pruning needs, an attribute shared by miniature roses. Pruning of these roses is generally limited to controlling the size of the bush, as well as removing dead, diseased or weak growth. Miniatures may be pruned with scissors, instead of secateurs.

light pruning is not recommended, except for very vigorous hybrid tea roses

hard pruning is recommended for newly planted bush roses, and to renovate neglected plants

roses respond wonderfully to efficient pruning, producing a multitude of flowers

miniature roses only need scissors to cut off spent blooms and diseased or damaged stems

Cutting out suckers

❀ Where plants have been produced by grafting, suckers may develop. These shoots grow from the original rootstock, not the required variety grafted on to it. If left unchecked, these suckers will eventually overwhelm the plant completely, reverting it to the rootstock variety.

❀ It is vital to remove the sucker properly at its source. You will probably need to remove some soil, before pulling off the sucker where it has developed on the rootstock. If you simply snip suckers off at ground level, they will thrive on this pruning and develop even more.

ABOVE: *Most hybrid tea and established floribunda roses require moderate pruning.*

Hybrid tea and floribunda roses

❀ Hybrid tea and floribunda roses are popular garden choices, and have broadly similar pruning needs.

❀ Hybrid teas have been used for around 100 years. Their flowers have what is often seen as a 'classic' rose shape. They are available in an amazing range of colours and are often well fragranced. However, there are drawbacks with some varieties.

❀ Many hybrid tea bushes are quite rigid in shape, producing a slightly stiff appearance that does not suit every garden, and hybrid teas generally bloom less frequently than floribundas. They are also more susceptible to rain damage, and are not tolerant of less-than-perfect conditions; so choose your breed carefully.

❀ Floribundas have been popular for around the last 50 years. Although the individual blooms may not be as choice as their hybrid tea counterparts, floribundas are chosen for their ability to flower continuously for long periods, for their increased disease resistance, their ability to thrive in less-than-ideal conditions, and for their rain tolerance.

❀ Prune these roses in early spring, when growth is just beginning, but to avoid the possibility of damage by wind rock cut back long shoots in autumn. Cut stems back to approximately half their length, and remove damaged, weak or diseased stems. For floribundas, hard prune some old stems close to the ground to encourage new basal shoots, while pruning last year's new shoots only moderately. This variable pruning will encourage a good coverage of flowers over the whole plant.

REGENERATING OLD CLIMBERS AND DEALING WITH SUCKERS

Suckers spoil the look and shape of any rose and should be dealt with firmly. Likewise, a neglected rose needs firm attention to encourage healthy and shapely regrowth.

shorten side shoots to just above a bud, facing in the direction that you want the rose to grow

when hard pruning, cut out unwanted stems close to their base for a good overall framework

remove suckers at their point of origin on the root, not at ground level

PRUNING CLEMATIS

THERE is a great deal of intimidating mystique about how to prune clematis correctly. In fact, there are just three basic methods. The choice of method appropriate for a particular clematis is the most important part of pruning this plant.

❀ Clematises are divided loosely into three groups, based on when they flower. These groups are widely referred to as Groups One, Two and Three type of clematis. When buying a new clematis, you will save yourself a lot of pruning indecision later on if you take the time to find out and note the group that your clematis falls into. Getting the type right is important. If you make a mistake in identifying the type of pruning required, you could unwittingly remove the next flush of flowers.

GROUP ONE: MINIMAL PRUNING NEEDS

THESE vigorous clematises flower in spring or early summer, directly on last season's ripened stems. They typically have quite small flowers. Clematises in this group need to be pruned hard when planted, but subsequently need only minimal pruning. If the plant becomes tangled, untidy and congested, you can prune it after flowering to control it.

❀ Popular Group One cultivars include *Clematis montana, C. macropetala, C. alpina* and *C. armandii.*

ABOVE: *Group One clematises, such as C. Montana, are very lightly pruned after flowering.*

GROUP TWO: LIGHT PRUNING NEEDS

THESE clematises produce large flowers early in summer or in midsummer. Some varieties continue flowering through into autumn. Group Two clematises flower on short stems produced in the current season, which grow on last season's ripe wood, and need only a light pruning in spring, before the plant starts active growth. Both Group One and Two clematises are sometimes referred to as 'old-wood' flowering clematis.

❀ Given their attributes of large flowers and an often prolonged flowering season, it is no wonder that Group Two contains many of the most popular hybrid clematis cultivars such as 'Nelly Moser', 'The President', 'Mrs Cholmondely' and 'Lasurstern'.

ABOVE: *Lightly prune Group Two varieties, such as 'Nelly Moser', in early spring.*

GROUP THREE: HARD PRUNING NEEDS

GROUP Three clematises flower late in the season – from mid- to late summer, and possibly through to autumn – producing blooms on the current year's stems. In early spring, before the plant starts active growth, cut back all last season's growth to just above the lowest pair of healthy buds, approximately 30 cm (12 in) above soil level. Tie in the new stems as they grow in late spring and summer. Take great care when training, as the stems are extremely brittle and prone to breakage.

❀ Group Three clematises include 'Ernest Markham', 'Jackmanii', 'Ville de Lyon', 'Perle d'Azur' and 'Gipsy Queen'.

RIGHT: *C. 'Jackmanii' and other Group Three clematises need hard pruning in early spring.*

CLEMATIS GROUPS

GROUP 1

ABOVE: *Prune Group 1 clematis if needed after flowering, removing a minimal amount of foliage.*

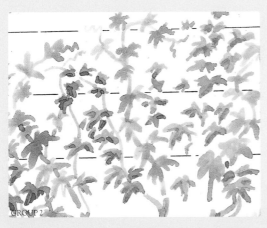

GROUP 2

ABOVE: *Prune Group 2 clematis only if the plant needs neatening up straight after flowering.*

GROUP 3

ABOVE: *Prune Group 3 clematis in late winter or early spring, taking them back to the lowest healthy shoot.*

Pruning and training clematis and other climbers on an arch or pergola

❀ Any climber looks best on a pergola or arch if it has been encouraged to produce a good, even coverage, with flowers over the whole plant, not just a few at the top, out of range of eye level. The key to producing a good climbing display is to train horizontally while the stems are flexible, and to prune main stems to encourage side shoots to develop.

❀ Always take care to tie in shoots gently, leaving room for movement and growth. Prune at the time of year appropriate for the type of clematis grown, removing diseased, damaged or dead wood. When the main shoots have climbed to the top of the support, prune them – again at the appropriate time of year – so that they do not become congested, untidy and susceptible to windrock.

BELOW: *Climbing flowering plants need careful pruning in order to keep the whole plant in bloom.*

PRUNING HEDGES

THE type of pruning a particular hedge requires depends on two things – the type of overall effect you are trying to create and the individual requirements of the plant.

❀ A dense, formal hedge like privet will need regular pruning if it is to maintain its neat good looks, whereas an informal flowering or fruiting hedge such as snowberry will need much less attention in order to achieve a desirable look.

Shaping a hedge

❀ A common mistake in trimming hedges is to produce a straight-sided form, or one that tapers towards the bottom. This will eventually yield the type of hedge that is an all-too-common sight in front gardens everywhere – the hedge that is leafy at the top and bare, twiggy and brown at the base. The reason is simple. The foliage at the base of the hedge has died due to a lack of light from being in the shade of the upper leaves and stems. Happily, there is a simple technique for preventing this.

❀ Always trim a formal hedge into a slightly pyramidal shape – so that it is approximately one-third narrower at the top than at its base – so as to allow plenty of light to reach all parts of the plant. This sloping angle also encourages greater wind resistance and helps the plant shed snow. In areas of high snowfall it may be advisable to make a more exaggerated A-shaped sloping cut at the top of the hedge, to further discourage snow from settling and ice forming on the plant.

❀ When the hedge has grown to the desired height, make yourself a cutting template from plywood to give you a clear, easy-to-follow guide to the shape and height required.

❀ When you start work from the base of the hedge, make sure that you work upwards so that clippings are discarded from the path of progress. A power trimmer makes light work of what can otherwise be an arduous task if you are dealing with hedges on a large scale. Always use the correct safety precautions and equipment, including gloves, goggles and, if using an electric trimmer, a residual current device (RCD).

Informal hedges

❀ Informal hedges are much less demanding than their neatly clipped formal counterparts. They generally need pruning only once a year, and maintaining a precise finished shape is not necessary for their visual success. These hedges are generally pruned in order to control their size and spread, to cut out any disease or decay, and to encourage new shoots to appear.

❀ Pruning is usually done after the plants have flowered, but do check the needs of individual species before pruning. For example, berrying hedges are generally left unpruned until the berries have finished fruiting, or the birds have eaten them. As a rule, simply cut out any congested or weak areas, shorten old shoots and cut back some shoots almost to the ground in order to encourage basal shoots.

FORMAL HEDGES

Formal hedges – ones that are clipped into precise shapes – need regular trimming to maintain a good appearance. A neglected formal hedge is a very depressing sight. Just as unkempt hair on an otherwise well-dressed person gives a generally scruffy impression, an untidy formal hedge transmits an air of neglect throughout the whole garden. The aim of pruning a formal hedge is to produce a dense mass of compact shoots that will form a bushy hedge, which grows evenly within its desired shape. Clipping side shoots will remove the growing tip of each shoot to promote this bushy growth. Many formal hedges can be trimmed when they look untidy – between spring and autumn – but always check the individual pruning needs of any hedge before picking up the trimmer. Fast-growing hedges may need several cuts a year; slower growing types will look perfectly respectable with just one or two trims during that time.

a pointed top helps shrug off heavy snowfall in especially vulnerable sites

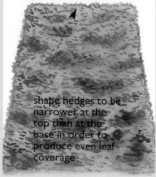

shape hedges to be narrower at the top than at the base in order to produce even leaf coverage

HEDGE-PRUNG METHODS

Decide which tools to use for cutting a hedge according to the area that needs trimming.

1 *Secateurs will suffice for lightly trimming the occasional shoot.*

2 *Sharp shears are adequate when quite small areas of hedge need trimming.*

3 *Power tools make light work of hedge trimming. Always use the appropriate safety equipment when using power tools in the garden.*

RENOVATING A NEGLECTED HEDGE

It is tempting to ruthlessly prune a very unsightly, neglected hedge, but severe cutting can over stress the plant and recovery will be slow. Initially, working at the time of year appropriate to the plant, trim only one side hard to encourage new growth from the centre of the hedge. You may repeat this drastic pruning in the following year on the other side of the hedge, and only lightly trimming the new growth on the other side.

the following year, trim new growth on the opposite side

in year one, trim one side of the plant hard

MAKING A HEIGHT GUIDE

A string line gives an accurate cutting guide for trimming a formal hedge. Fix a taut, brightly coloured line at the required finished height of the hedge as an easy-to-see guide for level.

coloured string line for easy viewing

desired height of hedge

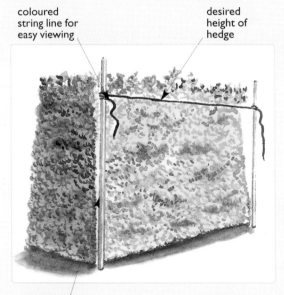

poles holding sting line

TOPIARY

TOPIARY is pruning elevated to an art form. Plants have been trained and cut into artificial shapes for decorative effect since Roman times. Topiary has a place in many gardens, not only the grand, formal settings with which it is normally associated.

❀ Topiary can visually anchor a more informal setting and provide valuable, year-long structure and colour in a garden. Even the smallest garden, perhaps little more than a flight of steps leading to a doorway, can look more imposing when embellished with a neat pair of clipped, container-grown plants.

TOPIARY SHAPES

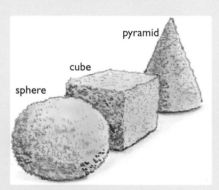

pyramid

cube

sphere

NOVICE topiarists are advised to start with a simple, geometric shape. Rigidly geometric shapes, such as cubes, are less forgiving of inaccurate cutting than slightly softer forms, like pyramids and spheres. More figurative shapes, such as teddy bears and peacocks, are not necessarily difficult to produce, particularly if you form them using a ready-made rigid frame as a guide. However, they can take many years to reach a size at which they can attain a recognisable shape, because the plants are generally slow growing, and are therefore not for the impatient topiarist.

Initially, young plants are snipped to shape by eye to form a loosely geometric shape. As the plant grows in subsequent years to a sufficient size, place a cutting guide over the plant and trim to shape. Canes, held together with wire at the top, make a simple and inexpensive pyramid 'template'. When the plant has reached the required shape and size, simply clip it lightly at intervals appropriate for the topiary shape and type of plant used, to maintain a crisp, outline and dense growth pattern.

❀ Low box hedging has long been used to contain herb gardens, which can, by the very nature of the plants, be quite unruly. Not only does the clipped hedging define and neaten the overall appearance of the area, but it also helps to protect the plants within its borders from the elements, and contains and intensifies the fragrance of the herbs in the local environment.

❀ Topiary can consist of very simple geometric shapes, such as spheres and cubes, or it can be extremely fanciful, such as chess pieces or a whole menagerie of animals. It can be used to add interest to a long run of hedging, or as stand-alone pieces of living sculpture. Slow-growing plants are generally chosen for topiary – species that can withstand regular clipping, but do not grow so rapidly that they lose their outline overnight.

The technique

❀ Topiary is not a low-maintenance form of pruning, although many of the plants used for topiary are chosen for their resilience and dense growth patterns. With just a little attention to some basic guidelines, successful topiary is not difficult to achieve. The results are impressive and extremely satisfying to produce.

❀ Always use very sharp, clean tools for topiary, as the soft shoots you are cutting are sappy and will be vulnerable to disease if torn. It is also very difficult to make decisive, accurate cuts on this flexible growth with blunt tools.

❀ Sheep-trimming shears are excellent for producing a light, accurate cut, but are not suitable for heavy work. Cutting little and often is the key to successful topiary. Dramatic, inexpert cutting can create an unbalanced shape, which will take at least a season to settle, and it is all too easy to cut inaccurately when making severe cuts. Cut large-leaved evergreens, such as laurel, with secateurs to prevent the unsightly halving of leaves, which can occur if clipping with shears.

Frequency of cut

❀ How frequently to clip topiary depends on the speed at which the plant grows, the intricacy of the topiary shape and the degree of finish required. Simple shapes in slow-growing plants will need relatively little clipping. For example, a yew pyramid will need only an annual trim, whereas a complex abstract geometric shape in box may need cutting at four- to six-weekly intervals during the growing season, in order to maintain its definition.

SIMPLE TOPIARY FRAMES

There is no need to buy purpose-built frames to produce topiary shapes.

1 *Canes secured together at the top to form a pyramid make an inexpensive and effective guide.*

2 *Trim back excess growth until the plant is level with the guides.*

3 *Wire spheres look attractive even partially covered with foliage. Tie in shoots to encourage even coverage of the shape.*

❀ As always when pruning, check the individual needs of a particular plant before planning clipping. Clipping times will also depend on your local climate. In cooler climates, do not clip after early autumn as the young shoots produced will not be tolerant of low winter temperatures. Milder environments, in which the plants grow almost continuously, may necessitate regular clipping throughout the year. Most topiary plants should be clipped as thier summer growth begins, however, the exceptions to this are hornbeam and beech, which should not be clipped until the late summer.

SHAPING A HEDGE CORRECTLY

EFFECTIVE topiary needs even leaf coverage, which is hard to achieve on shapes that have a lot of leaf shade shielding the lower parts of the plant. Do not allow hedges to become top heavy, flat-topped or tapering towards the bottom, with a twiggy base. Slope the hedge from a narrow top to a wide base for greatest ease of pruning, healthy growth and an attractive appearance.

tapered sides to hedge

flat top to hedge

bare, brown twiggy base

healthy broad base

Acacia

Laurel

Bottle brush

Scotch heather

Camellia

PRUNING ORNAMENTAL PLANTS

GIVEN below are the pruning requirements of some popular plants, with advice on timing and the best method to employ to make the most of the plants.

Mimosa (*Acacia*)

❀ No regular pruning is required for mimosa except cutting back the dead wood after a severe winter. If you need to restrict the height of the shrub cut it right back to a third of its size following flowering.

Laurel (*Aucuba japonica*)

❀ No regular pruning is needed for laurel unless it grows beyond its allotted space, in which case it can be cut back in spring.

Bottle brush (*Callistemon*)

❀ No regular pruning is needed but it is sensible to thin out the old branches and shoots at the base of the plant from time to time.

Scotch heather, ling (*Calluna*)

❀ Heather quickly becomes straggly and untidy if left unpruned for any length of time. Luckily, it is easy to prune, merely requiring a quick clip over with shears in the early months of spring. Do not cut right back into the old wood, as bare patches will appear.

Camellia

❀ No hard pruning is required for camellias; any straggly shoots can be taken off following flowering in mid-spring. Deadheading on varieties with masses of blooms will increase growth for the following year.

Convolvulus

Dogwood

Daphne

Bell heather

Fuchsia

Convolvulvus

❀ To create a bushy appearance, remove about two thirds of this shrub annually in late summer. This will encourage new growth of the pretty silvery leaves and flowers the following year.

Dogwood (*Cornus*)

❀ Dogwoods grown for their coloured stems need pruning regularly to promote new growth. For winter colour, the stems should be cut right back to the basal level in late spring.

Daphne

❀ No routine pruning is required for any of the many species of *Daphne*, but cut the straggly shoots out in early spring to keep a pleasing and neat appearance.

Bell heather (*Erica*)

❀ Clip off dead flowerheads to encourage new growth aand prune during the spring months when new growth is about to start.

Fuchsia magellanica

❀ The hardy fuchsia dies back in the winter as the top growth is killed by frost and low temperatures. Cut it right back almost to ground level in the spring and a profusion of new shoots will soon appear.

Hebe

Helianthemum

Laburnum

Lace-cap hydrangea

Lavender

Shrubby veronica (*Hebe*)

❀ Some varieties of these plants are not very hardy and will need attention after the winter. Do not prune the plant until spring, even if the leaves are brown and the stems bare, as they offer some small protection against the elements. Cut the damaged shoots off when the new growth begins to appear and cut back for shape if needed after about a month.

Rock rose, sun rose (*Helianthemum*)

❀ Cut two-thirds of the new shoots in the summer months to encourage new growth the following year.

Tree hollyhock, Tree mallow (*Hibiscus*)

❀ Very little general maintenance is required for this hardy species. Remove old branches to restrict size and prune back any frost-damaged shoots in early spring.

Lace-cap hydrangea (*Hydrangea macrophylla*)

❀ Leave the dead brown heads on many varieties of hydrangea during the winter months to protect flower buds from damage. Instead, remove the dead heads in spring, when the weather is warmer and the first green shoots appear. Remove straggly shoots at the same time.

Laburnum

❀ As these plants grow so abundantly, train them into shape when they are young. If necessary, remove crossing or over-large branches in the later summer, but in general it is preferable not to prune them, as the wounds tend to bleed excessively.

Peony

Lupins

Cistaceae

Lavender (*Lavundula*)

❀ Prune lavender to promote a neat appearance, since it can quickly become straggly and tatty. Cut right back to the new shoots in early spring as soon as the new shoots begin to appear. Keep lavender beds tidy by pruning them lightly with shears after flowering. Take cuttings for propagation in the summer.

Lupins (*Lupinus*)

❀ Lupins are short-term, fast-growing perennials that should be deadheaded after flowering to prevent reseeding. For bushy growth, cut one stem in three.

Oleander (*Nerium*)

❀ Oleander is not a hardy plant and should be placed in a greenhouse in winter. Remove half of the year's new growth after the plant has flowered in early summer. As Oleander is poisonous, always wear protective gloves when pruning.

Oleander

Peony (*Paeonia*)

❀ Remove all dead wood in mid-summer and cut off dead pieces of stem once the fruit-bearing shoots have died back.

Rhododendron

❀ This spring-flowering shrub requires no regular pruning until it is fully grown, which takes around 10–15 years. At this point, cut one stem in every three in the summer to promote healthy growth and an attractive shape. Deadhead the flowers anually.

Rhododendron

LOOKING AFTER LAWNS

The lawn is the centrepiece of many gardens. It remains green when much else in the garden is dormant, and sets off plants and hard surfaces beautifully. It unites diverse garden elements, harmonising planted and unplanted elements. As a practical garden floor, as well as a major visual feature, we make huge demands on our lawns. It is often a children's play area, family recreation area and hardworking everyday surface, trampled on regularly as we hang out washing or walk across it to reach the shed.

ATTENDING TO YOUR LAWN

CONSIDERING how demanding we are of our lawns, and how prominent they are in the design of most gardens, it is surprising that most gardeners expect lawns to perform at their best with very little attention, save mowing and perhaps an occasional weed or feed treatment when problems arise.

❀ Perhaps it will help to remember that a lawn is not a solid material, but is composed of millions of tiny plants, all of which need air, food, light, moisture and good drainage as much as any other garden plant.

❀ The list of tasks required to keep a lawn at bowling green perfection is rather daunting, and probably too time consuming for all but the most perfectionist lawn owner to undertake. However, most gardeners will find that increasing the level of lawn attention from mowing alone to include just a few more specific tasks will not be too onerous, yet will reward them with a much improved lawn.

BELOW: *A lush green lawn can be as rich and welcoming as a deep pile carpet if it is well maintained.*

TYPES OF LAWN

THE type of lawn you have is determined by the type of grasses it contains.

The luxury lawn

❀ Luxury turf comprises fine-leaved, compact grasses – bents (*Agrostis*) and fescues (*Festuca*). It is free of broad-leaved grasses such as perennial ryegrass. Luxury lawns are kept closely mown in order to prevent coarse-leaved grasses colonising the lawn. Although undoubtedly a thing of great beauty, a fine, ornamental lawn is not easy to achieve or maintain.

❀ Getting luxury lawns off to a good start is neither cheap nor quick. Turf and seed are more expensive than utility grades, turf particularly so. Starting such a lawn from seed requires meticulous preparation, as the closely cut finished lawn cruelly reveals any discrepancy in level. Fine grasses are also slow to germinate, so establishing this sort of lawn is a lengthy process.

❀ Luxury-grade grass will not withstand heavy wear, so is definitely not recommended as a lawn for gardeners with children. Nor can this type of lawn tolerate neglect, so unless you are a lawn hobbyist, choose a grade of grass that you can realistically maintain.

RIGHT: *To keep your lawn up to scratch in the warm summer months, iinvest in a good sprinkler system.*

LEFT: *If your lawn is going to be functional rather than decorative, it is best to choose a more hard-wearing type of grass that can stand up to constant use.*

The utility lawn

❀ Most gardeners will find utility-grade grass a far more user-friendly option than the luxury choice. The utility lawn contains broad-leaved grasses, combined with some fine-leaved varieties, which will withstand the rigours of family life.

❀ Most of us use the lawn as an extended living area, not merely as a showpiece to be viewed from a distance. Utility lawns cope admirably with the requirements of modern living, such as being regularly walked and played on.

❀ Very importantly for the busy gardener, utility lawns will also tolerate a certain amount of neglect without suffering irreparably. Utility-grade grass, whether seed or turf, is less expensive than luxury grades, and also establishes much more easily and quickly. The broader leaves also conceal the sort of coarse grasses that frequently invade lawns, and which would be very visible and unsightly on a luxury lawn.

❀ The chief disadvantage of a utility lawn is that it needs regular mowing from spring through summer. However, since this necessity springs from its resilient, fast-growing nature, most gardeners would agree that it is worth putting up with being moderately enslaved to the mower in order to escape the petulant demands of the luxury lawn.

SEED

SEED is an economical and popular way of producing a new lawn. Unlike turf, seed does not deteriorate quickly after purchase, so you have more flexibility about when you sow.

❀ On the downside, however, preparation of the ground is especially critical, and is a time-consuming process. In addition, lawns are best sown in spring or early autumn, which are already busy times in the garden. All weeds must be removed, and the emerging lawn seedlings are vulnerable to attack from new weeds, birds, disease, overly dry or wet weather and cats.

❀ You will need to keep a watchful eye on the new lawn for a few weeks as it germinates, in case it needs watering, so do not sow a lawn and go on holiday, expecting a faultless sward on your return. It might have died entirely if the weather is too dry. Another drawback of growing from seed is that the lawn is not ready for normal use for approximately 9 to 12 month.

TURF

TURF is very much more expensive than grass seed, particularly if you are buying luxury-grade turf. Turf laying is also heavy work. However, it has several advantages over growing a lawn from seed.

LEFT: *Most gardeners would not be too happy if weeds such as common sorrel appeared in their lawn; however, through regular lawn maintenance such occurences can be kept to a minimum.*

❀ Turfing is usually done in late autumn to winter, or in early spring, which are not especially busy times in the garden. It is therefore comparatively easy to incorporate turf laying into the gardening schedule. The most significant advantage over seed is that turf produces a mature-looking lawn almost immediately, and is generally well established within two to three months.

❀ Turf is not as vulnerable to problems as germinating seedlings and so requires much less attention after laying than a seeded lawn. Finally, although good ground preparation is important when laying any sort of lawn, there is no need for the time-consuming finely tilled seedbed when laying turf.

Choosing standard turf

❀ Hopefully, you will need to buy lawn turf only once in the life of your lawn, so it is worth considering the choices carefully before purchasing, and worth buying the best quality you can afford, from a reputable supplier.

BELOW: *Daisies are one of the most common weeds to grow in lawns, although many people do not mind, as they give the lawn a natural look.*

❀ Economising at this stage could create problems for years to come. For example, some cheap turf looks healthy enough, but may be rough, farmland meadow turf, containing a high proportion of weeds and coarse grasses, which will never look good, despite a lot of attention. Specialist turf suppliers have their reputation to protect, so it is well worth paying a little extra for their products.

❀ Turf needs to be laid as soon as possible after receipt, as it degenerates quite quickly. If you have turf delivered, intending to lay it at the weekend, but the weather is unsuitable, you need to be able to make time during the next week to lay the turf as soon as the weather allows.

❀ For busy, working gardeners, this may simply not be feasible. If, for example, the weather causes delays and you cannot rearrange your schedule, make sure you have a contigency plan. It may be that you have to get someone else to help you lay the turf.

❀ If a delay of more than three days is expected, you can unroll the turf and keep it damped down in a shady place, but it is much better to arrange to lay it promptly after delivery.

❀ Order approximately five per cent more turf than the exact amount required, to allow for wastage. Before delivery, remember to plan and clear the area where the turf will be stacked until needed.

Seeded turf

❀ Professional landscape gardeners have used seeded turf for many years, and it has become an increasingly popular method of producing a new lawn domestically. A major advantage of seeded turf is that it has been produced to a specific 'recipe' and should therefore be of uniformly high quality, whereas it is very hard for the lay person to ascertain the content and quality of standard turf.

❀ Particularly desirable lawn grasses are sown on to a substrate, so you know exactly what you are buying, and the turf is weed free. Seeded turf is also much lighter and easier to lay than standard turf. It may even be cut with ordinary scissors.

❀ However, seeded turf is more expensive than standard turf. It is also less forgiving of undulations in the underlying surface, so more careful site preparation is needed before laying to ensure that the soil is absolutely level.

BELOW: *Three of the most common lawn weeds (from left): dandelion, greater plantain and white clover, all of which can require a great deal of effort to remove permanently.*

ESTABLISHING A
NEW LAWN

PREPARATION is the key to a good-looking lawn that will be easy to maintain – no bumps and hollows to distort mowing, no perennial weeds to deal with, just even, level, healthy green grass. Keep this image in mind as you embark on the laborious, but very necessary process of preparing the site.

❀ Site preparation is essentially the same, whether you are sowing from seed or are laying turf. You should follow the general directions given below until you reach the individual directions for seed sowing and turf laying (see p. 406).

❀ Ideally, you should start preparing the site for a new lawn at least three months before seeding or turfing. There is quite a lot of initial work to be done, and you need to allow the soil time to settle.

Clearing and grading the site

❀ Clear down to bare earth. Remove tree stumps and roots, seeking professional help if necessary. Dig out perennial weeds and treat the area with weedkiller.

❀ You may need to alter the contours of the site to reach an approximate final level for the lawn. Whether the site slopes or is almost horizontal, there should be no bumps or hollows in its surface, as these will naturally lead to problems in the finished lawn – both visually, and when you eventually come to mow it.

❀ When correcting bumps and hollows, always keep the topsoil and subsoil in consistent positions. For example, to level a major bump do not be tempted to scrape away the topsoil only. You will need to remove the topsoil, put it to one side, then excavate the subsoil to the required depth, before replacing the topsoil.

Levelling the site

❀ To produce a level surface, take some wooden pegs – their length dictated by the degree of unevenness of the ground – and make a mark on each, 10 cm (4 in) down from the top. Insert the pegs in the soil at 1.8 m (6 ft) intervals in a grid formation.

❀ Place a length of wood, topped with a spirit level across each pair of pegs and hammer until level. Add or remove soil from between the pegs to bring the soil surface level with the marks you made on the pegs.

Draining the site

❀ Lawns need good drainage. Most sites can be sufficiently prepared by digging that incorporates soil improvers.

❀ Heavy clay soils may need more intensive consideration. The topsoil will need to be removed, and layers of drainage material added on top of the subsoil, starting with a 15-cm (6-in) layer of rubble, progressing through to a 15-cm (6-in) layer of small stones, coarse sand or grit, to the top layer of topsoil.

❀ Very waterlogged soils with impervious clay subsoils may need proper drainage systems installed if you are intent on having a lawn.

Preparing the soil

❀ Digging an area big enough for the average lawn is extremely hard work, and you may find it worthwhile to hire a mechanical rotovator. Remove large stones and perennial weeds. Dig when the soil is reasonably dry. Incorporate sand if the soil is heavy, well-rotted organic matter if the soil is light.

Firming and raking
the site

❀ On a dry day tread the soil evenly, using tiny steps with your weight on your heels. Rake the soil level and remove stones and debris. Alternately you can tread and rake until the site is level, with a fine, crumbly surface.

Leaving the site fallow

❀ When sowing seed, it is vital to prepare a weed-free seedbed. Turf will also benefit from a weed-free site, but this stage is not as critical for turfing as it is for seed sowing. Leave the site until annual weeds germinate, then apply weedkiller. After a few days, when the weeds have died, rake them off, taking care to remove all the roots.

Fertilising the site

❀ A few days before sowing or turfing the site, lightly rake in a good-quality compound fertiliser, following the manufacturer's directions precisely.

LAWN DISORDERS

Some of the most frequently found lawn problems are illustrated below. Regular care and maintenance of your lawn can help avoid these problems.

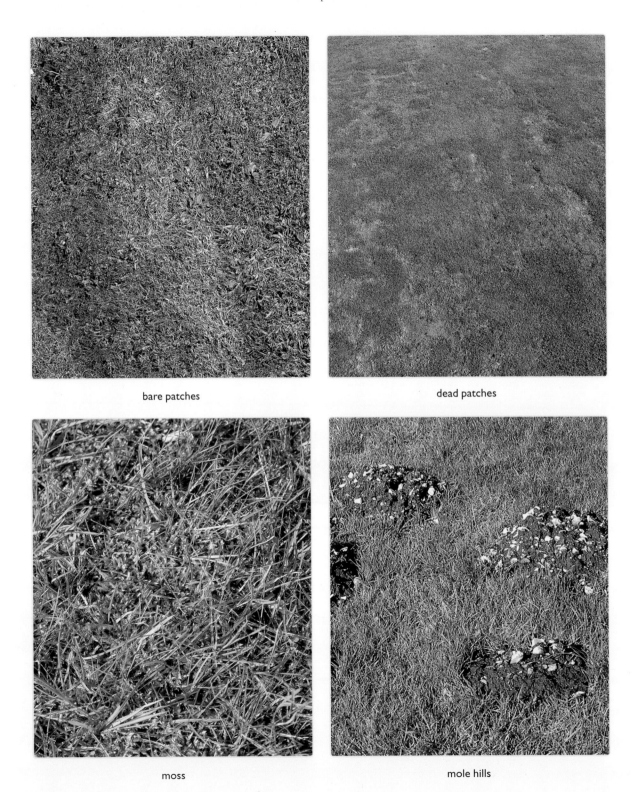

bare patches

dead patches

moss

mole hills

SOWING BY HAND

If sowing by hand, begin by marking out the site into equal areas.

1 *Divide the amount of seed accordingly and sow as evenly as possible, working first in one direction, then at right angles to this, as for sowing by machine.*

2 *Lightly rake in the seed and water with a sprinkler to avoid disturbing the seed.*

GROWING A LAWN FROM SEED

FOLLOW the manufacturer's directions regarding sowing rates. Too much seed can encourage damping off in the emerging seedlings; too little will produce an uneven effect, and will allow weed seedlings through to compete with the emerging grass.

❀ Always shake the seed container well so that the different types of seed are evenly mixed before you start sowing.

Sowing by machine

❀ A mechanical seed distributor is very helpful in sowing a medium to large lawn accurately. It is very important to sow evenly and at the correct rate for the area covered. The most even spread will be achieved by using half the seed to sow in one direction, then sowing the second half at right angles to the first.

Caring for a seed-sown lawn

❀ Water the site regularly with a sprinkler if conditions are dry. Cover the site with netting to protect the emerging seedlings against birds. Shoots should appear in approximately one to three weeks.

RIGHT: *Turf produces a neat lawn quickly and with comparatively little effort.*

Cutting a seed-sown lawn

❀ When the grass is approximately 5 cm (2 in) high, cut it to about 2.5 cm (1 in), using a rotary mower. If you have sown the seed in autumn you will not need to cut again until spring. If you have sown in spring, continue mowing regularly throughout the growing season, gradually lowering the mower's blades.

LAYING TURF

Laying turf is labour-intensive and more expensive than sowing a lawn but produces a mature-looking lawn much more quickly.

1 Start laying the turf along a straight edge, ensuring that each new turf butts closely to its neighbour. Stand on a plank as you lay the next row, gently but firmly tamping down each turf using the back of a rake head. This ensures that there are no air pockets below the turf.

2 Stagger the joints between the turfs in the second row equally between the joints in the first row, like brickwork. Never finish rows with very small pieces of turf, which will be unstable and vulnerable to damage and drying out. Instead use as large a piece as possible at the end of a row, filling in any gap between this turf and the next with a small segment of turf.

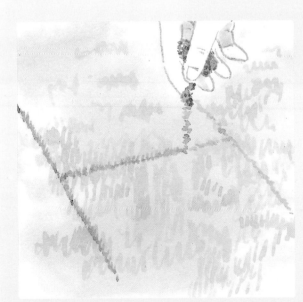

3 Sprinkle a top dressing of sieved sandy loam into the joints to help bind the turfs together.

4 Water the turfs in using a fine spray. Ensure that you keep the turfs moist so that they will root properly in the topsoil.

EDGING A LAWN

Crisp edges make a huge difference to the overall appearance of a lawn. Shaggy edges on lawns may be rectified with sharp edging shears or a power edger. To create neat edges on a new lawn use a clean, sharp half-moon edging iron driven vertically into the turf. Do not be tempted to use a spade, which would produce a scalloped effect.

1 *Always protect newly laid turf from undue compression by standing on a plank to distribute your weight evenly as you work. To cut a straight edge, use the plank as a guide. Align the plank with a string held taut in the required position. A long nail driven through the plank into the lawn will help keep it in position as you work.*

2 *A hose or rope secured in place with bent wire pegs assists in marking out a curved edge.*

3 *Trim any ragged edges with shears. Always remove clippings after edging, so that grass does not start to take root in your flowerbed.*

LEVELLING A BUMP

Uneven bumps or hollows in the lawn quickly become unsightly. Raised bumps become scalped by the mower, causing bare patches to develop on the lawn, while hollows do not drain freely, causing an increased risk of disease and producing patches of grass that are greener than the rest of the lawn.

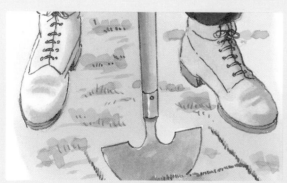 

1 *Make an H-shaped cut across the bump or hollow with a half-moon edging iron or sharp spade.*

2 *Gently peel back the turfs. Add soil to raise the level of a hollow or remove soil from a bump. Tread down the soil evenly. Roll back the turf and check that all is level before treading down the turf. Sift soil over the cracks created by cutting.*

NATURAL LAWNS

SOME sites may be more suited to a less manicured look than a traditional lawn. For example, if your garden backs on to fields, you may want to visually blur the transition from your garden to the surrounding countryside by allowing part of your lawn to grow longer so that a more natural effect is acheived.

Natural lawns are alive with wildlife and are low maintenance. However, if planted in the wrong place, such as a small, otherwise formal front garden, a natural lawn can easily look unkempt, as dying bulb foliage rots down in the shaggy grass. Natural lawns are generally best reserved for quite large areas, away from the house, where their wild beauty looks most at home.

NATURALISING BULBS IN A LAWN

1 Scatter the bulbs randomly across the lawn in the sort of drifts that they would naturally grow in. For larger bulbs make planting holes using a bulb planter, which neatly removes an appropriately sized piece of turf.

2 Plant each large bulb, roots down, at the recommended planting depth, making sure there is no air pocket beneath it in which water could collect. You may wish to add a shallow layer of grit or moist peat beneath the bulb to assist drainage. Replace the removed soil.

1 Small corms and bulbs are easily planted by partially lifting an area of turf. Make an H-shaped incision and fold back the turf. Lightly fork a little slow-release fertiliser into the exposed topsoil.

2 Scatter the small bulbs or corms randomly on the soil, root side down, and replace the turf. Gently but firmly tamp down the turf and ensure that the ground is level. Do not allow the cut edges of turf to dry out.

MAINTAINING A LAWN

Established lawns need regular attention, and not only from the lawn mower. There are specific tasks you can do, according to the season.

Spring

❀ As soon as the grass starts growing and the weather allows, rake the lawn to remove leaves and other debris.

❀ Give the lawn its first cut with the mower blades set high so that only the very tips of the grass are removed.

❀ Use a half-moon edging iron to neaten the edges of the lawn.

❀ Feed and weed the lawn.

❀ As spring turns to summer, gradually lower the blades of the mower to produce a closer cut.

Summer

❀ Apply summer feed.

❀ Weed the lawn.

❀ Continue mowing once a week. Ideally, rake before mowing to keep clover under control.

❀ At the height of summer, when the grass is growing vigorously, cut it twice a week.

❀ Keep the edges of the lawn neatly trimmed.

❀ If the weather is very dry, water the lawn and cut only once a week.

❀ As summer draws to a close, gradually increase the height of the mower blades for a longer cut.

Autumn

❀ Early autumn is an excellent time to sow a new lawn.

❀ Reduce the mowing frequency to once a week with the mower blades set high.

❀ Kill moss a couple of weeks before scarifying the lawn.

❀ Scarify the lawn to remove debris and promote good grass growth.

❀ Spike any compacted areas to aerate, and top dress the area.

❀ Top dress the lawn with a mixture of loam, sand and peat or peat substitute.

❀ Brush fallen leaves from the lawn.

❀ Returf or seed bare patches.

❀ Trim the edges of the lawn ready for winter.

❀ Clean and lubricate equipment ready for winter storage.

❀ Late autumn/early winter is a good time for turf laying.

Winter

❀ Stay off waterlogged or frozen turf.

❀ Check that mowing equipment is in good repair ready for spring.

BELOW: *Drifts of flowers in a natural lawn add irresistible spring colour.*

VICTORIAN GARDENS

WITH the Industrial Revolution, power and money moved from the landowners to the industrialists, who became the new creators of grand gardens. But the up-and-coming prosperous middle classes all wanted gardens, too. Numerous nursery gardens sprang up to supply the new demand. A spate of new gardening magazines appeared, many written by head gardeners. Although these were somewhat dictatorial in their approach, they were certainly widely read.

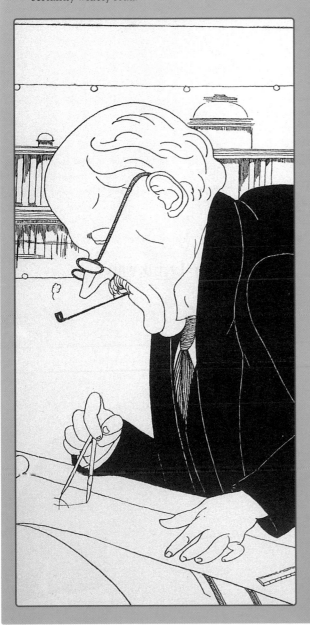

❀ The most striking aspect of Victorian gardens was 'bedding', which meant filling flowerbeds with patterns of brightly coloured annuals and exotics. Head gardeners had to propagate all the necessary plants in enormous greenhouses, and often had to plant a completely new scheme overnight to surprise weekend guests. Meanwhile, a man called E.E. Budding invented the lawn mower, giving rise to the closely cropped, highly groomed, green English lawn.

Growing flowers naturally

❀ The extravagant Victorian floral displays inevitably brought a reaction – in the form of William Robinson, a cantankerous Irishman who started off as a gardener and ended up a journalist. His philosophy was to plant 'perfectly hardy exotic plants under conditions in which they will thrive without further care'. He insisted on informality and introduced the idea of naturalising bulbs in grass. He used colour with great sensitivity and preferred permanent planting to the labour-intensive 'bedding' system. Not surprisingly, his ideas are incorporated into many of today's gardens.

The Jekyll/Lutyens partnership

❀ Gertrude Jekyll was a friend of Robinson's and the most influential garden designer in England before the Second World War. In 1889 she met a young architect called Edwin Lutyens and they collaborated on many gardens. He worked on the architectural aspects and hard landscaping and she on the planting. She had trained as a painter and was influenced by the sophisticated colour theories of the day. She developed single-colour and graded colour schemes, quite different from the earlier brash bedding colours. Her naturalistic approach was particularly successful within the formal framework of Lutyens' bricks, steps and paving.

LEFT: *Cartoon of the architect Edwin Lutyens, whose partnership with Gertrude Jekyll produced some of the most influential gardens in the late nineteenth and early twentieth century.*

PLANTING YOUR GARDEN

There is a lot more to gardening than simply popping a few plants into the ground at random. Too many gardens are populated with overgrown specimens that dwarf the rest of the plants. Other times plants are placed in the wrong position and become straggly and neglected-looking.

❁

To create an interesting garden you need variety of colour, height, form and texture as well as balance and simplicity. It is vital to consider the overall structure of your garden before you buy so much as a packet of seeds.

❁

Take a little time to choose the right place for the right plant and pay some attention to its planting requirements and your garden will reward you magnificently.

STARTING TO PLANT

Planting is one of the most enjoyable areas of gardening.
Placing something in the ground and watching it grow and
change with the seasons is incredibly satisfying, whether you are
planting seeds, shrubs, food crops, decorative perennials or trees.
Choosing the right plant for the right situation is at the heart of good
gardening practice. Every plant has its own individual feeding,
pruning and soil requirements. Some are easier to maintain than
others, but whatever you are growing, take time to absorb some basic
information about the needs of the plants in your garden.
This will enable you to enjoy consistently successful results.

Planting shrubs

❀ Deciding exactly where to plant shrubs is the most
important, yet often overlooked, part of the planting
process. Shrubs are the backbone of the garden, and
deserve very careful consideration in positioning. What
looks like a charming small plant in the garden centre
may quickly reach a size that will dwarf your garden, so
take care to research predicted size before purchasing.

❀ Shrubs are often planted far too close together, their
eventual spread having been disregarded at the planning
stage. The result is a messy jumble of intertwined plants.

It is far better to plant at the recommended planting
spacing, and fill in any initial bareness with perennials,
which can be moved as the shrubs grow.

❀ Naturally, also plant according to the type of soil you
have and any particular demands of the individual
shrub. There is no point planting a sun-loving shrub in a
shady spot for example, or a shrub that needs very rich,
moist soil on a dry, rocky site.

BELOW: *Shrubs can provide as much texture and interest as perennials and
annuals if chosen with care.*

Preparing the soil

❀ Although container-grown shrubs may be planted at any time of the year, they are easiest to establish in autumn or spring. These are the ideal times for planting bare root shrubs, when the ground is warm and moist. If planted in very hot weather, your shrubs will need vigilant watering after planting.

❀ Shrubs are hopefully destined to live in the garden for a long time, so the soil needs to be adequately prepared to give them their best chance of survival. It is not sufficient simply to dig a hole the same size as the pot and drop in the plant.

❀ You must encourage the roots to spread into the surrounding soil by avoiding a sudden change between the environment in the pot and the garden soil. Container-grown roots will be reluctant to grow from the peat in the container into mineral soil, so add organic matter to an area approximately 10 cm (4 in) bigger than the pot all round to counteract this.

MOVING SHRUBS

Occasionally it may be necessary to move an established shrub. Some shrubs, such as gorse, particularly dislike being moved, so try to avoid doing so if at all possible. If overcrowding is the problem, move a neighbouring, more resilient plant instead.

PLANTING A CONTAINER-GROWN SHRUB

1 *Water the plant thoroughly at least an hour before planting. Fork over the soil where it is to be planted and remove any weeds. Incorporate a slow-acting fertiliser in the soil.*

2 *Dig a hole at least 10 cm (4 in) wider and deeper than the rootball. Mix organic matter such as compost with the removed soil, and replace a layer of this planting mixture approximately 10 cm (4 in) deep in the base and around the sides of the hole.*

3 *Place the plant in the hole while still in its pot, to check the planting depth. A cane or stick laid across the top of the pot should lie flush with the soil surface.*

4 *Ease the plant from its pot and place it in the hole. Backfill with the planting mixture, taking care to firm the soil sufficiently as you fill, to avoid air pockets forming.*

5 *Firm the soil around the plant with your hands, and water thoroughly, before adding a layer of mulch approximately 7.5 cm (3 in)*

deep and 46 cm (18 in) wide around, but not touching the stems of the shrub, as this would encourage rotting. Mulching helps conserve moisture and control weed germination.

Staking shrubs

❀ Most shrubs do not need staking, but where a shrub has been planted in a new border, and does not have the benefit of other plants to support and protect it from wind rock, it may be necessary to provide additional support. This is particularly important when planting a top-heavy standard shrub. If the wind rocks the tall, vulnerable stem, the rootball may move, severing the roots as they try to spread out into the surrounding soil.

❀ By anchoring the base of the shrub, the top of the plant is permitted to move in the wind, encouraging the plant to grow stronger. Whatever staking method you use, consider it at an early stage, rather than when you notice damage or movement. Any instability you notice above the ground will probably indicate movement and possibly damage to the roots below the ground.

Staking when planting

❀ It is always advisable to stake when planting. Some stakes may be removed after they have performed their initial supporting role. For example, when a bushy shrub has been protected with short stakes while it settled into a new, exposed border, the stakes may be removed after a year or so when the roots are established and surrounding plants have grown to protective sizes. Very top-heavy shrubs, such as standard roses, are best left staked, as they are too vulnerable to breakage without support.

Staking established plants

❀ Staking an established plant may inadvertently cause root damage. If it is necessary to stake an established shrub, do not be tempted to knock in a stake close to the stem. The risk of damage to the root system is too great. Instead, knock in two stakes a good distance from the stem and connect them to the stem with heavy-duty rubber ties, to avoid chafing damage to the stem.

Types of support

❀ Tall standard shrubs will need sturdy wooden stakes made of rot-resistant timber, or wood treated with preservative. A selection of purpose-made plastic or wire supports is available in garden centres, alongside the traditional staking supports, canes. Twiggy sticks, simply pushed into the ground around a shrub, are also simple and effective.

❀ Purpose-made ties are available and, although it is possible to use string, these ties are a worthwhile investment. They incorporate spacers, which hold the stake taut against the stem, but which prevent chafing and can easily be adjusted as the plant grows.

BELOW: Most shrubs will not need staking, but if it has been planted in a new border it may need additional support.

STAKING A STANDARD SHRUB

1 Prepare the planting hole as normal. Use a rot-resistant, thick timber stake, or one of wood treated with preservative. Place it firmly in the hole and knock it in until it is stable.

2 Plant the shrub as normal, in planting mixture lining a generously excavated area. Push the rootball up against the stake. The stake

and rootball should now be approximately 10 cm (4 in) apart, and the top of the stake level with the lower branches of the shrub.

3 Firm the plant into the soil with your hands or your heel.

4 Fix a proprietary tie with spacer to connect the stem to the stake approx 15 cm (6 in) above soil level.

5 Fix a second tie around the stake and stem, just below the head of the shrub. Water in the shrub well and apply mulch as usual, taking care not to apply the mulch right up to the stem as this will encourage rotting.

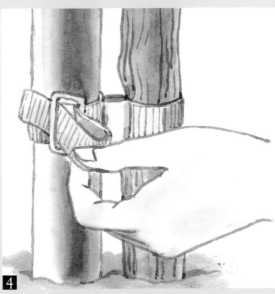

PLANTING TREES

TREES have a place in every garden. Even a tiny garden will benefit from the added height, colour and shape of a small tree. Some, like acers, are even happy in containers. Since trees are generally intended for permanent planting, it is critical to research the anticipated final height before purchasing. You will need to find out the expected height of the tree after 10 years before committing yourself.

Siting a tree

✿ Careful positioning will save much heartache later, and may help keep you on good terms with your neighbours. Consider carefully whether that adorable 'miniature' conifer will in fact grow to block out large amounts of light from your or your neighbour's home.

✿ Also, check that you are not planting too close to the house. Some trees, such as poplars, are particularly notorious for damaging foundations and lifting paving, so research your choice carefully. Plants grown in the lawn look attractive, but deciduous trees will shed leaves, which will need to be raked up each autumn.

✿ Planting a tree towards the back of a border, where leaves are allowed to slowly decompose and add to the organic content of the soil, is a lower maintenance option.

BELOW: *Trees provide year-round structural interest as well as seasonal colour.*

STAKE HEIGHT

For many years, the advice given on staking a tree was to have the top of the stake level with the base of the head of the tree. However, contemporary thinking is that a shorter stake, which allows the head of the tree to sway in the wind, encourages better root growth and a sturdy trunk. You should therefore use a stake that reaches only one-third of the height of the tree.

❀ However, you may still wish to remove some of the fallen leaves if the tree is particularly large and the leaf fall significant.

❀ Research the degree of spread and coverage the mature tree will provide, as this will obviously affect the amount of shade beneath its canopy, and the type of plants that you will be able to plant under it.

Planting a tree in a lawn

❀ The same general guidelines that apply to shrubs apply equally to tree planting. The planting hole must be sufficiently deep and wide to allow a good amount of planting mixture to be incorporated into the hole. Most young trees will need support for at least the first two years of their life, particularly in windy areas.

❀ The stake should be applied vertically, close to the stem of a bare-rooted tree, but at an angle of 45° when planting a rootballed or container-grown tree. The guidelines here apply only to newly planted trees. If you are considering moving a mature tree, it is advisable to consult a professional tree surgeon.

PLANTING A TREE IN A LAWN

1 Using sand, mark a circle approximately 1.2 m (4 ft) in circumference on the grass in the desired position. Cut into the turf with a spade and remove approximately 15 cm (6 in) depth of soil with it. Dig a planting hole deep enough to be at or just below the existing soil level on the tree stem, and wide enough to allow the roots of a bare root tree to spread out well. If you are planting a container-grown tree, plant at the same depth as the tree when in its container, and allow an area approximately half the diameter of the container all around the rootball.

2 Mix plenty of organic matter, such as well-rotted farmyard manure or compost, plus a general-purpose fertiliser with the soil removed from the hole.

3 Securely place a sturdy, rot-resistant stake in the hole, just to the windward side of where the tree will sit. Add a layer of planting mixture to the base of the hole. Place the tree in the hole, gently spreading out the roots if you are planting a bare-rooted tree. Use a

cane or spare stake to check that the soil level on the stem is level with the surrounding soil – approximately 5 cm (2 in) below the grass. Adjust the planting height by excavating further or adding more soil as necessary.

4 Backfill the hole and firm in the tree with your heel or hands. Secure the stem to the stake with a tree tie. Water the tree in thoroughly and add a generous mulch around the stem to suppress weed growth and help conserve moisture in the soil.

PLANTING CLIMBERS

THERE is a vast variety of climbers available, suitable for disguising or enhancing any number of vertical surfaces – from fast-growing Virginia creeper covering an unsightly old garage, to delicate annual sweet peas that can scramble prettily up a willow obelisk.

Siting a climber

❁ As with all planting, it is important to consider positioning carefully. Check that your intended climber will suit the soil, will receive the sunshine it needs and is appropriately sized for its location, support and your gardening habits when fully grown.

❁ Wisteria, for example, is very vigorous and needs regular tying in and pruning to keep it under control, so would not be a wise choice for a small area that you would prefer to be low main-tenance. A self-clinging climber such as an ivy would be a better choice.

❁ Although container-grown climbers can be planted at any time when the ground is not frozen, water-logged, or in extremely hot and dry conditions, autumn and spring remain the best times for planting – when the ground is warm, but the sun will not dry the soil out too quickly. It is advisable to plant bare-rooted climbers in autumn.

Types of climber

❁ Climber is a term used to describe a wide group of plants. Their common attribute is that they rely on some-thing other than their own stem for support. Some, like ivy, have aerial roots, which attach themselves to solid surfaces, making them easy to grow up walls and fences.

❁ Clematis have leaves that twine around stems, leaves, wires or other narrow supports, while passion-flowers have tendrils that coil around their supports, pulling the plant upwards. Ramblers, such as rambling roses, use thorns almost as crampons to attach themselves.

❁ There is also a group of climbers such as ceanothus, which do not actively climb, but which have lax, trailing stems that benefit from additional support.

Types of support

❁ The type of support needed will vary according to the individual plant and its climbing method. Annual climbers with twining tendrils, such as morning glory, need only light support, such as wires, willow, or even netting.

❁ Woody climbers such as wisteria and vigorous, scrambling climbers like honeysuckles need sturdy supports. It is always advisable to consider support at the planting stage; trying to apply support to an out-of-control established climber is a difficult task.

LEAVING A GAP BETWEEN A CLIMBER AND ITS SUPPORT

A common mistake is to plant a climber directly beside its support. The plant needs to be approximately 46 cm (18 in) away from the support so that the ground around the roots receives enough rainfall. Lean the plant gently towards the support and carefully spread out the roots before backfilling with planting mixture.

PLANTING A CONTAINER-GROWN CLIMBER

1 Dig over the site and remove weeds. Add shrub fertiliser to the area to be excavated.

2 Dig a planting hole approximately 30–46 cm (12–18 in) away from the wall, fence or support, following the general guidelines on planting all shrubs. Mix in a generous amount of organic matter with the excavated topsoil and line the planting hole with this mixture.

3 Water the plant well at least an hour before planting.

4 Place the plant, still in its pot, in the hole, and check the planting height with a cane. The soil level in the pot should be level with the surrounding soil. The exception to this rule is clematis, which needs its stems planted approximately 5 cm (2 in) deeper than its soil level in the container, to enable it to grow basal buds. These will give it an opportunity to renew itself if it is attacked by diseases or pests such as slugs.

5 Add or remove soil as needed to bring the plant to its correct height. Gently remove the pot and place the plant in the hole. Lean the climber against the support, and carefully spread out the roots. Add canes to the hole, leaning them towards the support and taking care not to damage the roots of the plant.

6 Backfill the planting hole with the planting mixture, making sure that there are no air pockets in the soil. Water thoroughly and firm in the plant with your heel or hands.

7 Train the stems up individual canes towards the supporting wall or fence. Secure the stems to the canes with purpose-made ties or garden twine. Even self-clinging plants or plants with tendrils will benefit greatly from this initial help. Add a generous depth of mulch around the plant, spread in a similarly generous area around it, leaving the stem itself clear so as not to encourage rotting.

2

3

4

5

7

Training methods

❀ Care in choice, positioning, planting and pruning all help you grow climbers successfully. However, training is also important, particularly on visual grounds, and you should consider training requirements at an early stage, while the plant is young and pliable.

❀ Left to their own devices, climbers will scramble upwards towards the light. Thus a climber that has been left untrained for many years may be very unattractive, with a mass of naked stems patchily covering the support, and a few small flowers way out of sight at the top of these stems. Such climbers will need drastic attention, which as well as being a major task, will temporarily denude the support.

❀ The surface beneath may not be in the best condition to accept new supports either, so in short, plan your training method early in the growing process. Spread out the stems of young climbers and tie them into the supports laterally, rather than letting them grow upwards in a single bunch of stems, which will be difficult to separate without damaging the plant later. Training the main stems horizontally thus allows all stems to reach the light and the plant is encouraged to flower at every level.

Training to control

❀ Although a climber scrambling crazily over an arch or around a doorway looks attractive, you may need to rein it in slightly to allow a smooth passageway for pedestrian access.

❀ Concentrate training efforts on those parts of the plant directly hampering easy movement, perhaps around the inner edge of an arch only, allowing the plant to spill prettily from its supports elsewhere. Some climbers may need training to encourage them to grow across a wall or other supporting surface, rather than outwards.

Training to encourage flowering

❀ When the climber has thrown up some good, long, pliable shoots from the main stems, bend these lateral shoots over in gentle curves and tie them on to the support. Flower buds will appear on the top edges of these curving branches, resulting in a support covered evenly in flowers, rather than just at the ends of the stems high above the support.

❀ As these trained shoots grow, new shoots will develop from them. Bend these over in the same way, while they are still flexible, and secure to the support. Continue in this way so that eventually the whole support becomes covered in an increasing series of arching stems. When training roses in this way, take care to cross over some of the stems rather than fan training, so that there is a good coverage of flowers all over the support.

Training to conceal

❀ Climbers are wonderfully useful for concealing unsightly features such as refuse areas, garden buildings or ugly fences. The same general rules about tying down lateral shoots apply. Depending on the area you

ABOVE: *Wall-clothing climbers can soften the edges of a building and make it blend effortlessly with the garden.*

are covering, and the plant you have chosen, you may need to install supports in addition to those on the vertical surfaces.

❀ Ivy and other self-clinging climbers are an excellent choice for concealing awkward shapes, as they clamber in all directions, attaching themselves by their suckers or aerial roots. You will need to install a structure, such as a network of wires between the eaves of a building and the wall below the edge of the roof, on to which to tie a less obliging plant.

Choosing ties

❀ In theory, all plant ties should be checked regularly to ensure that they are still holding the plant securely, but are not cutting into the bark as the plant grows.

❀ In reality, particularly on larger, woody climbers, it is not always practical to check every tie regularly. It is therefore best to use natural products for tying in, like raffia or soft twine, which will break under strain as stems thicken, rather than cut into the plant in the way that unyielding plastic or metal would.

TYPES OF CLIMBING PLANT

The particular support required depends largely on the type of climbing plant. Climbing and fixing methods are divided into the following categories:

AERIAL ROOTS: self-clinging climbers such as ivy and climbing hydrangea develop aerial roots from their stems, which clamp on to flat surfaces, making them generally self-supporting.

SUCKER PADS: other self-clinging climber types like Virginia creeper have sucker pads, which stick firmly on to flat surfaces.

TWINING TENDRILS: twining climbers, such as grapevines, climb by wrapping tendrils around other plants or purpose-made supports.

TWINING LEAF STALKS: clematis has leaf stalks, which entwine themselves around their supports.

TWINING STEMS: some climbers entwine their stems around neigh-bouring plant stems or artificial supports. Honeysuckle is the most popular example and needs a sturdy support system.

GROWING CLIMBERS ON WIRES

IF you want to train climbers up a wall, and have not selected a self-clinging climber such as ivy, you will need to plan your support at an early stage. Although it is possible to use trellis, it would detract from the beauty of a particularly nice brick or stone wall, as well as being relatively costly to install. Wires provide a good, unobtrusive support for a wide range of climbers, and can be painted to match the wall for even greater discretion.

Choosing wire and fixings

❀ Although many gardeners simply bang a few nails into the wall and tie in whatever pliable wire is at hand, these measures are inadequate for a climber that is going to occupy an area of any sort of prominence in the garden.

❀ Cheap wire will quickly rust, leaving unattractive rust marks on painted walls, and is also susceptible to breakage. Although your climber may look undemanding when it is first planted, it will quickly grow in both height and weight. Thin wire will simply bend, and possibly even snap, under the strain of a heavy plant.

❀ Choose a strong-gauge galvanised wire. Plastic-coated wire is liable to lose its smart coating eventually and looks very untidy. Any makeshift measures that need to be renewed later are difficult to replace. The plant will have grown significantly, making access difficult and damage to the plant likely. Therefore it is best to invest in good-quality wire and sturdy, properly applied fixings.

❀ Fixing a tension bolt at one end of the wire is a good idea if you feel that the wire may stretch. The wire may then be easily tightened if necessary.

ABOVE: *This seaside garden makes the most of its situation by growing the old-fashioned bright pink, pompon rambling rose 'Dorothy Perkins' up a pergola so that it is seen almost in silhouette against the blue ocean.*

TRAINING A CLIMBER ON A WIRE

1 First attach vine eyes to the wall. Although it may be possible to hammer these directly into soft masonry, a firmer fixing will be made by first drilling a pilot hole.

2 Insert wallplugs into the wall and screw in the vine eyes. The length of vine eye selected will depend on the type of plant grown. For example, a large-scale climber such as wisteria will need to be held away from the wall on wires, and needs long vine eyes to support the wires at the appropriate distance. Where the demands on a wire supporting system are not so great, for example when you are not planning to clothe an entire wall with a very large-growing, woody-stemmed plant, you could use wedge-shaped vine eyes. These are simply hammered directly into the wall.

3 Continue fixing vine eyes at the same height along the wall or fence, spacing them no more than 1.8 m (6 ft) apart. Fix parallel horizontal runs of vine eyes up the wall at intervals of approximately 50–60 cm (20–24 in). If the wires are too far apart, plants with tendrils may struggle to find the next wire and will need more frequent tying in than if the wires are more sympathetically spaced.

4 Thread galvanised wire through the hole in the first vine eye and wrap it tightly around itself, forming a secure fixing. Pass the wire through all the intermediate vine eyes until you reach the vine eye at the other end of the wall or fence and have completed the first horizontal run.

Pass the wire through this end eye and secure it so that the wire is held taut.

5 Curve over the stems of the climber and attach them in front of the wires using your chosen ties, such as raffia or string. Fix at as many points as necessary to ensure that the climber is held securely.

6 Continue tying in the plant in this way, pulling down and training in lateral shoots as they develop so that eventually the wall or fence is covered in a series of arching stems. These will produce a multitude of flowering buds, as well as clothing the surface evenly.

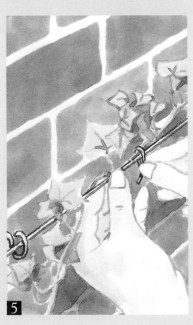

Growing climbers on trellis

❀ Wooden trellis has much to offer the gardener. Panels of timber battening nailed into squares or diamond formations may not seem very exciting in themselves, but trellis has a multitude of uses, particularly when combined with careful planting.

❀ It can add height to an existing wall, screen off the less attractive aspects of the garden, such as compost heaps, form part of existing garden structures such as arches, arbours, obelisks and pergolas, or simply be attached flat against a wall or fence to provide a convenient and sturdy support for climbing plants. The grid pattern is perfectly spaced, with the bars not too far apart, so that all kinds of climbers are encouraged to reach upwards without vast amounts of tying in.

Choosing trellis

❀ Trellis is available in many shapes and sizes, for example fan shaped, rectangular or square with an arched top edge. It is also possible to have trellis made to order to fit a particular area.

❀ It is worth buying the best-quality trellis possible, as the sorts of plants often grown on trellis, such as honeysuckle, can become quite heavy and unwieldy as they mature. Trying to clear a fully grown climbing plant in order to gain access to repair collapsing trellis is not an easy task. Timber that is approximately 2.5 cm (1 in) thick should be sufficiently sturdy, without appearing overwhelming.

❀ All trellis should be made of rot-resistant wood, or timber that has been treated with wood preservative. A wide range of shades for external wood are now available, which both colour and protect the timber.

❀ Generally, the more subdued shades of slate grey, sage green and dusky blue are the most successful colour choices, as they complement planting rather than fight against it visually. If you are attaching trellis to a flat surface, it is easier to paint it before it is fixed in position; but if the trellis is to form a freestanding divider, it is more convenient to paint it *in situ*.

ABOVE: *Hanging baskets are a popular way of increasing the growing area of a garden when all the horizontal and vertical surfaces have been filled with plants.*

BELOW: *Trellis is an inexpensive and versatile support for all kinds of climbing plants.*

Using trellis discreetly

❀ Because trellis is such a strong graphic shape, with its grid patterning, it can appear quite overwhelming if used in large quantities. In some cases, this may be a problem only initially. For example, where the trellis is being used as a screen, a vigorous climbing plant will eventually conceal the trellis almost entirely. In this instance, annual climbers such as sweet peas could augment the permanent planting until it is established.

❀ If you are planning to grow deciduous climbers over the whole of a house wall, wires may be a more subtle choice than trellis, which would compete with the strong lines of the brickwork when the leaves fall.

Fixing trellis

❀ Trellis may be permanently or semi-permanently fixed to walls and fences. If the wall or fence needs to remain accessible for maintenance, fix the trellis with hinges along its lower edge, and secure with a catch at the top. The whole trellis, with climber attached, may then be gently levered away from the vertical surface to allow repainting of the wall or fence.

❀ Whether permanent or hinged, the trellis needs to be held approximately 2.5 cm (1 in) away from the wall or fence on spacers for ventilation. The main stems of the climber can be trained into this space, and side shoots will grow out through the trellis towards the light, providing good overall coverage of the trellis.

FIXING TRELLIS PERMANENTLY TO A WALL

1 *Mark the position of the trellis on the wall. You will need battening level with the top and bottom of the trellis. If the trellis is over 1.2 m (4 ft) high, have an extra batten across the wall, behind the middle of the trellis. Drill the holes that will take the horizontal battens and insert wooden or plastic wallplugs in the wall.*

2 *Drill corresponding holes in the wooden batten spacers themselves and fix them to the wall. Drill and screw the trellis on to the battens, starting at the top. Use a spirit level to check that the trellis is horizontal.*

3 *Continue fixing the trellis on to the supporting battens, checking that the level remains true. Make sure that the finished trellis is firmly attached to the battening, and that the whole structure is securely fixed to the wall.*

ABOVE: *This beautiful climbing* Rosa Phyllis Bide *decorates the walls of the house with its delicate pink blooms.*

Growing climbers on netting

✿ Netting is an inexpensive way of evenly supporting a climber over a wall or fence. It is, however, not sufficiently strong enough to support a very large-scale woody-stemmed climber such as wisteria over an entire house wall.

✿ Netting is not the most attractive nor the toughest support for climbing plants, but it does have particular uses, such as wrapping around awkwardly shaped objects where trellis would not be an option, and when planting climbers around tree stumps or poles.

✿ Netting is available in a variety of gauges, from quite sturdy rigid square steel mesh, to very flexible, lightweight plastic mesh. The lighter gauges are perfect for fixing between upright posts with straining wire, as temporary supports for annual climbers such as nasturtiums or morning glory, as well as beans, peas, cucumbers and tomatoes.

✿ Although netting is not as good looking as wooden trellis, it can be used as an economical and easy-to-fit support in small-scale applications where it will be quickly concealed by planting, for example when it is fixed to support a vigorous climber over a small fence.

✿ Choose a coloured netting that tones inconspicuously with the support, and attach it well above ground level, so that the netting is not visible around the bare lower stems of the plant.

Leaving a growing space

As when attaching trellis, it is important not to simply nail netting directly on to a wall. Apply spacers between the netting and the wall, so that the plant will be able to climb between the two, as well as attach itself freely up and around all surfaces of the mesh, encouraging a good overall coverage of the wall.

Choosing fixings

Netting clips, which are widely available from garden centres and do-it-yourself stores, are not only easy to apply; they also incorporate a spacer, which holds the netting at an appropriate and uniform distance from the wall without recourse to battening. They are therefore an excellent fixing choice.

FIXING NETTING TO A WALL

1 Plan exactly where the netting will be. Position the first clip just below what will be the top level of the netting and hammer in a masonry nail to secure it in place. Alternatively, drill a pilot hole, plug it and fix the netting clip with a screw. Mark the position of the neighbouring clip, using a spirit level to ensure that the netting will be horizontal. Hammer or drill, plug and screw the second clip in place as before. Continue applying fixing clips along the wall at roughly 60 cm (24 in) intervals.

2 Position the netting so that a horizontal strand is within the jaws of the clip and push it firmly home. Continue to press the netting into position along the remaining line of clips.

3 Smooth the net down against the wall and mark the position of the next row of clips, approximately 60 cm (24 in) below the first row. Roll the net up out of the way and hold it in place temporarily with string, enabling you to fix the next line of clips. Continue marking and fixing clips in this way, working down the wall. Although you may need to continue a long way down the wall initially to get a climber going, it might be possible to remove some of the netting at the base of the climber, should it prove unsightly when the plant is more established.

4 When all the netting is fixed securely, train the climber into it and tie in place to secure. Even self-supporting climbers with aerial roots, like ivy, will benefit from a little help as they start the ascent, and may need to be trained along canes from their position in the ground, towards the netting.

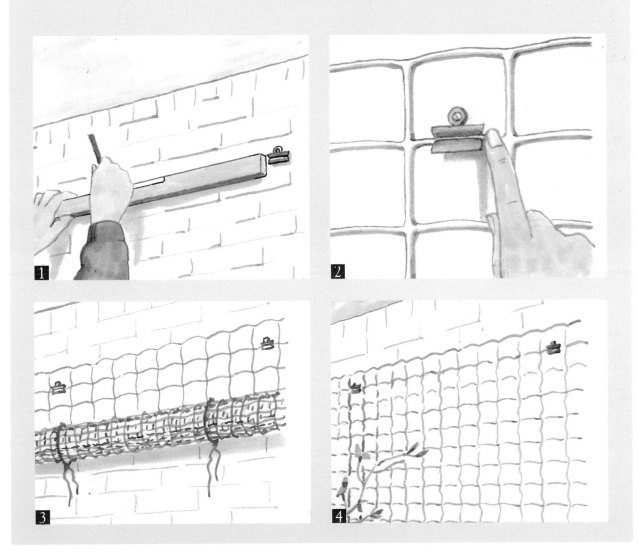

PLANTING BORDERS

THERE is a plant available to suit every space and climate and, with careful research and planning, you can produce borders that are alive with colour and interest all year long. Always select plants appropriate to their location in terms of soil, sun and space requirements. Research carefully, to plan for visual interest throughout the year.

Choosing plants

❀ The selection of plants for a border is vast – from shrubs and trees to perennials, biennials, annuals, bulbs, tubers and even vegetables. Most garden borders benefit from a permanent background of shrubs, which provide form and structure throughout the year, supplemented by perennials, which will return year after year to provide their seasonal brilliance.

❀ It is tempting to overplant a new border with many varied specimens, all crammed closely together to cover the bare soil. However, you will achieve a far more cohesive effect if you plant in groups of threes and fives, aiming for a smooth, drifting look rather than the dotted impression created by lots of individual impulse buys scattered randomly throughout the garden.

❀ Remember that what may look like small plants when first purchased can grow at an astonishing rate, so read labels carefully and allow your plants room to grow. Any initial unsightly bareness can be filled with colourful annuals.

Planting perennials and annuals

❀ Container-grown perennials may be planted at any time of year, but to give them the best possible start, avoid planting in very hot, dry, wet or cold weather. Spring is a good time to buy perennials, as their foliage and roots can be thoroughly examined and the plant has an excellent chance of establishing well, provided all risk of frost has passed.

❀ Mix organic matter and fertiliser into the surrounding soil when planting, and the roots will be encouraged to grow out freely into it. Most perennials need to be planted at the same depth in the soil as they are in their pots, although a few plants prefer either deeper or shallower planting, so always read plant labels

carefully before planting. Most annual plants should be planted in late spring, when the danger of frost has passed.

❀ Buy healthy-looking specimens that are not pot bound nor showing signs of having been insufficiently watered. Check that the roots are not congested, and are plump and pale in colour, not blackened and thin. The surface of the soil should be moist but not waterlogged, and free of algae and weeds.

Planting bulbs

❀ Although bulbs, rhizomes, tubers and corms are botanically different, they are generally considered together. All should be firm to the touch when purchased, with unblemished exteriors free from insect attack. If growth points are visible, they should not reveal any active growth, and there should be no fresh root development. Always keep this type of plant cool and dry between purchasing and planting.

PLANTING HEIGHT

As a general rule, bulbs are planted at a depth between two to three times their height, but there are some exceptions, so always check the packaging of your bulbs. Bulbs that are planted at the incorrect depth may fail to flower at all, a problem known as bulb blindness.

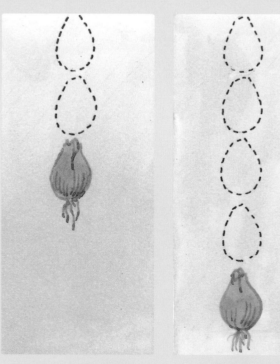

correct planting height   incorrect planting height

✿ After flowering, bulbs need to take in food for the next year's flowering from the dying foliage, so never be tempted to remove it prematurely or tie it off in an attempt to speed the process.

✿ In a border, this decaying foliage is not attractive, so plan your planting so that the leaves will be concealed by plants that begin active growth just as the bulb foliage is dying back. Alternatively, you could plant the bulbs in baskets, allowing them to be lifted out after they have flowered; they can then be moved to an inconspicuous part of the garden as the dieback process is completed.

PLANTING BULBS

1 Plant bulbs as soon as possible after purchase as they deteriorate quite quickly. Dig a planting hole and take care to place the bulbs the right way up.

2 Replace the soil in the hole, mixing it with grit to help drainage if your soil is heavy.

3 Once the hole has been filled, mark the planted area with sticks and water.

PLANTING A PERENNIAL

1 Soak the root ball thoroughly before planting. Tease out the plant without disturbing the root ball.

2 Dig a hole approximately twice the width of the root ball, and deep enough for the plant to sit level with the surface when in the hole. Incorporate plenty of organic matter with the surrounding soil before planting, so that the roots are encouraged to spread.

3 Firm in and water the plant. Continue to water in dry periods until well established. Adding a mulch around, but not quite touching, the plant will help to conserve moisture and suppress weeds.

PLANTING CONTAINERS AND HANGING BASKETS

CONTAINER gardening is a fantastically versatile and enjoyable aspect of gardening, and offers year-round opportunities for bringing colour and texture to all areas of the garden. Containers have a place in every garden, whether you live in an apartment with a tiny balcony or window box, or a house with a sizeable garden and patio. Container planting can visually blur the boundary between the lush greenery of the garden and the hard surfaces of the house itself, as well as paving or other hard external flooring.

The benefits of container gardening

❀ With container gardening, you can indulge your penchant for plants that would not thrive in your garden soil. While it is impractical to transform your garden soil permanently, for example rendering an alkaline border acidic so that you can grow camellias, it is perfectly possible to fill and maintain a container with precisely the right soil type that the plant needs to thrive.

❀ Containers can also be moved around to take full advantage of particular lighting and climatic conditions, which makes them even more adaptable. Plants that are too tender to be grown in the more exposed parts of your garden will appreciate being nurtured in containers close to the shelter of the house, and can be protected easily in extreme weather conditions.

❀ Containers enable you to ring the changes throughout the year. Underplanting containers with bulbs will lift your spirits as the dark days of winter give way all too slowly to spring. Containers come into their own during summer when bedding plants burst into life and blaze away well into autumn. Lilies and fuchsias add an autumnal glow, while heather, pansies and berried evergreens provide cheery colour all through winter.

Increased options

❀ Container gardening also extends the growing area. When you have planted up every spare inch of soil in the garden and have run climbers up every vertical surface, baskets hanging from wall-mounted brackets or even from the ceilings of pergolas and other structures, contribute yet another level of interest.

❀ It is becoming increasingly fashionable to plant edible plants in containers too, such as tomatoes, strawberries and herbs. Not only is this pretty, but practical, too. There is no need to stray down into the depths of the garden on a winter's lunchtime to collect a sprig of thyme, when you have a well-stocked herb basket just outside the kitchen door. Window boxes and troughs add even more planting opportunities.

ABOVE: *A successful hanging basket requires a subtle and balanced blend of flowers.*

Choosing containers

❀ Almost any type of container is suitable for planting, provided it is weatherproof and can have drainage holes added to it if they are not already present. It is advisable to raise containers slightly off the ground, using purpose-made feet or bricks, so that water can run freely away from the base.

❀ A wide range of purpose-designed containers is on offer at any garden centre, in a whole spectrum of shapes, sizes and materials and at all price levels. There is also great satisfaction to be had in adapting containers for planting, for example drilling drainage holes into an old copper wash boiler that has long ceased to serve its original purpose, but which would look wonderful when imaginatively planted.

Planting a hanging basket

❀ As with any form of planting, check that the plants you intend growing will thrive in the site chosen. For example, there is no point planting sun lovers in deep shade – they will grow leggy and not flower well, so read labels carefully before purchasing. Loam-based compost is advised, as it holds moisture well and is easier to re-wet than peat-based products should it dry out completely.

PLANTING A HANGING BASKET

1 *Remove the basket chain using pliers. Place the basket on a flower pot to hold it steady as you work. Press the basket liner into position.*

2 *Combine water-retaining granules with the compost and add water. The granules will swell, making the compost more bulky, so do not fill the basket until the gel has absorbed the water and appears jelly-like. Add a layer of compost to the basket.*

3 *Trailing plants will soften the lines of the basket and provide all-over interest. Make an X-shaped cut in the liner for each plant.*

4 *Very gently compress the rootball of each small plant in order to feed it through the liner into the compost.*

5 *Continue planting the container, building up the layers of compost and plants and firming in well, until the basket is almost full. Plant upright plants towards the centre of the top layer, surrounded by trailing plants. Leave sufficient space for watering.*

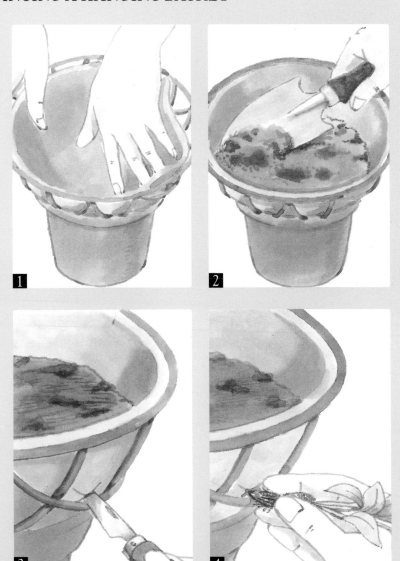

CANDLE POTS

These terracotta flowerpots gain a shot of glamour with a shimmering of gold around their rims. Not only does the candlelight add sparkle to outdoor entertaining, but a generous dash of citronella essential oil in the candle wax deters annoying insect invasion as dusk falls.

TOOLS AND MATERIALS

⊤ Small paintbrushes
⊤ Acrylic gold size
⊤ Terracotta flowerpot
⊤ Scissors
⊤ Gold-coloured Dutch metal leaf
⊤ Soft bristled brush
⊤ Amber shellac
⊤ Modelling clay
⊤ Wick
⊤ Pencil or thin twig
⊤ Candle wax
⊤ Bain-marie (double boiler)
⊤ Candle colourant (optional)
⊤ Citronella essential oil

1 Brush acrylic gold size around the rims of the flowerpot and leave to dry until transparent, but not so dry that it has lost its adhesive property. The length of time this takes will depend on the ambient temperature and humidity and may be anything between 10 and 30 minutes – some acrylic size has an indefinite 'open' or working time, making it foolproof to use.

2 Cut the metal leaf into manageable pieces. Place the metal leaf on the sized area and gently ease into place using a soft bristled brush. Gently brush away excess leaf. Continue until all of the sized area has been gilded.

3 Apply a coat of amber shellac to the gilded area to form a protective seal. Leave to dry, following the manufacturer's directions.

4 Push a small piece of modelling clay into the drainage hole at the bottom of the flowerpot to seal it. Suspend the candle wick centrally in the pot by attaching the upper end of the wick to a pencil or twig laid across the top of the pot. Embed part of the bottom of the wick in the modelling clay, allowing the remaining part to lie across the bottom of the pot so that the finished candle will burn for as long as possible.

5 Melt the candle wax in a bain-marie (double boiler). Add candle colourant if desired, and a few drops of citronella essential oil.

6 Pour the molten wax into the flowerpot and leave until set, then snip the wick with scissors.

WIRE HOOP BORDER EDGING

Wire hoop edging is sold commercially on a roll, but is generally too flimsy to serve any real purpose as a border edging. Its colour range is very limited and, if single hoops are available, the cost of edging an entire garden with them is prohibitive. These hoops solve the problem. They are economical and quick to make, using a reel of fencing wire and spray paint in a soft pastel shade to complement planting.

TOOLS AND MATERIALS

- Tape measure
- Small length (15–20 cm/ 6–8 in) of hardwood or metal, for twisting handle
- Drill and 3 mm (⅛ in) drill bit
- Stout protective gloves
- Wire cutters or hacksaw
- 3 mm (⅛ in) galvanised fencing wire
- Bench vice
- Small metal floristry bucket (optional)
- Spray can of exterior primer
- Spray can of light grey exterior paint
- Sheets of newspaper
- Protective face mask

gloves, cut three 1 m (39 in) lengths of galvanised wire and secure one end of each in a bench vice. Pass the free end of each wire through one of the three holes in the drilled bar and secure by twisting it around itself.

1 Measure the length of the hardwood or metal bar that is to be your 'handle' for twisting the wire, and drill a 3 mm (⅛ in) hole at the halfway mark. Drill two more holes, 30 mm (1¼ in) from each side of the central hole. Wearing protective

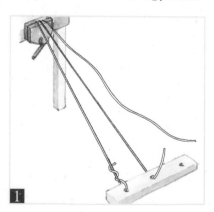

2 Holding each end of the bar and maintaining an even tension on the wires, twist the bar clockwise until all three wires become a single twisted piece – there will be 30–40 mm (1¼–1½ in) at each end that you are unable to twist.

3 Remove the wire from the vice and drilled bar and make more twisted lengths of wire in the same way. Trim each twisted wire to the same length, removing the untwisted sections.

4 Bend the trimmed, twisted wires into open-ended hoops, using a former such as a small metal floristry bucket.

5 Spray priming and painting can be done before or after the hoops are 'planted'. Protect the surrounding areas from overspray with sheets of newspaper. If working indoors, work in a well-ventilated area and wear a face mask.

6 'Plant' the hoops at the edge of the border by pushing them into the earth at a uniform height.

WIRE BASKET WALL PLANTER

It is easy to make a whole collection of wall planters that are
cost effective and also easily outclass their plastic-coated, mass-produced
counterparts. The gentle tones and textures of wire
and hessian are a natural, understated partner to any planting.
You should always wear stout protective gloves when working
with chicken wire, which has very sharp edges.

TOOLS AND MATERIALS

⟊ Pencil and paper, for template
⟊ Scissors
⟊ 12 mm (½ in) exterior-grade plywood
⟊ Jigsaw
⟊ Stout protective gloves
⟊ Protective eye goggles
⟊ Floristry scissors or wire cutters, for cutting chicken wire
⟊ Chicken wire
⟊ Hessian
⟊ Netting staples
⟊ Staple gun or hammer
⟊ Length of wire

1 Draw a symmetrical basket shape on a piece of paper, slightly shallower than a semicircle. Cut out the paper template. Place it on your piece of plywood and draw around it. Cut out the wooden shape, using a jigsaw.

2 Wearing protective gloves and eye goggles and using floristry

scissors or wire cutters, roughly cut out a piece of chicken wire to fit the plywood, allowing plenty extra to wrap around behind the wooden shape, as well as sufficient to make a pocket at the front. Cut a piece of hessian to the same size as the chicken wire.

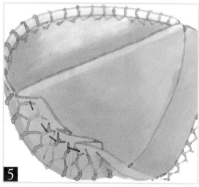

3 Cut a second piece of hessian large enough to wrap around the plywood. Wrap it around one face of the shaped plywood and staple it in place on the back, tucking the edges of the hessian under neatly as you work. (The stapled side will be inside the back of the basket.)

4 Take the remaining piece of hessian and fold under one long edge twice to form a neat 'hem'. Fold the raw edge of one long side of the chicken wire around the folded edge of hessian to produce a tidy, firmly rolled 'hem', which will be the top edge of the basket.

5 Shape the hessian and chicken wire roughly to produce a pocket of the desired size ion the front face of the plywood (i.e. the one that is not completely covered by hessian). The bare plywood will be inside the basket and therefore concealed as the pocket is filled with compost.

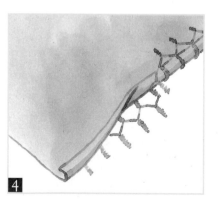

6 Secure the pocket in place by stapling the edges of the hessian and wire on to the wooden shape. Keep placing your hand inside the pocket as it is formed to ensure that you produce an even, symmetrical shape.

7 Trim away excess hessian and chicken wire. Staple the ends of a length of wire to the back corners of the basket to make a loop for hanging the planter on the wall.

WINDCHIME

This pretty, seashore-inspired windchime makes a softly musical sound with each passing breeze, and is incredibly simple to make from odds and ends. The terracotta shapes used here were Christmas decorations bought from a garden centre. Floristry supply shops are also a good source of unusual objects that would work well, for example miniature flowerpots, shells and seashore shapes intended for inclusion in pot pourri. The antiquated-looking piece of 'driftwood' used here is actually an old hammer handle, found while digging over a garden border. Be inventive and cast a careful look over your button box, garden shed, bathroom and garage shelves before stepping into a shop. You probably have almost everything you need for this project already, and searching for alternatives is a major part of the fun. Some objects will need small holes drilled in them – the type of drill sold for miniature work is inexpensive, widely available and easy to use.

TOOLS AND MATERIALS

- Jute twine
- Clothes peg
- Instant bonding glue
- Scissors
- Piece of driftwood, branch, well-worn hammer handle or similar
- Selection of objects for hanging, such as shells, terracotta shapes and old buttons
- Drill and small drill bit

1 To make lengths of hairy jute twine easier to thread through objects, grip one end of the jute in a clothes peg and twist the twine tightly to reduce its diameter close to the peg. Drip instant bonding glue on to this tightly twisted end and hold the peg for a minute or so until the glue has dried and the twist is secure. When the glue is totally dry, cut through the glued twist and you will have a rigid, neat, unfraying end, which will thread smoothly through your chosen objects.

2 Tie the un-neatened ends of several lengths of twine on to the piece of driftwood, branch or hammer handle that is to form the top support of the windchime. Tie a further length of twine to the wood to form a loop for hanging the finished chime.

3 Drill a small hole in each object to be threaded as necessary – for example in the bottom of each miniature flowerpot and in any shells that do not have naturally occurring small holes.

4 Thread your chosen objects on to the lengths of twine, knotting them in place to secure. Knot collections of shells and buttons suspended from the pots to produce 'bells'.

5 Continue threading objects on to the twine until you have a well-balanced windchime. Add new lengths of twine to the wooden support, if necessary, checking that they are sufficiently well spaced to appear uncrowded, yet close enough together to knock gently into each other when the wind blows.

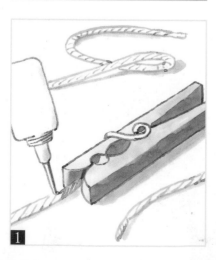

1

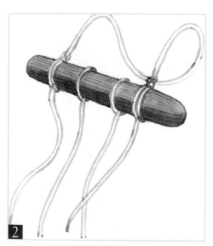

2

TIE-ON SEAT CUSHIONS

❦

Folding garden chairs are wonderfully inexpensive and practical for impromptu al fresco dining, but are not always sufficiently comfortable to invite a lengthy stay. This pretty cushion is designed for simplicity of making and laundering. Natural piping cord adds a jauntily nautical feel and removes the need to make and insert fiddly covered piping and fabric ties. The whole cushion may easily be washed with no need to remove the cover.

TOOLS AND MATERIALS

- Pencil and tracing paper, for template
- Garden chair
- Tape measure and/ or ruler
- Scissors
- Pins
- Needle and thread
- Sewing machine and thread to match fabric
- Iron
- Thick wadding
- Piping cord

1 Place a large piece of tracing paper on the seat of the chair and trace the outline of the seat. Mark a 2.5 cm (1 in) seam allowance all around the outline of the seat and cut out the template.

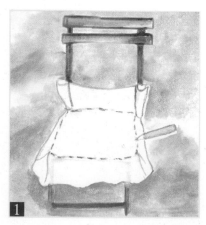

2 Pin the pattern on the fabric and cut out two pieces, taking care to match any obvious patterns such as the large checks shown here.

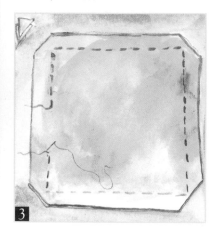

3 Pin the two pieces of fabric together, right sides facing. Tack then stitch along the seams, leaving a gap in the centre of one side to allow for turning the cushion cover the right side out. Snip diagonally across the corners of the seam allowance so that the finished cushion cover will have neat, sharp corners when turned right side out. Press the seams open.

4 Turn the cover the right side out and press. Cut away the seam allowance from the paper pattern to leave the original outline of the seat. Cut a piece of thick wadding to this size and insert in the cushion cover. Slipstitch the opening closed.

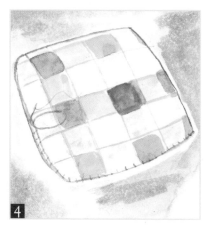

5 Pin then stitch piping cord around the edge of the cushion. Cut two lengths of cord for the cushion ties. Knot the ends of each length to prevent fraying and fold the lengths in half. Securely stitch each cord at this half-way point on to the rear edge of the cushion, at the point where they will be tied to the chair back.

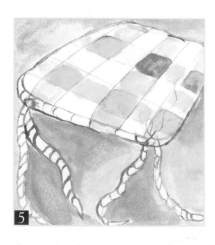

WITHY OBELISK

A little extra height is always welcome in the garden border, adding another level of interest to large, bland expanses, and providing a valuable further planting surface in a smaller plot. You can use any attractive straight sticks instead of the hazel, their length determined by how tall you want your obelisk to be. Flexible willow stems are increasingly available in do-it-yourself stores and garden centres, as well as being a popular mail order item from specialist growers. If fresh ones are not available, soak older, dried-out willow stems in a large container of water overnight or longer, until pliable.

TOOLS AND MATERIALS

- Hazel or other non-branching straight stems, approx. 1.5 m (5 ft) long
- Twine
- Scissors
- Pliable willow stems (withies), for weaving
- Knife or secateurs

1 Stand an uneven number of rigid hazel poles together – 19 were used here – to form a wigwam shape. Temporarily tie a short length of twine around the poles near the top to secure them while you complete the rest of the process.

2 Wrap two or three pliable willow stems around the group of poles approximately 10 cm (4 in) down from their tops to bind the poles tightly to each other. Push the end of the willow securely into the wrapping to fix in place. When a tight binding has been formed, remove the temporary twine.

3 Take two pliable willow stems and twist them loosely together before wrapping them around and weaving in and

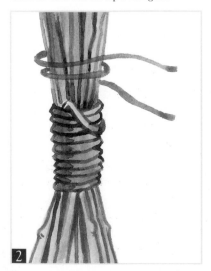

out of the upright poles to make bindings about 5 cm (2 in) wide in two places – roughly one-third and two-thirds the distance between the top binding and

ground level. Trim, and tuck any loose ends of willow to the inside of the obelisk as you work.

CHIMNEY POT PLANTER

This elegant planter started life in a much less sophisticated guise – as an orange-coloured plastic chain store bargain. A simple paint technique transforms the fake terracotta into a deceptively realistic faux lead finish, which complements plants beautifully.

TOOLS AND MATERIALS

- Medium grade sandpaper
- Plastic chimney pot planter
- Spray can of white acrylic primer
- Matt emulsion paint in white and charcoal grey
- Paintbrush
- Acrylic scumble glaze
- Plastic carton
- Spray can of exterior acrylic varnish, in matt or satin finish

1 Using medium grade sandpaper, sand the plastic planter well so as to provide a 'key' for the paint, enabling it to adhere well. Working in a well-ventilated area, spray the planter evenly with white acrylic primer – all over the outside and on the inside at the top of the planter.

2 When the first coat of primer has dried sufficiently (follow the manufacturer's directions for drying

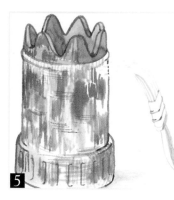

and re-application times), apply a second coat of white acrylic primer – sufficient to cover the planter uniformly. Leave to dry thoroughly – preferably overnight.

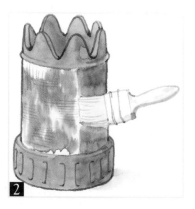

3 Paint the planter evenly with charcoal-grey emulsion paint and leave to dry for at least 3 hours.

4 Place a little acrylic scumble glaze in a plastic carton and tint it with white emulsion paint. Add water until the glaze has a runny, milky consistency. Briskly brush the glaze all

over the planter, allowing the glaze to run unevenly down the surfaces, forming pools that are opaque in some areas and watery and translucent in others. Wash randomly over the glaze with a little water, taking care not to dislodge the glaze in areas where it has formed naturalistic patterns. Leave to dry for several hours.

5 Add more of the same glaze to some areas of the planter to give an impression of age-encrusted salts. Add water to soften any hard, unnatural lines. Flick splatters of the glaze randomly over some parts of the planter to give a further weathered impression. Leave to dry thoroughly – preferably overnight.

6 Working in a well-ventilated area, finish the planter by spraying it with acrylic varnish. Apply several coats, following the manufacturer's directions for drying and re-application times.

PLANTED BUCKET

Metal complements plants beautifully and it weathers attractively, too. For impromptu entertaining, this hanging bucket can be filled with cut flowers arranged in wet oasis to enliven a garden wall, then later planted up for a more permanent display. The project is as ecologically sound as it is pretty, since this bucket has been recycled, now enjoying a new lease of life after its initial incarnation as a candle pot.

TOOLS AND MATERIALS

† Hammer
† Long nail
† Small galvanised bucket
† Wallplug plus masonry screw, or wood screw, as appropriate
† Screwdriver
† Plants and compost or cut flowers and wet oasis (florist's foam)

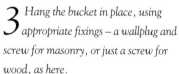

1 Using a hammer and a long nail, punch a hole in the side of the galvanised bucket near the rim for hanging the planter.

2 In the same way, punch drainage holes through the base of the bucket.

3 Hang the bucket in place, using appropriate fixings – a wallplug and screw for masonry, or just a screw for wood, as here.

4 Plant up the bucket or arrange cut flowers in well-soaked wet oasis for a temporary, colourful display.

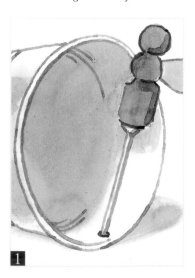

HURDLE BORDER EDGING

Modern border edging is a quick and simple way of containing soil and providing a neat mowing line, but the unnatural tones of pre-formed concrete edging are not always compatible with a romantic garden style. This rustic miniature fence adds definition to a garden border, and is as pretty as it is practical. If fresh willow stems are not available, soak older, dried-out ones in a large container of water overnight or longer, until pliable.

TOOLS AND MATERIALS

⊤ Mallet
⊤ Hazel sticks, 40–45 cm (16–18 in) long, 2–3 cm (³/₄–1¹/₈ in) in diameter
⊤ Long pliable willow stems (withies), for weaving
⊤ Knife or secateurs

1 Hammer hazel sticks firmly into the ground approximately 15 cm (6 in) apart along the border, so that the tops of the sticks protrude from the ground level with one another – approximately 30 cm (12 in). Hammer them into the ground only moderately firmly if a removable panel is desired.

2 Working with a handful of withies – about 10–12 – at a time, weave them in front of and behind alternate hazel uprights.

3 When you reach an end upright, go around the stick and back to the next, as in a figure of eight. Keep the withies compacted towards ground level as you work.

4 Continue adding bundles of withies until you reach the top of the uprights, always starting and finishing each bundle at the rear of the panel, trimming ends and tucking them in as necessary.

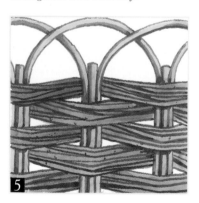

5 Cut single withies to lengths of about 90 cm (36 in). Starting at one end of the woven panel, push the ends of the single withies into the gaps beside alternate uprights to make the decorative overlapping hooped top.

VERSAILLES-STYLE PLANTER

Supermarkets and do-it-yourself stores are great places to pick up inexpensive growing kits, which come complete with compost, bulbs or seeds and even a planting diagram to ensure a naturalistic display with minimum effort. However, the containers supplied with these kits are all too often unsightly orange 'terracotta-effect' plastic. This smart wooden cover pops neatly over the cheap and cheerful container, has just enough space left around the base for excess water to drain away and is sturdy and attractive enough to use year after year. If using paint rather than woodstain, use an all-in-one formulation, which combines primer, undercoat and topcoat.

TOOLS AND MATERIALS

- Tape measure
- Plastic planting trough
- Pencil
- Straight edge
- Panel saw
- 12 mm (½ in) exterior-grade plywood
- Exterior wood glue
- 50 x 50 mm (2 x 2 in) planed softwood
- 8 corner joining blocks
- 32 x 12 mm (½ in) No. 6 wood screws
- Screwdriver
- Carpenter's square
- 50 mm (2 in) diameter turned knobs
- Hot melt glue and glue gun (optional)
- Medium/fine sanding block and sandpaper
- Damp rag
- Exterior paint or woodstain
- Paintbrush

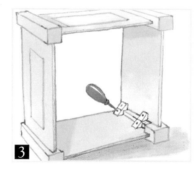

1 Measure the height and width of the plastic planter to be disguised. Cut four plywood panels 10 mm (⅜ in) wider and 20 mm (¾ in) taller than the plastic planter. Cut four plywood panels smaller than the first panels by 100 mm (4 in) all round and glue these in the middle of the first panels, using exterior wood glue.

2 Cut four corner posts of 50 x 50 mm (2 x 2 in) planed softwood, 60 mm (2⅜ in) taller than the height of the plastic planter.

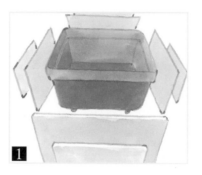

3 With the smaller decorative plywood panels facing outwards, fix the panels to the corner posts, using corner joining blocks and wood screws. Align the bottom edge of the panels 10 mm (⅜ in) up from the bottom of the corner posts, to leave a small gap at the base of the planter so that the water can drain away.

4 When all four panels and corner posts have been assembled, glue a decorative knob on the top of each corner post, using hot melt glue or exterior wood glue.

5 Sand all surfaces lightly and smooth off any rough edges with a sanding block. Rub off sanding dust with a damp rag.

6 Paint the planter using exterior paint or woodstain. Apply at least two coats, allowing drying times between coats according to the manufacturer's instructions.

GLOSSARY OF GARDEN DIY TERMS

To the uninitiated, hardware stores and builder's merchants can seem to use a confusing maze of abbreviations and terminology, understood only by expert construction workers, plumbers and electricians. This glossary will help you navigate the do-it-yourself (DIY) jungle.

Aggregate

A mixture of sand and gravel, combined with cement and water, to make concrete. Types of aggregate are distinguished by the size of the gravel pieces, which range from fine to coarse.

Alkali-resistant primer

A primer/sealer that prevents the attack on subsequent layers of paint by an alkaline substrate, for example, medium-density fibreboard (MDF).

Ballast

Naturally occurring aggregate (sand and gravel mix) used for making concrete.

Bond

The way in which bricks overlap to provide strength and load-bearing capacity.

Capping strip

A timber strip fixed to the top edge of a fence panel, shaped so as to shed rainwater and prevent its ingress into the end grain of otherwise exposed timber.

Cavity wall

Two walls built side by side 75 mm (3 in) apart (a double wall), connected only by 'butterfly' or other galvanised metal ties that are cemented in at regular intervals as the walls are built up. The cavity is for insulation and moisture protection and can be filled with fibreglass or foam insulation.

Coping

The top course of a brick or block wall, often made of shaped concrete slabs designed to shed rainwater from the top of the wall and protect the mortar joints from moisture damage.

Countersink/counterbore

The enlargement of the top of a screw hole to allow the screw head to be driven flush with the surface. Counterboring is where the hole is deep enough for the screw to be driven below the surface; the hole can then be filled with a plug of the same diameter.

Damp-proof course (DPC)

A layer impervious to water, inserted between two of the lower courses in a brick wall to prevent damp rising through the brickwork.

Damp-proof membrane (DPM)

A layer impervious to water, spread beneath a concrete floor to prevent damp rising through the floor.

Efflorescence

The appearance of moisture-borne salts on the surface of brick or plasterwork.

Expansion joint

A flexible joint between large

areas of brickwork or concrete to allow for expansion and contraction with changes in temperature.

Featherboarding
Tapered, section timber, overlapped to make fencing panels.

Footing
A simple foundation to support a wall.

Hard core
Bulky, solid matter such as old bricks or blocks, used to form a sub-base below concrete.

Marine ply
Plywood impregnated and bonded with waterproof adhesive, suitable for use in moist situations.

Masonry bolt
Heavy-duty fixing for brickwork (see 'Wallplug').

Mastic
A flexible, non-setting jointing compound.

Microporous
Allowing the passage of small molecules, i.e. microporous paints allow the wood to 'breathe out', while preventing moisture from passing into the wood.

Pale
A wooden fence upright.

Paver
A brick or block specially made for paved surfaces. Pavers should be water-resistant and therefore frostproof.

Piers
Upright brick columns at the ends and at regular intervals along a run of brickwork.

Prefabricated
Made off-site and simply installed in one or more larger pieces.

Primer
The first coat in a 'paint system', often preservative, which seals and bonds the subsequent paint layers.

Render
A thin coat of plaster; a sand and cement render is often applied to brickwork in a thin layer to form a smooth finish.

Retaining wall
A wall constructed specifically to hold back a weight of soil from an upper level.

Scalpins
Ballast with a clay content, compacted to form a substrate for pathways.

Scratchcoat
An undercoat of sand and cement render, scratched or 'keyed' so that a subsequent layer will bond firmly.

Sett
A small, regular-sized paving block.

Soakaway
An underground pit filled with rubble or sand into which surface water can drain.

Spur
A length of electrical cable connected to a ring main or other main cable.

Subsidence
Sinking of the ground.

Tamp
To compact material, usually concrete, with repeated 'taps', thereby excluding air pockets and forcing the material into cavities.

Wallplug
A fixing for masonry, which works by expanding to a tight fit in a pre-drilled hole as a screw is fastened into it.

Weep hole
A small hole in the exterior of a cavity wall for any accumulated interior moisture to drain from.

INDEX

ACKNOWLEGEMENTS

AUTHOR & PHOTOGRAPHER'S ACKNOWLEDGEMENTS

Martin Mansfield for his patience in demystifying soil science, disseminating the underlying principles of plantsmanship and general good advice. Pat and Chris Cutsworth for their unfailing tolerance in being used as a garden photography location. Bob Sawyer, manager of the Swindown branch of Jardinerie, for his trust and patience far exceeding the call of duty. Derek Guy for having the trust to allow us to spontaneous access to his beautifully maintained garden for photography.

PUBLISHER'S ACKNOWLEGEMENTS

The publishers would like to thank the following for their kindness in allowing us to photograph their gardens Anne Birnhack, Ken Baker, Michael Clark, Derek Guy, Graham Hopewell, John and Dorothy Knight and Gae Oaten.

Thanks also to the following companies have been more than generous in loaning equipment. props and plants for photography Chairworks, Clifton Nurseries, Draper's Tools Ltd, Idencroft Herbs and Queenswood Garden Centre. Extra special thanks to Jardinerie in Swindon, Wiltshire for allowing us to shoot within the garden centre.

PICTURE CREDITS